Laura Bieger
Belonging and Narrative

Lettre

Laura Bieger is Professor of American Studies, Political Theory and Culture at the University of Groningen. She held teaching and research positions at Universität Freiburg, FU Berlin, UC Berkeley, Universität Wien and IFK Wien. Her essays have appeared in *New Literary History, Amerikastudien/American Studies, Studies in American Naturalism, Narrative* and *ZAA*. She is currently working on reading publics in U.S. democracy.

Laura Bieger
Belonging and Narrative
A Theory of the American Novel

SFU LIBRARY

[transcript]

Bibliographic information published by the Deutsche Nationalbibliothek
The Deutsche Nationalbibliothek lists this publication in the Deutsche Nationalbibliografie; detailed bibliographic data are available in the Internet at http://dnb.d-nb.de

© 2018 transcript Verlag, Bielefeld

Cover layout: Maria Arndt, Bielefeld
Typeset by Dominik Fungipani
Printed by Majuskel Medienproduktion GmbH, Wetzlar
Print-ISBN 978-3-8376-4600-9
PDF-ISBN 978-3-8394-4600-3
https://doi.org/10.14361/9783839446003

Contents

	PREFACE	7
1	**BELONGING, NARRATIVE, AND THE ART OF THE NOVEL**	13

Uses of Narrative. Life and Narrative (and) Art. Subjects of Belonging. Historical Trajectories.

2 POISONED LETTERS FROM A GOTHIC FRONTIER — 41
Charles Brockden Brown's *Edgar Huntly*

Frontier Paternalism Meets Liberal Capitalism. Epistolary Transgressions. Belonging as *Unterhaltung*. The Power of Narrative and the Limits of the Narratable.

3 THE ART OF ATTACHMENT — 73
Sarah Orne Jewett's *The Country of the Pointed Firs*

Topophilic Dispositions. The Sketch and the Journey. Receptive Agency. Consecutive Endings, Editorial Care, and the Book as Dwelling Site

4 DWELLING IN WHAT IS FOUND — 105
Henry Roth's *Call It Sleep*

Childhood as Immigration. Space as Felt, Storied, and Scripted. Found Stuff as Narrative Foundation. Yearnings for Autonomy and the Aching Limits of Belonging

5 OF CRANES AND BRAINS — 135
Richard Powers's *The Echo Maker*

Connecting Midwest and Medial Cortex. Being No One. Colliding Narratives, Conjoint Map-Making. Back in Oz Again.

WORKS CITED — 163

Preface

This is a book about the intricate ways in which belonging and narrative condition each other, and about the ways in which their relation can elucidate our understanding of narrative art and of the art of the novel in particular. Belonging as I conceive it is not an anthropological given; it is continuously produced in and through narrative. I like to think of it as basic constituent of human being—the yearning for a place in the world without which both place and world would crumble. Moreover, I think that much of narrative's sweeping allure (it can be found in any culture) stems from its capacities to emplot and emplace our lives. The traction that narrative has gained in recent theories of identity is a powerful testimony to the fertile relation between belonging and narrative that is the concern of this book. And while life-stories are becoming more and more novelesque in our thoroughly mobilized, digitalized, and crisis-ridden age a popular fantasy of the self as a writer (enhanced by new possibilities of self-publishing) is that of the novelist.

We tell and we listen to stories because we yearn to belong, and ever since its modern inception the novel has become a viable testing ground in this matter. With its endlessly malleable form, its preferred tropes of quest and trial, and its oddly detached characters in search for meaning and mooring, the novel is a perfect candidate for such exploitation. If and how we belong—by way of leaving home, building new homes, dwelling in multiple homes (some of which might be imaginary), or dismissing the idea of home all together—depends largely on narrative. This book argues that the novel, with its generic affinities to troubled states of belonging, has incessantly shaped both the yearning for a place in the world and the narrative vectors and affective currencies in which such a place can be forged. The final stretch of writing this book in the winter of 2015/16 coincided with the daily realities and reports of staggering numbers of refugees leaving their homes in search for a more salient future—mobilized by war, social injustice, and electronic media. Today's world is a world in which rumors, news, stories, and images circulate in the blink of an eye to even the remotest corner of the globe, with vast impact on our sense of the near and the far, the neighbor and the foreigner. The geopolitical consequences of the recent upheavals are still unforeseeable, but from redrawing maps to charting itineraries and (de)regulating borders, and from restructuring places and communities to mending broken biographies narrative will play a crucial role in the outcome. For better or for worse, the world we will inhabit in the future depends on the stories that we tell ourselves today.

Among scholars of literature and culture, however, narrative has yet to recover from the bad reputation that it gained in the wake of poststructuralism. As a "structure of desire, a structure that at once invents and distances its objects and thereby inscribes again and again the space between signifier and signified" (Stewart ix) narrative is thought to be generative of symbolic order, and symbolic order is viewed as the executive branch of ideology. No doubt, narrative and ideology are natural allies (not least because all ideology asserts narrative form). But narrative is also a practical component of dwelling in the world. We use it to connect sense impressions and memories; to orient ourselves in the world and familiarize us with places and people; to draw boundaries between inside and outside, public and private; to build institutions and regulate our attachments. Both socio- and psychogenesis relies on it. From an anthropological perspective narrative has been aptly described as "one of the large categories or systems of understanding that we use in our negotiation of reality, specifically [...] with the problem of temporality; [wo]man's time-boundedness, and [her] consciousness of existence within the limits of mortality" (Brooks xi). This is a useful starting point to think about the fertile relation between belonging and narrative for sure. But is narrative not just as invested in our existence in space? Our relation to space may be more tangible than our relation to time, more pragmatic and this-worldly than our quarrels with mortality and the existential unknowability of our own death, but it is just as crucial to our sense of belonging, and certainly no less reliant on narrative.

My interest in narrative as a practical component of dwelling in the world thrives on my wish to complicate, and perhaps even move beyond representational assumptions about narrative that dominate our understanding of what narrative is and does to this day. I have learned much from structuralism and narratology, especially from their shared tendency to view literature as an integral and quantifiable part of human signifying practice, and I owe a considerable debt to Peter Brooks's psychoanalytic approach to narrative as a system of understanding that progressively unfolds over time, driven by the dynamics of memory and desire in its creation of meaning and form. But I disagree with a bedrock assumptions of these theories; namely, that narrative is superimposed retrospectively on an experience (or an entire existence) that is on some deeper level unmediated, and as such part of the non-narrative flux of the real. Based on my understanding of media as something that we both use and are—yes, our bodies are media, and they are places, too—I believe that no matter how deeply we delve into the fabric of our being, our experiences are never unmediated. Against the rigid oppositions between subject and object, or life and narrative that such (often tacit) implications about raw experience and secondary mediation bring to bear on our understanding of narrative, this study assumes that being in the world always entails being engaged with the world; that narrative is a basic mode and mediator of this engagement;

and that living and telling our lives are continuous and interdependent because of our deep-seated need to belong.

In short, this book is invested in moving beyond narrative as a mode of representation to learn more about narrative use. Its job is to put forth an understanding of narrative as an endlessly useful resource of orientation and emplacement that both feeds and is fuelled by narrative art. Like any work of theoretical ambition (and, as it happens, like any novel), this book searches and squabbles rather than posits and proves. My endeavors to chart a narrative theory based on the human need to belong have led me to traditions as divergent as philosophical anthropology, human geography and social psychology. Some of these traditions are explicitly engaged in ongoing efforts to rethink the relation of life and narrative. Others offer insight into the inherently progressive constitution of space and place, "the unutterable mobility and contingency of space-time" (Massey, *Space, Place* 5) that, in turn, prompts questions about narrative's stakes in both propelling and coping with these dynamics. But what does all of this have to do with art? And what is the role that literature plays in these narrative operations? Taking my cue from social psychology, I argue that the stories we live by draw from those artistic (and often fictional) narratives that we consume when we read novels and comics, watch movies and television, play computer games, etc. The widely shared hunger for narrative artifacts at work in this pattern made me wonder why our life stories gravitate so notably toward them. And when thinking about the matter in the light of this study it occurred to me that one thing that makes these artifacts so immensely attractive for someone who yearns to belong is an amplified sense of *narrative agency*. I use the term to describe the capacity to make choices about the telling of one's story and impose them on, relate with, and ultimately be in the world. A main claim that I unfold in this book is that the novel exploits this kind of agency (which happens to be just as endlessly malleable as its searching form) to the end of suturing troubled life-worlds. In fact, since its modern inception the novel has been so conducive to dealing with troubled states of belonging that it became the main provider of the narrative frames and formulas that modern individuals need to dwell in the world.

But this book does not attempt to cover all the varieties or even the basic types of narrative forms and agencies that have gained shape in and through the art of the novel. Instead of writing a survey of this development, I chose four iconic American sites—the frontier, the region, the ghetto, the homeland—to explore how four paradigmatic American novels give voice and form to concerns with belonging particular to these sites. Of course, there are other sites, novels, and concerns with belonging than those dealt with here, and as any student of narrative knows, a different selection and combination would have amounted to a different story. The story that I tell through my examples takes us to a series of conflicted sites of U.S. cultural history that are prone to bring out both the salience and significance of having a place in a changing world, and the proactive role that narrative assumes in the making und unmaking of this place. The letter, the sketch, the found object, and the brain-as-storytelling-machine are the main protagonists in this story, and their adventures revolve around mending and suturing troubled life-worlds. Charles Brockden Brown's frontier gothic *Edgar Huntly, or, Memoirs of a Sleepwalker* (1799) exploits its narrator's compulsive habits of letter-writing and sleepwalking to stage a narrative act of *re*covering a haunted ground previously traversed with no proper sense while *un*covering a state of impossible belonging. Sarah Orne Jewett's regionalist masterpiece *The Country of the Pointed Firs* (1896) endorses the "minor" art of the sketch in an exercise of familiarization and attachment that destabilizes both the medium of the book and the genre of the novel at a time when defamiliarization and detachment become the hallmarks of narrative art. Henry Roth's *Call It Sleep* (1934), written with the ambition that ethnic literature should absorb the experimental impulse of modernism, mediates the experience of immigration through a fearful Jewish boy with a rare gift of gathering objects, people, and stories to dwell in them. And Richard Powers's *The Echo Maker* (2006) depicts the Midwestern homeland as a product of two interactive eco-systems: the life-sustaining environment and the nonstop narrating human brain, one geological, the other neurological, one endangered by global capitalism and post-9/11 trauma, the other threatened by a brain disease that spreads through colliding storylines.

At the end of my story I hope to have made tangible how the human need to belong operates as a driving force of literary production, and vice versa; and how the American novel, because it comes from a place where belonging is even less of a given then in other parts of the modern world, makes for a particularly rich field of study in this regard. Hence, much will be said in this book about what narrative brings to the human need to belong, and how narrative art and the art of the novel are involved with this need. But even if my story persuades its readers that narrative is a practical component of dwelling in the world—can one actually be at home in it? My answer to this question is simple: To the tenuous degree that one can be at home at all, it is in and through narrative. There is no other way.

~

Writing this book in a language that is not my mother tongue has taught me a lot about not belonging, or not quite belonging—about the comfort that is lacking when being unable to tap into the secret wisdom of one's own language where thoughts turn in circles or come to a halt. Writing this book as a member of an academic institution made me aware of that institution as a place of support and care.

This book grew out of my *Habilitationsschrift* at Freie Universität Berlin, titled "No Place Like Home: The Ontological Narrativity of Belonging and the American Novel, 1799—1934—2006." I am grateful to Winfried Fluck, whose unwavering support and intellectual guidance have been instrumental not only to completing my *Habilitation* and this book but to my entire academic career. And I am grateful to Susanne Rohr, who has accompanied every stage of this book and the questions about belonging and narrative that it raised in its author, and who has become a close friend along the way. I also wish to thank my colleagues at the John F. Kennedy Institute for North American Studies at FU Berlin, where this book was conceived and most of it written, especially Heinz Ickstadt, Ulla Haselstein, Andrew Gross, Florian Sedlmeier, and Johannes Völz, for glorious years of collaboration. The German Academic Exchange Service generously funded a research stay at the University of California at Berkeley in 2011/12, and I am grateful to Anton Kaes for being an inspiring and generous host. Helmut Lethen invited me to IFK Internationales Forschungszentrum Kulturwissenschaft in Vienna in 2015/16, where I was able to revise my *Habilitationsschrift* for publication in conversation with him, Hartmut Böhme, Penelope Deutscher, Michael Hagner, and Katja Petrowskaja, and I am grateful for that. Sieglinde Lemke and Wolfgang Hochbruck have provided a home at the University of Freiburg for me at a crucial junction in my career, and I am immensely grateful for that as well. Over the years of working on this book, I have benefitted from the generous support of many people, among them Charles Altieri, Rita Felski, Frank Kelleter, Günter Leypoldt, Philipp Löffler, Ruth Mayer, Donald Pease, John Carlos Rowe, Ramón Saldívar, Joshua Shannon, and Hayden White. I am fortunate that many of those mentioned here not only offered their guidance in giving feedback on chapters and talks, writing support letters, and drawing my attention to unknown texts but also their friendship. Dominik Fungipani, Kalina Janeva, Rieke Jordan, Evelyn Kreutzer, and Anirudh Sridhar have been indispensible in proofreading and setting the manuscript in its various stages. And Daniel Bonanati and Anne Poppen at transcript have been miraculously suave and efficient in getting the manuscript published.

Some of the material in this book has appeared elsewhere in earlier form and is reprinted here with permission. A shorter version of Chapter 1 appeared in *New Literary History* 46.1 (2015). Portions of Chapter 5 appeared in *Re-Framing the Transnational Turn in American Studies*, ed. Winfried Fluck, Donald E. Pease and John Carlos Rowe (Dartmouth, NH: University Press of New England, 2011), and in *Ideas of Order: Narrative Patterns in the Novels of Richard Powers*, ed. Antje Kley and Jan Kucharzewski (Heidelberg: Winter, 2012). And a previous version of Chapter 2 appeared in *Towards a Post-Exceptionalist American Studies*, ed. Winfried Fluck and Donald E. Pease, *REAL* 30 (2014).

This book is dedicated to Dustin Breitenwischer, who is familiar with every thought processed in it, and who has shaped its final form through countless conversations in our various homes and en route between them. Belonging has gained a brighter and broader horizon with him in my life, and I thank him for that with my whole being.

1 Belonging, Narrative, and the Art of the Novel

Having mastered her adventures in Oz, Dorothy learns the secret of the ruby red slippers: There is no place like home. Repeating the phrase over and over, she calls her home into existence. There is indeed no place like home unless one calls for it. And there is no reason to call unless that place seems uncertain. But something is curious about this lesson, and this something becomes tangible in its repetition. Does the phrase mean that there is *no* place like home? This would attest to an almost sacred exclusiveness. Or does it mean that there *is* no place like home, which would attest to its elusiveness or even sheer absence? As one meaning dovetails the other, there is an eerie sense that home may be forever gone, or, once seen from Oz, turn out to never have existed. Alas, the return that stands at the end of Dorothy's story does not put an end to the concerns with where, how, and to whom she belongs that made her leave home in the first place—and that are perhaps the single most powerful generator of narrative.

Belonging as I conceive it is an inescapable condition of human existence—"not just being, but longing" (Bell 1), the desire for a place in the world without which both place and world would crumble. To feel and direct this longing we need a mediating structure; narrative is that structure. Just think of the many people who write diaries in times of trouble, and stop once things have smoothened out. In turning to narrative, we grapple with unsettling experiences and conduct the semantic, psychic, and geographic movements unleashed by them within the shifting parameters of space and time. Narrative's sweeping allure (it can be found in any culture) thrives on its promise to give meaning and mooring to our lives (which may include the dissolution of old and obsolete ties). Where, how, and to whom we belong depends on the stories we tell (or do not tell) ourselves. Today, matters of belonging are most rigorously debated in the contexts of transnationalism, postcolonialism, and queer and gender studies, usually to highlight states of troubled belonging caused by experiences of migration, diaspora, racist or sexist discrimination. These debates have brought out the centrality of these experiences in the formation of modern cultures, and they have been crucial in replacing notions of belonging as set (and saturated) in stable (and unjustly distributed) correlations of place and self with an understanding of belonging as inherently fabricated and provisional. Salman Rushdie's "imaginary homelands," Homi Bhabha's "third space," Mary-Louise Pratt's "contact zones," Paul Gilroy's "black Atlantic," Iain Chamber's "impossible homecomings," and James Clifford's preference of "routes" over "roots" capture this critical impetus.

I have learned much from these debates, and I fully subscribe to their insistence on the tenuous, quintessentially performative nature of belonging, its contested and often precarious relation to space, race and gender, its nostalgic inclinations and cosmopolitan potential. For my own purposes, however, the (identity) political framework of these debates is limiting. Rather than focusing on particular sets of experiences, their proper recognition, and their capacity to resist hegemonic renderings of belonging (the national homeland, the nuclear family), I want to consider belonging as an anthropological premise of narrative. Yet pursuing this interest against the backdrop of these debates throws into sharp relief the racist, sexist, and imperialist implications that are couched in the notion of the human in part through its relation to narrative. In fact, narrative art, and the art of the novel in particular, were essential to creating the sense of self that (with its enlightened capacities of inner growth, rational conduct and critical interrogation) has come to define what it means to be human in the modern age. So yes, the human is a haunted point of reference, far easier dismissed from a position of white privilege than from one of systematic exclusion (to this day black activism gains force by insisting on its share of the human)—and hence vexed with the very dynamics of belonging that this book sets out to explore.[1]

In pairing belonging and narrative I hope to gain a new angle from which to address what narrative is and does; or rather, what we do with it, what it does with and for us, and why we are so endlessly inclined to engage with it.[2] With this focus, I am less concerned with narrative as a mode of representation and more with narrative use. In foregrounding the practical and pragmatic dimension of narrative, my study aligns itself with the work of scholars such as Barbara Herrnstein Smith, James Phelan, and, more recently, David Rudrum, in its conviction that "any definition of narrative that ignores the importance of use is […] incomplete" (200). While our engagement with narrative can certainly not be reduced to use in a utilitarian sense, it always occurs "on a particular occasion" and "for some purpose" (Phelan, *Rhetoric* 218). This also means that engaging with narrative always

---

1   From the first slave narratives written in support of the abolitionist movement to Ta-Nehisi Coates's recent protest essay *Between the World and Me*, "being human" serves as a rallying point against racial discrimination and injustice. The main reason for this insistence is, of course, the fact that modern slavery was based on a systematic denial of humanity to those degraded to the status of property. I discuss how Edward P. Jones's neo-slavery novel *The Known World* exploits these vexed aspects of belonging in my essay "Property, Community, and Belonging."

2   The heightened attention that narrative has recently gained in theorizing identity, social action and agency is a powerful testimony to the conundrum of belonging and narrative that is the concern of this book. See Somers, Ezzy, Gergen and Gergen, Taylor, Ricoeur, "Narrative Identity," Cavararo.

has practical value—a value that exists in relation to those who use it and their everyday needs. Based on these premises, what I put forth in this opening chapter is an understanding of narrative as an endlessly useful resource of orientation and emplacement on which we draw to shape, order, and sustain our relation with the world and everything in it. I argue that we engage in narrative to reach a more adept state of belonging; and that, in this basic sense, narrative is foundational to our being in the world, especially to our practical need for emplacement.

Moreover, building on this anthropological approach to narrative, I propose an understanding of narrative art in which the novel, with its endlessly malleable and searching form, assumes a special place. The following four chapters are meditations on this place, each based on one novel with its own situational and formal ramifications for the project of theorizing narrative use based on the human need to belong, and conjointly reaching across four centuries in probing narrative modes of emplacement and agency. These novels are American novels, which means they come from a place where belonging is even less of a given then in other parts of the modern world. They will take us to four iconic and conflicted sites of U.S. cultural history—the frontier, the region, the ghetto, the homeland—that are prone to bring out both the salience and significance of having a place in a changing world, and the proactive role that narrative assumes in the making und unmaking of this place.

Uses of Narrative

In a most basic sense, narrative is a kind of language use in which an act of telling serves the end of interconnecting dispersed elements across space and time, generally to reconstruct what has happened. And just as any other kind of language use, narrative is inherently dialogic—which is, of course, crucial to its use. It is geared toward a receiver with the hope of engaging her in an act of exchange. This exchange is never neutral; on the contrary, it always entails a desire for change in the receiver, be it of opinion, feeling, or mood. But change will not occur unless the receiver gets in on the narrative act. Participation can be light and wavering, a cruising through a narrative to grasp the plot and indulge in select passages (Barthes, *Pleasure* 10-13), but ideally it takes the form of playing along with the demands put forth by a specific mode of exchange. Yet no matter how we participate, it is the particular and concrete form of a narrative that regulates the terms of participation and exchange.

Theorists have described the dialogic dimension of narrative in terms of contract, transfer, transference, transaction, and feedback loops (Barthes, *Pleasure* 95-96; Iser, *Fictive* 236-48; Fluck (building on Iser), *Romance* 365-84; Brooks, *Reading* 216-37; Schwab, *Subjects* 22-48; Phelan, *Fiction* 5), and they have defined its purpose or use in terms of pleasure, desire, imaginary self-extension, and inner growth.

In all of these cases, time is the implied measure of purpose and use. Engaging in narrative can yield a pleasure that either confirms or disrupts the continuity of one's self (Barthes, *Pleasure* 14). It can keep the boundaries of the self open over time (Iser, *Prospecting* 242-248; Schwab, *Subjects* 22-28). And in progressing from beginning to end, it can cultivate of judgment (Phelan, *Fiction* 133-148), advance fictional justice and recognition (Fluck, *Romance* 389-400; 446-449), and endorse and suspend the death-bound logic of time (Brooks, *Reading* 107-112). Given the widely accepted understanding of narrative as a representation (and hence reconstruction) of events that have happened in the past, and given the vast body of theoretical work dedicated to the structural and philosophical problems that arise from this retrospective mode of engaging with the world, this inclination is hardly surprising.[3] Some of the most sweeping and philosophically ambitious narrative theories (Paul Ricoeur's *Time and Narrative*, Peter Brooks's *Reading for the Plot*) conceive narrative as a dialogical model of understanding that is especially useful to grapple with the problem of human temporality and time-boundedness. They examine, for instance, how narrative, in both structuring time and progressively unfolding over time, teaches us basic lessons about the difference between past, present and future, or time and memory; and how narrative provides a virtual playing field for staging conflicts between Eros and the death drive, ultimately to the end of confronting our mortality (Ricoeur, *Time and Narrative*, Vol. 3.; Brooks, *Reading* 90-112).

So yes, narrative is an immensely useful resource when it comes to grappling with the complex and intangible realities of time, and in unfolding over time it can generate such marvelous things as insight, awareness, affirmation, and joy. But are the ties to human temporality as exclusive in determining narrative use as it appears through the lens of this scholarship? Consider, for instance, that narrative creates spatial (with Mikhail Bakhtin we may say "chronotopic") orders without which it would be incomprehensible. Such orders are always symbolically laden through hubs of power, areas with restricted access, conflicting regions (country vs. city), or journeys to foreign places. According to Jurij Lotman, whose narrative theory displays a rare awareness of matters of space, "[a] plot can always be reduced to a basic episode—the crossing of the basic topological border in the plot's spatial structure" (*Artistic Text* 238).[4] But space not only organizes narrative, it also drives and directs it. Moreover, and crucially, the medial and material form in

---

[3] If Lessing arguing in the *Laocoon* that literature a temporal, and hence more sophisticated art than the spatial art of painting is an early expression of this conundrum, Seymour Chatman's *Story and Discourse* and Paul Ricoeur's *Time and Narrative* are narratological and philosophical monuments. For more recent work on the topic see Currie, *About Time*; Grethlein; "Narrative Configuration."

[4] The works of Bakhtin and Lotman are two notable exceptions to the negligence of space by narrative theorists. See Zoran, "Space" for an early attempt to assess the significance of space for narrative theory.

and through which we engage with narrative is always extended in space. The size of a book in our hands, the layout of letters on a page or a screen, the space between individual words, paragraphs or images, all this directly affects our mode of engagement. Narrative's relation to space becomes even more basic when we consider that storytelling presupposes emplacement. Narrative acts are always conducted from somewhere, and this somewhere has a concrete spatial form (the face-to-face situation of oral storytelling, a particular desk at a particular place in time). And because narrative is inherently dialogic, it reaches out from that place toward an interlocutor who engages with it at an equally particular place (a favorite reading chair, a beach, a subway car, a prison cell). The transformative effects aimed for by any narrative act materialize in the space unfolding from this extended "narrative situation."[5] They are bound to change the mode of emplacement on either side of the dialogical bond, and the storyworld harbored by a narrative is the space in which the terms and trajectories of this transformation are laid out. There is indeed a complex network of spaces and places produced and interlinked in any narrative act that determine its use.

Hence, an important claim that I make in this book is that narrative does not merely engage us in ways that resemble real-life experience.[6] Positing that one's state of belonging can effectively change through narrative engagement implies that life and narrative are somehow continuous, that the boundaries between the storyworld and the actual world are more porous and permeable than it is usually assumed. Rethinking the relation between space, place and narrative is key to substantiating this point, which Edward Casey squares as: "No implacement without implotment" (461).[7] Perhaps inspired by the heightened currency of matters of space and place in literary and cultural studies, yet certainly under the influence of "postclassical" extensions of their field, narratologists have recently begun to pay more attention to the underrated relation between space and narrative.[8] Sparked by the advance of cognitive narratology, there is, for instance, a sizable interest in the spatial metaphors that we use to describe what narrative is and does. Scholars

---

5   The term is drawn from Stanzel, who uses it strictly to describe structural features of a narrative text.
6   This would be the constructivist approach embraced by narratologists such as Monika Fludernik, Ansgar Nünning, and Meir Sternberg, and recently reinvigorated in the burgeoning field of cognitive narratology, especially by David Herman and Manfred Jahn.
7   As much as I like how Casey's formula captures the first-person-perspective of phenomenology through the repeated "i," for the purpose of theorizing narrative it makes more sense to stick with the term "emplotment" and the corresponding "emplacement."
8   Among these extensions of classical narratology are inclusions visual and oral media, non-fictional genres such as memoir and autobiography, and rhetorical theory and cognitive sciences. The term "postclassical narratology" was first coined by David Herman in his book *Narratologies* and quickly gained traction thereafter. For a recent overview of this development see Alber and Fludernik, *Postclassical Narratology* and *The Living Handbook of Narratology*.

have described the cognitive work of expressions such as "plotline," "thread," and "circularity" as translating the notorious elusiveness of time and meaning into the more tangible realities of distance and direction, and they have described the "narrative is travel" metaphor as converting temporal progress into spatial sequence and as mobilizing space under the impact of reading and writing it.[9] Yet sage and important as these revaluations are in broadening our understanding of narrative use by complicating narrative's privileged relation to time, in the end they remain limited in the degree to which they shed light on narrative's spatial dimension. The main reason for this is that they stick to a representational model of narrative that, due to its core premise of narrative being a retrospective mode mediating objects and events across time, does not allow for any direct transaction between physical space and narrative use.[10]

Bridging this divide is key to the project to theorizing narrative based on the human need to belong. Step one in this endeavor is to complicate, and possibly part with received notions of narrative as a stable backdrop to the messiness of life.

Life and Narrative (and) Art

Approached in the traditional way, narrative's capacity to mend troubled states of belonging is strictly retrospective. Categorically removed from life, it elucidates what already *has* been lived; in fact, it can only function as a basic form of human understanding because it *re*-creates (and thus recovers) life from a safe distance. This also means that narrative is viewed as a cognitive instrument to impose meaning and order on the natural disorder of human existence.[11] But recently scholars

---

9 See Kemp, "The Inescapable Metaphor;" Mikkonen, "The Narrative as Travel Metaphor." I discuss their positions at greater length in my article "Spatial Forms."

10 This tendency also persists in more general reassessments of the significance of space in our understanding of narrative, of which Marie-Laure Ryan may be the most prolific proponent. Her work on the topic offers a typology of different manifestations of space in narrative, it traces these manifestations across different media, and it explores the relation of space and narrative together in collaboration with two geographers. But throughout this series of comprehensive and nuanced studies, and especially in the most recent, interdisciplinary one, the two domains remain clearly separated: There is space as an object of narrative representation, and there is narrative as a means of dealing with space. See Ryan, "Space;" "Narration in Various Media;" "Space, Place;" *Narrating Space*. I discuss her position at greater length in my article "Spatial Forms."

11 This understanding of narrative, which Metetoja aptly calls "epistemological" for its primary focus on understanding the world, rejects assumptions about "the nature of reality" including the ontological dimension of narrative, while indeed making a strong ontological claim in positing "a deeper level at which human, lived experience is immediately given, and human existence in general—as part of the flux of the real—is nonnarrative in character" ("Human Existence" 91).

from fields as diverse as sociology, anthropology, psychology, political philosophy, legal theory, feminist theory, and organizational theory have come to claim something vastly different about narrative; namely, that narrative is "an ontological condition of social life." In abrogating the received division between life and narrative, scholars aligning themselves with this position assert "that stories guide action; that people construct identities (however multiple and changing) by locating themselves or being located within a repertoire of emplotted stories; that 'experience' is constituted through narratives; [...] and that people are guided to act in certain ways, and not others, on the basis of the projections, expectations, and memories derived from a multiplicity but ultimately limited repertoire of available [...] narratives". And if "everything we know from the making of families, to coping with illness, to carrying out strikes and revolutions is at least in part a result of numerous cross-cutting story-lines in which social actors locate themselves" our common understanding of action and agency is in dire need of revision (Somers 613-14, 607).

For Margaret Somers, who I am quoting here, the "cross-cutting story-lines" that orchestrate social relations are strikingly spatial (as is Somers's entire "relational and network approach"). Addressing these same social relations from the perspective of human geography, Doreen Massey claims that they "always have spatial form and content: they exist, necessarily, both *in* space (i.e. in a locational relation to other social phenomena) and *across* space." In fact, Massey defines space as "the vast complexity of the interlocking and articulating nets of social relations." Conversely, "a 'place' is formed out of the particular set of social relations which interact at a particular location." Delving deeper into the social mechanisms of place-making, Massey expounds: "the singularity of any individual place is formed in part out of the specificity of the interactions which occur at that location [...] and in part out of the fact that the meeting of those social relations at that location [...] will in turn produce new social effects" (*Space, Place* 168). So yes, the places in which we dwell are formed out of ever-shifting sets and networks of social relations. But how do the social effects that, in altering these constellations, continuously make and remake these places materialize, take hold, and spread? Because social actors locate themselves and draw on an available repertoire of storylines—which is another way of saying that narrative plays a formative role in the production of space and place.[12]

See also Metetoja, *Narrative Turn*, which reconstructs the troubled career of storytelling from the postwar crisis to its recent return.

12 If it makes a lot of sense to assume that narrative plays a crucial part in the production of space and place it is important to stress that practically none of the thinkers of the spatial turn—Henri Lefebvre, Edward Soja and Doreen Massey come to mind—have given thought to this nexus. A notable exception is the opening chapter of Massey's *For Space*, which I discuss at length in my essay "Spatial Forms." The few works that do engage with both space and narrative—such as

Recent developments in social psychology confirm these ideas.[13] For Kenneth and Mary Gergen, two of its leading proponents, "[t]he present analysis stops short of saying that lives are narrative events. [...] Stories are after all forms of accounting, and it seems misleading to equate the account with its putative object. However, narrative accounts are embedded within social action. Events are rendered socially visible through narrative, and they are typically used to render expectations for future events." I find this argument highly compelling: Events "become laden with a storied sense" because our daily lives are immersed in narrative; they "acquire the reality of a 'beginning,' a 'climax,' a 'low point,' an 'ending' and so on," and in turn, they are experienced in accordance with how they are indexed, both individually and collectively. Tying this back to the question of how narrative participates in the production of place, the social effects that drive this operation materialize, take hold, and spread in part because life is imbued with narrative. "In a significant sense, then, we live by stories—both in the telling and the doing of the self" (18). And this is where narrative art enters the picture. According to the Gergens, the stories by which we live are taken more or less directly from the realm of art—not in the sense of life copying art but in the sense of art being "the vehicle through which the reality of life is generated" (18). The Gergens do not say more on this issue, but if art is assigned with the role of a privileged creator of scripts for our everyday use, it must be conceived as a separate realm in which we can experience things without pragmatic consequences (there is no need to call the police when reading about a mass murderer in a novel).

So yes, the stories by which we live are deeply pervaded with all those novels, memoirs, graphic narratives, films, television series, computer games, in short, with the narrative art and media that we routinely engage with. But how to account for the quizzical fact that the stories by which we live seem to gravitate toward these artistic forms, and what does this mean for the ties between belonging and narrative that are the topic of this study? It means, first and foremost, that narrative art is more directly invested in matters of belonging than it might seem at first sight. In being one step removed from the messiness of life (and thus committed to representing rather than living it), it stages and explores the narrative drive engendered by the need for a place in the world as a life-sustaining "need to tell." And by this I mean that human beings (for reasons to be further explored in the following section) interpret their surroundings and articulate their being in the world in relation to them, hoping that someone is listening. The most practical way in which

---

Nye's *Space and Narrative* and Psarra's *Architecture and Narrative*—refrain from conceptualizing their interlocking productivities. The Special Issue on "Space, Place and Narrative" of *Zeitschrift für Anglistik und Amerikanistik*, ed. by Nicole Maruo-Schröder and myself aims at filling this gap.

13 For further examples see *Narrative Psychology*, ed. Sarbin; especially Sarbin's own contributions to this volume; *Hermeneutics and Psychological Theory*, ed. Messer, Sass, and Woolfolk; *Advances in Experimental Social Psychology*, ed. Berkowitz.

concerns with belonging play out in narrative art is indeed in such interlocking acts of articulation and interpretation. These acts can take on an endless array of different forms, but they all share one basic feature: the assertion of narrative agency. And if agency is usually understood as the capacity to act within a given social world by making choices and imposing them on that world, narrative agency is the capacity of a narrating agent to make choices about the telling of her story and impose them on the (story)world.

Narrative agency is not unique to narrative art; on the contrary, it is an inherent feature of all narrative. But in the realm of art the choices that a teller has in terms of selection and combination multiply.[14] And if we conduct our lives in and through stories (rather than merely recounting them), social and narrative agencies converge in far-reaching ways. Think, for instance, of the forms of agency asserted through written correspondence, emails and text messaging in our present age, letter writing in earlier days and on special occasions still today. Early novels turned to the epistolary form to stage and explore this kind of agency. In fact, Charles Brockden Brown's *Edgar Huntly, or, Memoirs of a Sleepwalker* makes for such a productive read in the context of this study because the agency that comes with the form of the letter is both asserted and perverted in this novel (the letter-writing narrator is a sleepwalker). But narrative agency does not exist in a vacuum. As a mode of engaging with the world by imposing choices on the world, it brushes against given orders, be they real or imagined. And this is precisely how narrative agency is a staple of narrative art: Within the confines of a literary work, it takes shape against the backdrop of distinctive—chonotopic—conjunctions of psychic and spatial orders or imaginaries. Tracing these interlocking constellations and agencies is a primary aim of the following chapters, which take us to places as different as the post-revolutionary frontier, a remote and enchanted stretch of coastal Maine, an urban ghetto at the peak of immigration, and a Midwestern homeland haunted by environmental destruction and 9/11. And as my readings will show, four different models of the human psyche—based on the skeptical empiricism of John Locke and David Hume, Swedenborgian mysticism, Freudian psychoanalysis, and present-day neuroscience—are couched in these settings in ways that determine the actions performed in them and the dwelling places emerging from them.

---

14 While Butler conceded this much in her essay "Giving an Account of Oneself," she insists that this kind of (narrative) agency has severe limitations. Iser discusses the narrative *modus operandi* of selection and combination with regard to "fictionalizing acts," but the basic pattern of receptive engagement drawing from both the world of the text and the word of the reader to actualize a text and its meaning can be applied to reading in general. Fictionalizing acts, and by extension narrative acts in general, make themselves and their strategies of world-making "observable" through the necessity of selection and combination. See Iser, "Fictionalizing Acts."

In tracing how narrative agency evolves amidst the places and people in which and from whom belonging is sought, I assume that the forms that such agency gains within a literary text—in the novels considered here through the letter, the sketch, the found object, and the brain-as-storytelling-machine—can travel beyond the confines of the text. Caroline Levine has recently made similar claims about form. To assess form in both its social and aesthetic dimensions and capture the complex relation between the two, she borrows the concept affordance from design theory, where it describes "the potential uses or actions latent in materials and designs" (*Forms* 6) resulting from the limits and restrictions that make a particular form distinctive. Narrative agency as I conceive it is latent in narrative materials and designs in precisely this way—"*carr[ying] its affordances with it*" (19; emphasis in the original) when moving back and forth between the social and the literary world. However, my own thinking on the social relevance and mobility of narrative forms is invested in reception aesthetics rather than formalism, especially in Wolfgang Iser's notion of the articulation effect of fiction. For Iser, fiction has the power to express and make available to experience what would otherwise be diffuse and mute. If structuralism has taught us that these articulations are condemned to reiterate the codes and conventions in and through which they operate, I have no intention to refute this view. But giving account of uncertain states of belonging involves a struggle with the unsayable that almost by default pushes narrative toward and across the limits of the sayable. Narrative is, through this experiential disposition, equipped with an inherent drive toward exposing and transgressing its own conventionality, and this drive can unfold with fewer constraints in the depragmatized realm of art. Why? Because this realm is "bound to mobilize the imaginary in a different manner, for it has far less of the pragmatic orientation required by the subject, by thetic consciousness, or by the socio-historical, all of which channel the imaginary in quite specific directions" (Iser, *Fictive* 224).

The performative "play of the text" (Iser, *Prospecting* 249-61) that becomes tangible here opens up a space in between the world of the text and the world of the reader, between what is imagined and what is real. And when a reader inhabits this space, the two worlds become permeable. It is for this reason that engaging with fiction—which Iser defines as an activity, fiction as shorthand for "fictionalizing acts"—can lead to a revision of the narrative frames and formulas by which we live. Narrative thus reinvigorates itself in and through art, and in doing so, it perpetually refurbishes its potential use. Paul Ricoeur speaks of a "life of narrative activity" to describe this autopoetic thrust of narrative: Sustained by an ever-changing repertoire of experiences brought to language, it thrives on a tension between sedimentation and innovation that creates ever-new forms ("Life in Quest" 24). Note the point of convergence here: Both Iser and Ricoeur contend that new narrative forms become available beyond the realm of art in the fusion of the world of the text and the world of the reader. And this leads Iser to insist that narrative art is always invested in use. Its "pragmatic significance […] for action becomes unmistakable" once we acknowledge this dimension (*The Fictive* 168). Dorothy's call epitomizes this kind of action: it gets her home and ends the story. But if narrative is both produced and consumed out of the yearning for a place in the world, the main attraction of engaging in it may reside less in the promise to get home, and more in the promise to go on a journey—not necessarily to get home but to encounter new modes of dwelling, and to try out new forms of agency along the way.

In proposing that narrative is a practical component of dwelling in the world, the larger goal of this book is to unsettle prevailing views of narrative as a mere mechanism of ideology. To this day, such views dominate literary and cultural studies, especially my field, American studies, in which narrative is mainly of interest to find out how a literary text fits into a larger discursive field, and particularly how it collaborates in regulating the subject positions contained in this field. But this interpretive framework comes at a cost, for it presupposes a relation between a literary text and its reader that is located, first and foremost, on a conceptual (or cognitive) level. A resistant reception penetrates its object intellectually while affective mobilization is seen as manipulation. From such a perspective, aesthetic experience is reduced to a mere function of interpellation, and conversely, art produces "aesthetic regimes" that the critic must resist and unravel.[15] Yet if we have come to take it for granted that even the most idiosyncratic, incoherent, or open-ended account of where, how, or to whom one belongs is conducted within ideological constraints, how can radical proclamations of non-belonging (politically desirable as they may seem) be fundamentally different? Is the refusal to belong not just another narrative of belonging, another way of using the form-giving power of narrative to carve out a place in the world for oneself, tenuous and provisional as it might be?

Giving an account of where, how, and to whom one belongs is indeed nearly impossible to resist; it is too deep-seated a psychic and social need.[16] Suspicions of this need take us to a well-known terrain: As a subject-forming power to be exposed and disseminated at almost all costs, the prescriptive aspects of narrative are an all-too-familiar target in the "resistance paradigm." But while there can be no doubt that narrative is inclined to bring disparate elements into a socially intelligible (and thus at least somewhat coercive) whole, using narrative as the mediating structure through which we feel and direct our need for a place in the world is bound to extend and revise existing forms and norms simply because they do not seamlessly fit. In a narrative theory based on the human need to belong a

---

15 The term "aesthetic regime" is drawn from Rancière. For strong critiques of the resistance paradigm see Fluck, "Theories of American Culture;" Ickstadt, "Pluralist Aesthetics;" Voelz, *Transcendental Resistance*.
16 Judith Butler has taken up this issue in her aforementioned essay "Giving an Account of Oneself." See also Ricoeur, "Narrative Identity;" Ezzy, "Theorizing Narrative Identity." A good example of the critical desire for radical states of non-belonging is Pease, "Remapping the Transnational Turn."

double bind of coercion and transgression thus emerges as a motor force connecting narrative use and narrative art. From such a perspective, the need to tell that stems from and gives shape to the human need for a place in the world becomes a critical resource for tracing concerns with and limits of belonging at particular conjunctions of time, space, and social being. In confronting the subject-forming power of narrative as a symbolic structure with an interest in the human need to tell that operates in and through this structure, the experiential dimension inherent to any regimic mode of "distributing the sensible" (Rancière 13)—its eccentric involvement with making and unmaking this structure—gains critical weight.

Subjects of Belonging

If this theory defines narrative primarily in terms of use we need to know more about the *user* in this equation: about the human being—which is, almost by default, conceived in terms of its being a subject—engaging with narrative out of an existential need to belong, and about how this disposition defines its relation to the world. Acknowledged or not, assumptions about human being and subjectivity subtend any theorization of art and culture (either by way of endorsing or by way of rejecting notions of human expressivity). Narrative theory is no exception, and for one that is based on the human need to belong, spelling out these assumptions is a must. Moreover, it provides an occasion to explicate the anthropological premises of some other narrative theories. My own search for theoretical models has led me to the anthropological philosophy of Helmuth Plessner, especially to his notion of "eccentric positionality," which I want to briefly introduce before broadening the discussion.[17]

For Plessner, all matter can be defined by the ways in which it is positioned in the environment, and the first distinction he introduces is that between live and dead matter: Live matter has bodies, and these bodies not merely have contours, they have boundaries. Moreover, and crucially, the traffic across these boundaries defines their place (or positionality) in the world. Plants, for instance, are living

---

17 Plessner's work has been subject to a remarkable rediscovery in recent years, but remains little known outside of the German-speaking academic world because only a fraction of it has been translated. An English translation of Plessner's monumental *Stufen des Organischen und der Mensch*, originally published in 1928, is currently in the making. A first effort to present Plessner's philosophical anthropology to the English-speaking academic world is de Mul, *Plessner's Philosophical Anthropology*. See Horstmannshoff, *The Loop* for an insightful discussion of Plessner's model of subjectivity and its ramifications for the study of human space-boundedness. In stressing the "ecstatic" dimension that engenders human consciousness by pulling it out of itself, Judith Butler's recently republished reading of Hegel's *Phenomenology of the Spirit* in *Subjects of Desire* is engaged with related concerns.

bodies with no special relation to their boundaries, and this makes their positionality *open*. Animals do have a special relation to their boundaries; in fact, their high-strung nervous system makes their positionality *closed*. Human beings have a self-reflexive relation to their boundaries; they not only live and experience their lives, but they also *experience the experience* of their lives. And this decenters their positionality, making it *eccentric*. In Plessner's words, "[wo]man is not in an equilibrium, [she] is without a place, stands outside time in nothingness, is characterized by a constitutive homelessness (*ist konstitutiv heimatlos*). [She] always still has to become 'something' and create an equilibrium for [herself]." And because this state is "unbearable" it becomes the "ultimate foundation of the *technical artifact* (*Werkzeug*) and that which it serves: *culture*." In fact, the eccentric positionality of human beings is what makes them "artificial by nature" (*Schriften* IV 385; my translation, emphasis in the original).[18]

Based on this model, I contend that human beings are incomplete—non-sustained—without narrative; that in engaging with narrative, they assert— create, build—a place in the world. In substantiating this claim, I want to broaden the discussion. Defining human being via a fundamental lack, and assigning art and culture with a primary role in remedying this lack grew into a sprawling discourse in the twentieth century, with philosophical anthropology, phenomenology and psychoanalysis as its main intellectual venues. Plessner's "eccentric positionality," Martin Heidegger's assumption that human beings are "thrown" (*geworfen*) into a world without meaning, Jean-Paul Sartre's notion of the "absolute freedom" to which man is condemned, Sigmund Freud's notion of "the uncanny" (*das Unheimliche*) haunting us where we feel most secure and familiar, Jacques Lacan's "mirror stage" as a primal scene of a subject formation based on misrecognition, these are all figurations of the modern subject, uprooted and alienated, some of them "paranoid, even fascistic" (Foster, *Return* 226).[19] What they all have in common

---

18   In the final chapter of *Stufen des Organischen*, Plessner deducts three anthropological laws from human beings' eccentric positionality: (1) that human beings live in a state of "natural artificiality" that give occasion to the production of culture; (2) that they live in a state of "mediated immediacy," condemned to express themselves again and again to find themselves; and (3) being the animal with a utopian standpoint, they are always searching for a secure place—thus the monopoly of religion—yet unable to ever reach it.

19   "Ghosted in his theory," writes Hal Forster about this implicit historicity of Lacan's mirror stage, "is a contemporary history of which fascism is the extreme symptom: a history of world war and military mutilation, of industrial discipline and mechanical fragmentation, of mercenary murder and political terror. In relation to such events the modern subject becomes armored—against otherness from within (sexuality, the unconscious) and otherness without (for the fascists this can mean Jews, Communists, gays, women), all figures of this fear of the body in pieces come again, of the body given over to the fragmentary and the fluid" (*Return* 226). I find this observation more than apt. Set into perspective like this, Lacan's theory of subject formation becomes

is a conflicted and uncertain sense of belonging—and this tell us that theoretical vogues are bound up with concerns with belonging as well. One can only speculate about why poststructuralist models, with their alleged relativism and their respective marginalization of existential concerns have exhausted their explanatory power while materialist approaches such as object-oriented ontology, speculative realism and cognitive linguistics are on the rise today, but it seems safe to say that our thoroughly globalized, mobilized, and digitally mediated world has given new relevance to questions of belonging.

This book is part of this *zeitgeist*, but contrary to the new materialisms, which tend to deemphasize or even level the significance of the human, its goal is to think beyond the postmodern *without* eliminating its "residual humanism" (McGurl, "Geology" 380). And for this project, anthropological philosophy and phenomenological hermeneutics offer useful alternatives to the psychoanalytical models of subject-formation (grounded in Lacan's mirror stage and Althusser's notion of ideological interpellation based on Lacan) that have come to dominate critical discourse in the wake of the linguistic turn.[20] My point of departure in assessing these models is something they have in common: They all base their notion of what it means to be human on the idea of a constitutive lack. But this lack is conceived in different ways, with vast implications as of how human beings are shaped by this lack, and of narrative's role in shaping—constituting—human beings.

In psychoanalytic models, narrative springs from the experience of losing an undifferentiated state of wholeness: the state of being one with the nurturing mother. Driven a relentless desire (Peter Brooks even calls it a *narrative desire*) for something irretrievably lost, narrative generates projections that range from nostalgic regress to utopian transgression. As such, it is immensely productive, a force that coerces us to imagine and act in order to make up for what is perceived as lacking. These operations are irreducible to expressing and giving coherence to a mere want, for they are backed by a visceral need to belong not unlike the irreducible needs of the material body.[21] In fact, the primordial experience of loss creates a

---

tangible as a historically conditioned radicalization of the Freudian, narcissistic loss of undifferentiated wholeness—a conceptual move with far-reaching implications for the possibilities of entertaining a sense of belonging within the frame of this particular model.

20 See McGurl, "Geology" for a lucid discussion of how speculative realism and object-oriented ontology endorse an amplified antihumanism as a means of thinking beyond the latent humanism of the postmodern. For recent returns to Heidegger and Plessner see, for instance, the 2017 *Modern Fiction Studies* Issue on "Dwelling in the Global Age" and de Mul, *Plessner's Philosophical Anthropology*.

21 This need-and-demand structure of "narrative desire" follows Lacan's reinterpretation of the Freudian concept, in which desire is born from a split between need (for nourishment/the mother's breast) and demand (for love). It is "irreducible to need, for it is not in its principle relation to a real object, independent of the subject, but rather to a phantasy; it is irreducible to demand, in

psychosomatic sense of incompleteness that narrative seeks to mend, for Brooks by enlisting the rivaling forces (or desires) of Eros and the death drive for engendering plot. And since narrative desire is ultimately the desire for the end (death, quiescence, non-narratibility), narration serves as the tool with which to emplot one's life "toward [that] end under the compulsion of imposed delay" (Brooks, *Reading* 295).[22] Read along these lines, Dorothy's act of calling her home into existence promises verbal eloquence and psychic enchantment but no material gratification. And by the same token, maturing in matters of belonging increases the capacity to transform material need into psychic demand. But the underlying need is never replenished. It leaves "memory traces" (55) that seek—demand—realization in the realm of the imaginary, in places like Oz. From a Lacanian perspective, such places are imaginary in troublesome ways: As phantasmatic images of wholeness they reiterate (and thus keep alive) the primal scene of loss. Where a Freudian desire to belong is quintessentially the desire of one's death (prompting Brooks to argue that narrative desire is ultimately the desire for the end, for a promised state of quiescence), the Lacanian counterpart is essentially circular, leading to ever more desire, and never to more belonging.

So yes, there are different psychoanalytical models, but in one aspect they all agree: The yearning subject may dream of, yearn for, or even contest having a place in the world—but it cannot *build* such a place, for the place that is longed for is quintessentially phantasmatic. It may have been these implications that led Gabriele Schwab, in her psychoanalytical model, to D. W. Winnicott rather than to Freud or Lacan. For Winnicott, the mother's absence creates a "transitional space" that functions "as a space for the imagination's testing and mastering of the demands and tasks posed by the gradual development of intersubjectivity"—a process that makes this space potentially generative of poetic speech with the effect of alleviating the subject's entanglement with the symbolic order (*Subjects* 22-48; here 28).[23] In fact, the psychic space of "transference" invites the subject to continually reshape its boundaries through an imaginary encounter with others. This also means that narrative use does not necessarily create misrecognition (as it does for Lacan); it can indeed lead to valuable transformation. Narrative art assumes a special role in this model that points toward Schwab's affiliation with Wolfgang Iser and the Constance School. In providing protected versions of this psychic space,

---

that it seeks to impose itself without taking account of language and the unconscious of the other, and insists on being absolutely recognized by the other" (Laplanche and Pontalis, *Vocabulaire de la psychoanalyse* 122; quoted in Brooks, *Reading* 55).

22 Freud's *Beyond the Pleasure Principle* is the "masterplot" of Brooks's narrative theory. See Chap. 2, which was separately published before as "Freud's Masterplot."

23 See also Schwab, *Mirror* 1-46. Coming out of the Constance School, Schwab casts her notion of reading as an act of "transference" deliberately against Iser's notion of "transfer," which she finds too schematic in its intersubjective engagement with the other.

narrative art assures that the experience of breaking down the boundaries between the real and the imaginary can be reenacted throughout a person's life. For Schwab, narrative gravitates toward poetic expression and fictional boundary-crossing because human beings yearn for an "other." This understanding of narrative corresponds with a psychic structure that is highly amenable to change and explicitly geared toward imaginative culture. And yet, the transformation that it envisions remains confined to a logic of internalization and projection: The yearning subject may keep readjusting its boundaries when engaging with narrative art time and again, but it cannot transform what lies beyond them.

Peter Brooks argues along similar lines when proposing that all narrative acts are bound to "discover, and make use of" the intersubjective and inherently dialogic nature of language itself (*Reading* 60). Embedded in this discovery is the secret of "narrative transference"—Brooks's ruby red slippers. "The motivation of plotting is intimately connected to the desire of narrating, the desire to tell, which in turn has to do with the desire for an interlocutor, a listener, who enters into the narrative exchange" (216). Turning to Roland Barthes's notion of the "contractual" nature of all storytelling—its asking for something in return for what it supplies—Brooks contends that contract is too static a term to conceive of this exchange; unsuited to acknowledge the degree of transformation invoked by it. I could not agree more with this assessment, especially of the yearning for a receiving other that is both expressed and pursued in and through narrative. But I also cannot fail to notice how close these ideas are to the basic premise of reception aesthetics,: that narrative is incomplete without a willing receiver, and that theorizing narrative must thus account for the insurmountably (inter)subjective and provisional dimension of transfer and exchange. Schwab makes a similar move when combining Winnicott's transitional space with George Poulet's phenomenology of reading to substantiate the transformative capacities of consuming narratives (*Mirror* 25-27).[24] It is worth pondering over these phenomenological proxies here for another moment, for they bring out a striking disposition of the psychoanalytical model of subjectiviy: Without at least a hint of the decidedly spatial positioning of the subject envisioned by phenomenologists (and especially without the *thetic* move toward the world that this school of though tends to stress), engaging in narrative is a self-serving operation of desire. What it engenders is nothing but a mere symptom of an insurmountable state of lack. And while the results of this relentless process may be interesting or even innovative manifestations of the basic lack of and from which they speak, their only remedy is to "love" or "enjoy" one's symptom.[25]

---

[24] Another important point of reference for Schwab is Kristeva's *Revolution in Poetic Language*. In this early monograph, Kristeva, who is usually steeped in psychoanalysis and poststucturalism, turns to Husserl's idea of the "thetic" to conceptualize signification's inherent positionality, its indispensable and processual working across space.

[25] This last formulation evokes Žižek, *Enjoy Your Symptom!*

What, then, do phenomenological models have to offer? They, too, assume that narrative is born out of lack, but this lack is not the result of a primary experience of loss; it is in and by itself foundational. Human beings are not hardwired to the environment like other animals, and the lacking connectivity marks the world (when perceived by this "impaired" life-form) with a fundamental lack of meaning. Which is why human beings experience themselves as "thrown" (*geworfen*) into a world that is infinite and opaque. At the same time, however, realizing this lack of meaning and connectivity sets in motion a life-long activity of interpretation, to which the unknowability of one's death poses the greatest challenge.[26] This is the basic set-up of Heidegger's ontological hermeneutics and, acknowledged or not, it has vast repercussions on the works of Hans-Georg Gadamer, Paul Ricoeur, and the Constance School. All of them assume, in one way or another, that interpretation (which I view as a mode of narrative engagement) is a basic constituent, "an anthropological modality [...] that achieves a never-completed mediation between human beings and the world." For Gadamer, texts are the intermediary objects (*Zwischenprodukte*) of this activity, "their manifestation as writing operates as a temporary stasis in an ongoing dialogical process" (Schwab, *Mirror* 17). And although not a direct influence on these phenomenological hermeneutists, Plessner's model of "eccentric positionality" is seamlessly compatible with their ideas on this matter. Moreover, and crucially, Plesser's model links concerns with embodiment to the sources and trajectories of narrative use that become tangible here. To reiterate a point that I have made above, for Plessner, it is the self-reflexive relation of the human body to its boundaries that generates the recurring need to express its being in the world in relation to the environment. Narrative forms and practices exist for this very purpose.

It is important to stress that the lack of meaning and connectivity in phenomenological models is just as insurmountable as the lack of wholeness in psychoanalytical models. However, in not going back to a traumatic experience of loss (the lost state of wholeness with the nurturing mother), it is less inclined to produce hermetic states of mourning such as nostalgia or melancholia, or other self-enamoring desires. Rather, it is a type of lack that draws its bearer out of herself and into the world, forcing her to engage with the world. In Paul Ricoeur's words: "It is because there is first something to say, because we have an experience to bring to language, that conversely language is not only directed towards ideal meaning but also refers to what is" (*Interpretation* 21). The phenomenological type of lack thus leads directly to a yearning for voice and form—to language, which assumes its referentiality (and its narrative capacity) through the existential yearning to make the world over in terms that are meaningful. And because of this entanglement

---

26 See Heidegger, *Being and Time*, esp. chapters 4-6. *Da-sein*, Heidegger's term for this existential reality of human being, is not an unmediated basis of being, but in arising from its own projection, it is already the result of interpretation.

with the ontological condition of being in the world, human language is, according to Ricoeur, "not a world of its own. It is not even a world. But because we are in the world, because we are affected by situations, and because we orient ourselves comprehensively in those situations, we have something to say, we have an experience to bring to language" (*Interpretation* 20-21). (Perhaps we turn to etymology for precisely this reason: to decipher the changing character of experience brought to language from its shifting reference to what is.)

"Orientation," "situation," these are traces of narrative's spatial dimension. In Heidegger's notion of "dwelling," this dimension is much more pronounced. The experience of being thrown into a world that fundamentally lacks meaning (and thus lacks a securely given place) not only triggers a fundamental need for interpretation (and thus for narrative); it also leads to the realization that dwelling is not a given but a matter of *learning* to dwell. For Heidegger, being in the world assumes a place and sense of self through *building*—an activity that, if correctly performed, gathers dispersed aspects of the environment and sets human beings in relation to the world thus opened up for them to dwell. It is indeed the realization of this lack that "*calls* mortals into their dwelling" ("Building" 159; emphasis in the original).[27] And while it would, of course, be foolish to dispute Heidegger's deep-seated concern with human temporality, in his later work (starting in the postwar years) the experience of temporal contingency leads straight to an investment in place-making. But building may or may not succeed; in fact, it is the ability to *think* that enables both building and dwelling.[28] And this ability is tied to a sensuous mode of perception. Placed in a semantic field with terms such as "being let into" (*einlassen*), "being turned toward the world in a friendly manner" (*der Welt freundlich zugewandt sein*) and "nursing" (*hüten*) (Heidegger, "Was heißt denken?"; my translation), thinking is the primary means of becoming immersed in the world's lack of meaning.

---

27 In what reads like an anticipation of the spatial turn, Heidegger contends in this essay that we can only think of space as space used by human beings (and thus as social space), given to them through their need to dwell, and constantly changing under their building efforts. Here is one particularly iconic passage in this regard: "When we speak of man and space, it sounds as though man stood on one side, space on the other. Yet space is not something that faces man. It is neither an external object nor an inner experience. It is not that there are men, and over and above them *space;* for when I say 'a man,' and in saying this word think of a being who exists in a human manner—that is, who dwells—then by the name 'man' I already name the stay within the fourfold among things. [...] Spaces, and with them space as such—'space'—are always provided for already within the stay of mortals. Spaces open up by the fact that they are let into the dwelling of man" ("Building" 154-55).

28 See Harris, *Ethical Function* for an extensive discussion of Heidegger's trialectic of building, dwelling, and thinking.

Moreover, and crucially, thinking can make present what it perceives. In a later essay, "... Poetically Man Dwells ...," these romantic implications are amplified in the move from thinking to *poiesis*, a hermeneutic practice that is assigned with the capacity to transform the world into a suitable dwelling place by means of taking imaginative measures.[29] For Heidegger, Hölderlin's poetry exemplifies these forth-bringing capacities of verbal art (the title of the essay is borrowed from Hölderlin), but is Dorothy's act of calling not a similar attempt of taking measure? Of exploiting the imagination to express and direct her longing for that place called home, and to realize and embrace its inherently evocative, provisional, and mediated nature? Two correlated trajectories become tangible here that I will further explore in the final section of this chapter. If Dorothy's call gives voice to a quintessentially *modern* sense of being in the world, what we discover at the end of her journey is an enhanced tie between belonging and narrative *art*. And if one of the challenges of modern life is that home often lacks a stable referent whose evocation could make this place present (like a passe-partout), calling out for that place may not be not enough. More often than not, it has to be built, word by word, sentence by sentence, storyline by storyline.[30]

---

29 The forth-bringing capacitiy that *poiesis* brings to dwelling resonates with Heidegger's general notion of art making present that which is not yet present and can only become present through art. See Heidegger, "Work of Art."
30 If heightened concerns with belonging in our present age make it worth returning to Heidegger today, such a move must reject his reactionary longings to return to an Arcadian place untouched by modernity at all cost. Plessner provides a wholesome counterweight here. For him, yearnings for a place in the world should resist the bourgeois overexpansion of inwardness that looms large in Heidegger's thinking (and in existence philosophy in general), and instead turn the constitutive inscrutability of human being into a political obligation. Writing against the backdrop of the Great War, the faltering Weimar Republic, and the rise and fall of Nazi totalitarianism, his Jewish background made him an ardent cosmopolitan where Heidegger wrote and dreamt about preserving his Black Forrest hut. The fault line between the private and the political that become tangible here (and that Plessner explores in his later work, especially in *Macht und menschliche Natur* and "Schicksal der Deutschen") is resurfacing today from a vastly different constellation, yet with undeniable force. How to deal with the injustices inflicted upon so many by a rampant financial capitalism and environmental recklessness, with religious and expansionist wars, and with the millions and millions of people left anxious and uprooted under these circumstances, mobilized not only by immediate threat or hardship, but also by digitally mediated notions of a better life circulating around the globe? If living in today's world has indeed lent new relevance to existential matters, a return to existence philosophy is only feasible when its traditional concerns with private wellbeing and self-realization are opened up to larger social responsibilities. See, for instance, the conference on "Political Existence" at the Centre for Studies in Practical Knowledge and Philosophy Department at Södertörn University, Sweden in November 2015.

A hermeneutics of dwelling, in the poetic sense suggested here, is not a genuinely phantasmatic enterprise. It is a practical function of narrative, and perhaps even its primary use. That this use gravitates to the realm of art to give meaning and mooring to our lives makes it an especially potent remedy; in fact, without this drift, the stories by which we live would soon become stale and our dwelling places out of sync with our needs.[31]

Historical Trajectories

Expanding narrative into the ontological realm is a contestable enterprise, which is why I want to revisit and contextualize this claim. According to Stephen White, whom I will follow here for a moment, the recent "turn" toward ontology gained traction once the term no longer referred to a restricted field of philosophical scrutiny into matters of being but to a more general questioning of what "entities" are presupposed by our theories. Ontological concerns have hence migrated from philosophy to other fields, among them cultural and literary studies, where they have surfaced in claims about affect, language, narrative, objects and subjects.[32] And if the sense of uncertainty brought about by the crisis of late modernity has affected many of the things taken for granted in the modern world, the new interest in ontology may very well be "the result of a growing propensity to interrogate more carefully those 'entities' presupposed by our typical ways of seeing and doing" (4). In the proverbial front row of these interrogations are "enlightened" ideas about the human subject, sustained by the familiar subscriptions to its self-reliant and socially disengaged autonomy. Ontological commitments growing out of the waning certainty about the "Teflon" constitution of the modern subject hence seek to replace it with a "stickier" one, with the effect of stressing its manifold dependencies on natural, social, and cultural worlds. Conceiving the subject through an existentially imposed and narratively sustained need to belong is such a commitment.[33]

---

31 Riceour uses the term *pharmakon* to describe this alleviating, healing dimension of narrative. *Interpretation Theory* 43; quoted in Valdés, "Introduction" 6.
32 For the first development see, for instance, Hemmings, "Invoking Affect;" McDonald, "Language and Being," and "The Ontological Turn." Some key texts of the second development are Deleuze and Guattari, *A Thousand Plateaus;* Meillassoux, *After Finitude;* Gabriel, *Transcendental Ontology;* Bennett, *Vibrant Matter;* Latour, *Reassembling the Social;* Harman, *Guerilla Metaphysics.*
33 It is worth stressing that this line of reasoning is seamlessly compatible with posthuman revisions of this "entity," for it locates the life-form in question in a thoroughly hybrid space between its being and its environment. And if the network (with its familiar challenges to nature-technology and subject-object dichotomies) has become the dominant mode of life-world, the life-form in need to belong may or may not be human anymore; yet it is still quintessentially weak and mortal, and still inclined to use its narrative capacitates to deal with these basic vulnerabilities.

For White, the new commitments go hand in hand with a shift from "strong" to "weak" ontologies—ontologies that, rather than positing foundations of human being whose validity is categorically unchanging and of universal reach, operate upon a basic set of conceptualizations that are at once fundamental *and* contestable. Instead of postulating fixed ideas of "human nature or telos," they present context-bound "figurations of human being in terms of certain existential realities." And while these realities are "in some brute sense universal constituents of human being" (9), their meaning, even when analyzed in the most clearly defined correlations, is categorically indeterminable (no matter how closely we scrutinize language, life, or death, we will not find a discernible essence or terminal meaning). My contestable claim, then, is that human engagement with narrative is one of these existential realities; that narrative springs from the eerie feeling that we are weak and mortal, and that using its mediating capacities is imperative if life is to be moored and meaningful. The ways in which we feel weak and mortal are, of course, never fully articulable, and they change over space and time, place and lifespan. But modern life has amplified these feelings, and in doing so it has boosted narrative productivity. For when the old keepers of certainty (such as feudalism and theology) lost their coercive powers, narrative offered itself as a viable tool to counteract the vastly multiplying, accelerating, and often persistent feelings of uncertainty that people now had to face. An increased and increasingly metamorphosing engagement with narrative has thus been generated as the articulating, structuring, and implementing *agent* of belonging.

The etymological history of the term bears traces of these developments. At first, "belonging" was strictly used in the substantive plural to refer to objects of possession ("my belongings"), but by the mid-eighteenth century this use was complemented by the abstract singular ("belonging") that denotes the existential, emotional state that concerns us here. This semantic drift away from substantive, unilateral claims of ownership (and, by extension, to a secure and proper place in the world) points toward a profound restructuring in the social organization of property: In the emerging market economy, material possessions began to take on a supplementary rather than a stabilizing function; as "goods" they were perpetually consumed rather than securely possessed. In this situation, belonging assumes a new meaning ("to belong") that testifies to an increased need to make use of the verbal capacity to bind and cohere. This capacity was further enhanced by the fact that the new term was intransitive: It reaches out and moves toward something (a place, a person) to become complete, and this quality enhances its use for orientation.[34] In sum, the change was substantial. "Belonging" now functioned as a relative rather than an absolute marker of position, which also means that it became

---

34 This etymological assessment is based on *The Oxford English Dictionary* (Oxford: Oxford UP, 1933 reprint 1961); *The Barnhart Dictionary of Etymology* (H.W. Wilson, 1988); *The Oxford Dictionary of English Etymology*. Oxford: Oxford UP, 1966); *A Concise Anglo-Saxon Dictionary*, Second Ed.

inherently deictic. Indeed, the structural incompleteness marking it now served to enhance and proliferate the practical ties between belonging and narrative.

Once again, the relation between space and narrative offers itself as a viable trajectory along which to expound these ideas further. Following Edward Soja, I take the recurring "recomposition[s] of space-time-being in their concrete forms" that are the result of modernization as constitutive of the ever-shifting, heterogeneous fabric of social being that Soja calls modernity (*Postmodern Geographies* 27). And from this notion of modernity as modernization, and modernization as a dynamic compound of temporal, spatial and social forces, it is just a small step to arguing that the perpetual transformations thus unleashed are conducted to a substantive degree through narrative. Which brings me to Henri Lefebvre's famous model of space as produced in a trialectic of perceived space (*espace perçu*), conceived space (*espace conçu*), and lived (including represented) space (*espace vecu*): Lefebvre does not mention narrative in his model of spatial production, but from the perspective of this study there can be no doubt that it features prominently throughout. In the conceptual mode of producing space, it plays a key role in architectural planning, legal discourse, building instructions, and so forth. It pervades the perceptual mode of producing space in the manifold processes of cognitive mapping, especially the correlation of perceptions and memories. And it essential for the lived mode of spatial production, for instance in the fabrication of tales and images that charge space with habitual, symbolic, or ritualistic value, and that are indispensible to making it familiar and meaningful. Spelling out these transactions has vast repercussions for matters of narrative use, especially for the aspect of *narrative agency*. In fact, an important claim that I make in this book is that the frequent recompositions of time, space and social being caused by modernization have turned this kind of agency into a crucial skill—and, respectively, into a highly desirable good for consumption and consummation.

Even so, it would be wrong to assume that modernity invented belonging. Rather, it laid open a fundamental uncertainty in the human condition that was formerly covered up by the coercive epistemologies of religion and feudalism, and that now prompted a relentless narrative productiviy. The "modernized" need to belong is indeed thoroughly mobilized, inclined to build ever-new homes, often by turning inward rather than outward, or by attaching itself to a series of homes rather than to just one that is thought to be singular and irreplaceable. In our own—global, digital—age, the spatial correlatives of belonging have become increasingly vexed as geographical and social spaces are less and less congruent, and dwelling practices are potentially ever more deterritorialized.[35] In fact, modern life

---

(New York: Macmillan, 1916); *Dictionary.com Unabridged*, based on the Random House Dictionary, http://dictionary.reference.com; *Middle English Dictionary*, http://quod.lib.umich.edu.

35 See, for instance, Beck, "Vorwort." Arjun Appadurai goes so far as to argue that dwelling in the world has become so drastically deterritorialized and infused with imagining one's life based on

has gradually dematerialized the modalities of belonging, shifting them away from beloved and presumably stable landscapes, dwellings, and social bonds, away from a soil that has been cultivated by one's family for generations, away from durable and secure possessions, away from struggles over ownership and dispossession—and toward the world of letters and the imagination.

These claims are at once vastly general and decidedly limited. My argument is, first and foremost, an argument about the changing uses of narrative in the ever-changing fabric of modern life. Specifically, I suggest that within the uneven continuum of modernity, the advent of *Neuzeit* opened up new trajectories for the structural and practical ties between belonging and narrative. Powered by the "discovery" of the Americas, the emergence of global trade systems, the rise of individualism, instrumental reason, and the "enlightened" formation of knowledge, the conditions of life changed substantially in the Western world around the time of the Renaissance, with the effect of enhancing the need for orientation and emplacement on a massive scale. In this situation, the demand for new stories to live by leaped to unprecedented heights, causing a sheer explosion of narrative, "whether in fiction, history, philosophy, or any of the social sciences," which dethroned theology and established history "as the key discourse and central imagination" (Brooks, *Reading* 5-6). The pertinence that historical storytelling gains at this time is a powerful token of narrative's altered function to mend troubled states of belonging in the modern world. The development was driven by a loss of providential plots and their capacity to settle doubts about the existential constituents of human being, and it absorbed, as Hayden White has forcefully argued, the basic modes and conventions of *literary* storytelling, with the effect of blurring the line between factual and fictional narrative in its scientific quest for meaning.[36]

The other significant change occurred in the realm of literary storytelling, most notably through the emerging form of the novel. The story of the novel as the paradigmatic literary form of modern life has often been told—so often that

---

the offerings of globalized mass media that "ethnography must redefine itself as that practice of representation which illuminates the power of large-scale, imagined life possibilities over specific life trajectories" ("Ethnoscapes" 200). However, he then only gives a most rudimentary sketch of what ethnography as a practice of representation may amount to, leaving aside how notions of representation are currently rethought in ontological terms. Similarly, Doreen Massey who, when contemplating the present state of "[t]hat place called home" in the light of these current challenges, insists that it "never was an unmediated experience" (*Space, Place* 164), but then does not care to address any of the further implications that this basic *necessity* of mediation has for matters of emplacement and belonging.

36 Applying Northrop Frye's formalist model to historiography, White argues that writing history follows the same basic narrative modes as fiction (comedy, tragedy, romance, satire), which are, in turn, inclined to use different kinds of figurative language (tragedy to metonymy, romance to synecdoche, satire to irony). See White, *Metahistory*, and "Literary Artifact."

is has become deeply engrained into the history of modernity itself. For Walter Benjamin, the rise of the novel bears testimony to an emerging state of alienation, brought forth by the capitalist rationalization of work routines. The resulting death of oral (and thus communal) storytelling solidifies this unfortunate state.[37] Arguing along similar lines, Georg Lukács sees in the novel the quintessential expression of a "transcendental homelessness" (*Theory* 41), "the epic of a world that has been abandoned by God" (88), "of an age in which […] the immanence of meaning in life has become a problem" (56). Its prototypical hero is a "product of estrangement from [an] outside world" (66) that has become internally heterogeneous and fractured. The novel responds to this unhomely world by turning the search for form into its primary artistic end, and in doing so, it "transform[s] itself into the normative *being of becoming*" (72-73, my emphasis). Mikhail Bakhtin, although diametrically opposed—enthusiastic—in judgment, confirms these observations. For him, the novel is "a genre-in-the-making" that we find "in the vanguard of all literary development (11)." Its "peculiar capacity to change" stems from "a very specific rupture in the history of European civilization: its emergence from a socially isolated and culturally deaf semipatriarchal society, and its entrance into international and interlingual contacts and relationships" (11)—in short, from the modernizing processes launched by *Neuzeit*.

That the novel "is determined by experience, knowledge and practice (the future)" (15) must have compelled an audience struggling with a profound loss of familiarity, with finding new ways of doing and making while facing a structurally uncertain future. There is no need to venture further into these well-known accounts to grasp how unanimously they insist on the novel's *functional* relation to modern life. For all of them, the new genre springs from a heightened sense of

---

37 See Benjamin, "The Storyteller." To cite two iconic passages from the essay's well-known argument: "The earliest symptom of a process whose end is the decline of storytelling is the rise of the novel at the beginning of modern times [*Neuzeit* in the German original]. What distinguishes the novel from the story (and from the epic in the narrower sense) is its essential dependence on the book. The dissemination of the novel became possible only with the invention of printing. […] The storyteller takes what he tells from experience—his own or that reported by others. And he in turn makes it the experience of those who are listening to his tale. The novelist has isolated himself. The birthplace of the novel is the solitary individual, who is no longer able to express himself by giving examples of his most important concerns, is himself uncounseled, and cannot counsel others." (363). Respectively, the model situation of oral storytelling is a pre-modern, artisan workplace that becomes extinct in the modern age: "The resident master craftsman and the traveling journeymen worked together in the same rooms; and every master had been a traveling journeyman before he settled down in his home town or somewhere else. If peasants and seamen were past masters of storytelling, the artisan class was its university. In it was combined the lore of far away places, such as a much-traveled man brings home, with the lore of the past, as it best reveals itself to natives of a place" (364-65).

instability, which it sutures by means of its extraordinarily amendable capacities of narrative form-giving. A mechanically facilitated printing process, the rise of an aspiring class of professional writers, and a fiction-hungry (largely bourgeois and often female) audience paved the novel's road to success, soon turning its comparatively unrefined, long form of storytelling into the most popular literary genre of the modern age. There were, however, initial suspicions against the seductive power on which the rise of the novel to become the first modern mass medium thrived. Heated debates revolved around the unpredictable effects that reading novels might have on the imagination—which had until then been strictly synonymous with mere illusion, just as fiction (which meant mostly sentimental fiction at the time) had the reputation of transporting its readers to make-believe worlds with the looming threat of forever corrupting their sense of morals and reality. Now these assumptions became porous, and novelists had their share in overhauling them.

In the transatlantic world, a small yet influential group of writers—among them Mary Wollstonecraft, William Goodwin, Thomas Holcraft, Robert Bage, Helen Maria Williams, and, in America, Charles Brockden Brown—began to claim that fiction harbored, precisely because of the imaginative power that it invoked, vital capacities for creating a better society.[38] The reformist ambitions of these writers were inspired by contemporary efforts to rethink the human mind, particularly those of John Locke and David Hume, who began to envision an autonomous psychic realm with new "demands" for the imagination. A fundamental rift (uncomfortable for Locke, insurmountable for Hume) was now assumed to separate an individual's inner and outer worlds, and the imagination seemed perfectly suited to bridge this gap: to correlate perceptions (sensory data stemming from the outer world) with memories (sensory data stemming from the inner world) and to mediate present and past experience.[39] I read the the parallel success stories of the

---

38   The early phase of the American novel in the crossfire of these debates is discussed in Davidson, *Revolution of the Word*, and Tompkins, *Sensational Designs*. For the abovenamed writers, new ideas about the imagination and its relation to sentiment served as a touchstone for a reformist literature. Strong emotion, they came to believe, could encourage moral behavior, and imaginative literature could thus become instrumental in fostering democratic societies. For work on these writers and their beliefs see Kelly, *The English Jacobin Novel*, and *English Fiction*; Clemit, *The Godwinian Novel*; Shapiro, *Culture and Commerce*.

39   To briefly rehearse the basic steps of this "remodeling" of the human mind: In his *Essay Concerning Human Understanding*, Locke claims that the human mind does not process innate ideas (as it does for Descartes) but begins its life as a *tabula rasa* on which sensory perceptions leave immediate and lasting imprints. Yet if this shift in thinking about the human mind—from a safely enclosed, self-contained entity to a genuinely vulnerable target of random impressions—corresponds to an uncertain, irritated sense of belonging of the subject to whom this mind belongs, Locke also pairs the mind's new vulnerability with a strong instinct for survival. Not only can the

novel and the imagination as a remarkable token of the era's heightened stakes of orientation—which is, after all, a successful correlation of perceptions and memories. In a situation in which the outer world must have lost much of its familiar appearance (and perceptions were almost by default strange and distorted), the newly designated faculty of the imagination equipped the inner world (and thus the very site where memories and perceptions were to be meaningfully connected) with a powerful yet precarious tool of recovery.

When the novel emerged as the preferred food for the imagination at right around this time, it populated these inner worlds with a sheer endless roundel of characters in search for something that might give meaning and mooring to their troubled lives. And as we move through the nineteenth century and beyond, ever-new genres and sub-genres, artistic forms and devices emerged, with visual storytelling (in both still and moving images) becoming an increasingly pertinent and creative force of narrative production. That many of the new forms were serialized bears an obvious attraction in light of the continuous need for narrative that is a staple of modern needs to belong. Scholars have recently stressed the distinct forms of purpose and use afforded by serial narrative (Kelleter, *Serial Narrative*), and the serial publication of novels in popular magazines that often preceded their book publication underscores this point. In one of the texts considered here, Sarah Orne Jewett's *The Country of the Pointed Firs*, serial publication had a feasible impact on the shifting form of the tale (it first appeared in a magazine, then as a book, then in a number of editions, all with different chapter numbers and arrangements). *Pointed Firs* is indeed an especially interesting case for this study, for it brings into view how profoundly these material and medial aspects change the terms of the narrative use. More importantly, however, the new narrative forms were all children of the novel: They responded to the amplification and pluralization of modern needs to belong with a proliferation of narrative form. Ever since the novel's modern inception in the eighteenth century, its structurally unrefined, endlessly malleable form (for Lukács, its "normative being of becoming," for Bakhtin the

---

mind repeat the simple ideas that it derives from sense perception but it also has the capacity (albeit still quite mechanical) to rearrange, alter, and fuse the separate elements that it receives almost infinitely. Assessing the same set of problems a generation later in his *Treatise of Human Understanding*, Hume dismisses the stability of the external world, which was the last resort of certainty in Locke's model. The mind now responds to experiencing the world so strongly according to its *own* fears and desires that any certainty about it is rendered intangible. The "inner world," now the crucial site of gaining a sense of belonging, is assumed to have no rigid barriers, and the most significant mental activity occurred when "reason" and "passion"—stimulated by the imagination—mix so thoroughly that distinguishing them became impossible. As this quintessential enabler of mental life, the imagination could never *not* be part of human understanding, but its tendencies to exaggerate or tone down the emotional effect on an idea made it potentially treacherous. For further reading see Engell, *Creative Imagination*; Iser, *Fictive*.

contagious effect of "novelization") turned out so conducive to engaging with concerns with belonging that it became the main provider of the narrative frames and patterns that modern individuals use to stay orientated and emplaced in the world.

The history of the novel in the U.S. is an especially fascinating case. Perhaps it was because the New World contained so little that was familiar for its colonizers that not the novel but the more speculative genre of the romance was long viewed as the paradigmatic form in American literature.[40] Whether one agrees with this judgement or not, the romance-typical quest for elusive goals sought in unknown territories, the resulting move beyond everyday experience, paired with celebrations of common sense are emblematic of a life-world in which ways of doing and making (including the ways of doing and making literature) depended more than elsewhere on their capacity to creatively adapt and improvise in the face of the radically unfamiliar.[41] The romance, in its generic endorsement of the unknown, amplifies precisely those imaginative capacities to cope with change that, for Bakhtin, define the novel—with one crucial difference: In the American context, the "novelization" of narrative art in which romance and novel participated side by side was *not* engaged with a world that had shed itself from a previous state of cultural deafness and social isolation as it was the case in Europe. It was engaged with the vastly heterogeneous and genuinely modern contact zone opened up by colonizing the "world island" of the Americas.

The novels to which I turn in the following chapters all spring from disruptive moments in the social fabric that was the outcome of the encounters occurring at this site. A site that, from the moment of its inception existed both as spatial reality and as a mythical construct, with the nexus of belonging and narrative fueling the production of both. With novels that take us across four centuries and to four iconic sites in the cultural geography of this contact zone—the gothic frontier, the enchanted region, the immigrant ghetto, the Midwestern homeland—I aim to show how the searching form of the novel and the ever-shifting need to belong have shaped each other in and through this series of proto-modern settings. Specifically, I aim to show how the four novels assembled here are paradigmatic in

---

40 An important part of these claims was the assumption that the romance was a distinctively *American* literary form and thus a proper foundation for a non-derivative national literature. See Chase; Trilling.

41 Without downplaying the injustices of settler colonialism, Breen insists that "[t]he tale of peopling the New World is one of human creativity" (195). And while many settlers aspired to reproduce the life they had known, once removed from the "rich particularity of the past" (216), the familial ideals and communal norms were anything but well-worn traditions. In Europe, the advent of *Neuzeit* seemed to threaten a familiar and predictable world from the outside; in the American context, such an external threat was only conceivable for the indigenous population while all other groups were facing a radically unfamiliar world. For the corresponding situation in Europe see Kittler 153-68; Gebhardt, Geisler and Schröter 13-18.

their ways of exposing and transgressing contemporary limits of belonging in and through their artistic practice. Tracing the staged agency of the letter, the tactile agency of the sketch, the cyclical agency of the found object, and the networking agency of the brain-as-storytelling-machine within and beyond the storyworlds of the four novels is key to this aim. And it is key to making palpable how the need to belong operates as both a driving force of literary production and as an eminent, shape-shifting touchstone of narrative use.

2 Poisoned Letters from a Gothic Frontier
Charles Brockden Brown's *Edgar Huntly*

Published in 1799 and set in the mid-1780s, *Edgar Huntly; or, Memoirs of a Sleepwalker* speaks from a place of utter disruption. During Brown's short lifetime—he was born in 1771 and died of tuberculosis in 1810—the American, the French, and the Haitian Revolutions swept up the Atlantic world. The Declaration of Independence and the *Federalist Papers* were published. The Ordinance of 1785 and the Northwest Ordinance became the legal blueprints for colonizing the North American continent. The U.S. Constitution was signed, and soon thereafter Federalists and Republicans found themselves in a fierce battle over the nature of the democratic order that had just been ratified. Outside of established circles and political elites, dissatisfaction with the new order erupted in Shay's and the Whiskey Rebellions. The Fugitive Slave Law and the Alien and Sedition Acts were ratified to regulate undesired movements of non-citizens. The Napoleonic Wars broke out and produced a power vacuum that overseas tradesmen (many of them American) readily seized. The Louisiana Purchase multiplied the territory of the young nation, expanding it into parts of the continent completely unknown to its non-indigenous population, which were quickly settled due to increasing immigration.

What happened was indeed a "revolution of massive proportions" (Watts, *Romance* 3). Its perhaps profoundest effect was the breakup of a republican order that had rested on values such as the common good, the public sphere, and civil responsibility, and its replacement by a liberal-capitalist order inclined to promoting individualism, mobility, self-made success, and the private sphere.[1] For a short while, coinciding with Brown's most creative years (between 1797 and 1800), the two orders co-existed, forming a "culture of contradictions" (Hedges 107). *Edgar Huntly* responds to this situation by imagining a protagonist who falls out of his

---

1 Among the best historical works on this shift are those by Appleby. The republicanism-literalism debate has also become a major trajectory of scholarship on early American literature. Warner, Ziff, Gilmore, and Dillon stress the active role that the rise of the novel played in bringing about the gradual fading of the Early Republic's republican ideology and its publically oriented literary culture.

familiar life-world. After going to bed one night, he awakes in a pitch-dark cavern, barely dressed and miles away from his uncle's farm, where he has been living with his sisters since his parents were killed in an Indian raid. In one terrible instant, the world around him grows strange and unfamiliar. The shock of this "fall" haunts the tale, constituting a threshold of uncertainty, a liminal space where action—both physical and narrative—becomes imperative if life is to remain meaningful. The rehabilitation of the protagonist depends on restoring meaning and mooring, incoherence and unfamiliarity after his "fall," and he tells his story to this very end. Brown's novel bundles and personifies the need for narrative recovery in the figure of the letter-writing protagonist who must tell his story to resume his place in the world. But this protagonist is also a sleepwalker, and this means that the actions he performs to this end are in a quintessentially deviant, erring state.

The result is a letter of epic proportions. Addressed to his fiancée Mary and several hundred pages long, it tells the story of Edgar's adventures, including the trailing of a sleepwalking Irishman whom he suspects of having murdered Mary's brother and his beloved friend, killing and eating a ferocious panther, slaughtering numerous Indians, rescuing a girl from captivity, sleeping in an impressive number of beds, escaping an ambush by jumping into a river from impossible heights, and fainting several times out of exhaustion along the way. It also tells her about Edgar's encounter with a stranger named Weymouth who made credulous claims about the money that Mary had unexpectedly inherited upon her brother's premature death, urging her to return it. And eventually, it tells her that Edgar is also a sleepwalker, and that it was his sleepwalking that brought him into the wilderness and made him a stranger to himself. Loosely framed by the epistolary form, the tale is restless and inconclusive, containing stories within stories, changing narrators, characters that emerge out of nowhere, elaborate plotlines that are suddenly dropped. It is indeed "a charmingly, a maddeningly disorganized book, not so much written as dreamed" (Fiedler, *Love and Death* 157). For a long time, the lacking coherence of Brown's novels was viewed as a major weakness; the situation could hardly be more different today.[2] Brown is now widely celebrated for

---

[2] Conjointly fixed by New Criticism's normative aesthetics and the predominantly "exceptionalist" concerns of Cold War American studies, Brown's reputation as an artistically flawed writer remained firmly in place until the early 1980s. It was not until the transnational reconfiguration of early American studies that his reception underwent a profound revision. Three major shifts undergird this development: the breakup of the consensus view of early American ideological history and its underlying assumptions about the relation between the individual and society through the republicanism-liberalism debate; the programmatic reevaluation of formerly disregarded genres such as the sentimental and the gothic, and the general expansion of the literary field in the wake of the canon debates. Ironically, by 2009 the tides had turned to such an extent that Waterman, introducing an *Early American Studies* Special Issue on Brown, wondered if 'Brown studies' had taken over the field of early American studies.

the artful "complexity of his response and exploration of key concerns and issues in early national culture," among them the intersecting debates on republicanism, nationalism, and expansionism, the rise of bourgeois liberalism and its impact on gender dynamics. And he is praised as an author whose "achievement [...] lay in his ability to radically challenge both form and content of contemporary writing" (Barnard, Kamrath, and Shapiro x). In assuming that "Brown's work adequately, deliberately, and often intelligibly engages or represents a coherent early national culture," the revisionist scholarship inverts the assumptions of earlier criticism, which tended "to see Brown as a prototypical Romantic author and framed him as writing against his culture rather than typifying it" (Waterman, "Introduction" 236). In consequence, features such as the maddening incoherence and excessive sentimentality of Brown's novels are now read as historical symptoms whose "problematic" forms are artistically sound and innovative means of expressing a sense of disorientation engrained into their contemporaneity.[3]

Building on, and yet departing from these revisions, my own engagement with Brown's work does not aim at producing historical "evidence" about the larger discursive field in which it is situated and about the subject positions contained in it, nor does it seek to determine whether this novel is acting out or striving against the premises of its ideological context. Rather, in assuming that uncertain states of belonging create a need for narrative recovery that manifests itself in the realm of narrative art, this chapter traces how the novel gives voice and form to concerns with belonging at its time. Brown's fiction is, in fact, deeply entangled with the foundations and limitations of dwelling in its nook of the modern world: It quarrels with established authorities (Enlightenment ideas of reason, traditional gender roles, and the paternalistic order), and is anxious about material insecurity and moral corruption in a world mobilized by self-made success. But while all of these themes have a recurring presence in Brown's narrative universe, *Edgar Huntly* adds a new one: the frontier. In fact, the frontier enters American fiction with this novel—as a space with a guilt-ridden past that haunts all future prospects of dwelling.

---

3   Garbo's *Coincidental Art* was instrumental in bringing about this revaluation. His structuralist readings of Brown's major novels contended that, whatever one might think of Brown's prose style, his plots were intricately crafted rather than hastily improvised. Later critics extended this revision with the use of narrative discourse and performance theory. See, for instance, Wall Hinds, Barnard, Bellis, Downes, Hagenbüchle, and Hamelman.

Frontier Paternalism Meets Liberal Capitalism

Edgar Huntly's frontier is not the mere allegory of a disturbed psyche that a former generation of scholars has found in it. It is a "recognizable landscape" (Jehlen 162). Moreover, and crucially, this landscape is not portrayed as a "virgin land" innocently awaiting its defloration but as a site of bloodshed and dispossession.[4] Carefully modeled after the western parts of Pennsylvania at the time, *Edgar Huntly*'s frontier "provides the literal premises for the possibilities and trajectory of narrative action— inscribing, describing and circumscribing an extrapolative or speculative [...] world and giving that fantasized world a significant and visibly signifying shape and temporal dimension" (Sobchack 123). It has been rightly argued that the gothic gains psychological depth in Brown's fiction; this novel adds site-specificity. The brutal killings of Edgar's parents and infant sibling, the resulting move of the remaining Huntly children to their uncle's farm, which has been built at a site formerly occupied by a Delaware village, and the killings of Edgar's uncle and his close friend Waldegrave (a cartoon name *avant la lettre*) spring directly from the violence inflicted by settlers taking possession of their non-native land.

The troubled state of belonging engrained into this setting gains voice and form in the first-person account of a figure that becomes this story's narrator out of profound experiences of insecurity and loss. Coming to terms with this troubled state is the narrative's primary motivation, motif, and theme. Moreover, imagining the novel's setting in these concrete terms inscribes the dwelling places envisioned by it with historical remnants of betrayal and guilt that deeply trouble the ways in which these places are suitable dwelling places. It has often been pointed out how intensely *Edgar Huntly*'s depiction of frontier violence draws from historical record, most notably from the infamous Walking Purchase of 1737, a fraudulent land deal between European/Quaker settlers and a Delaware tribe, which took place precisely at the site Brown chose as the setting of his story, and which is known for having stirred a series of violent revenge raids.[5] But while the historical refer-

---

4   For Jehlen, the novel is "at once seminal and terminal, the first to envision a specifically American psyche and also more or less the last to represent taking possession of the continent not as destined fulfillment but [...] as conquest" (161). Earlier readings had valued it primarily for its psychological dimension. Ringe was the first to praise Brown for adding a psychic dimension to the gothic genre. In fact, for him the "Americanness" of Brown's fiction was not primarily a matter of its setting but of psychologizing narrative techniques. The most influential psychological reading of the novel stems from Fiedler, for whom the protagonist's destructive desires are forces of the id, which he, in turn, interprets as a token of the conservative underpinnings genuine to American gothic fiction in general.

5   Initiated by William Penn's sons John and Thomas, the Walking Purchase resurveyed a tract of land measured on the basis of what could be walked by a man along a windy river in a day and a half. Penn's sons manipulated these conditions by previously clearing straight paths into the

ences made by the novel are strikingly accurate and complex (and contemporary readers would have been familiar with them), it is important to note that these references are *implied* rather than *explicated*. In stressing this point, I do not want to dismiss the importance of tracing and contextualizing these historical markers. However, for the narrative operations performed by the novel, their muteness is just as significant. The violence, injustice, and guilt of conquest and dispossession with which they are endowed remain silent throughout the novel. In fact, it makes sense to assume that relegating these troubled aspects of belonging in between the lines was the only way of including them in the story; that they could indeed only become part of what was narratable at the time in this muted way.

This point is further underscored by the fact that the *mise-en-scène* of the frontier is one of gradual domestication. Whenever it is described, this is done by drawing on the picturesque, an aesthetic regime that correlates and binds seemingly random and irrelevant parts together with the effect of containing the "unruly" features of its object of depiction.[6] The houses that Edgar passes on his way from the cavern back to civilization illustrate this spatial logic of domestication. Scholars have read these houses as mirroring a progression in Edgar's behavior, which is most violent at the site closest to the wilderness (Garbo 65; Slotkin 384-93), as visual markers in the frontier landscape that enhance the domesticating implications of the picturesque (Berthold 79-83) that "symbolically reiterate the social order that they host" (Wall Hinds, "Brown's Revenge" 56), or as manifesting the process of remodeling the period's notions of national identity (Faherty 56-66). What I want to add to these interpretations is that these houses, all allegories of

---

wilderness, hiring several walkers in particularly good shape and equipping them with support teams. What would under regular conditions have added up to a walk of about twenty-five miles was thus extended to sixty-four miles and a resulting territory of 1,200 square miles of tribal land that the Delawares then lost to the Pennsylvanian settlers. Scholars have identified "the Elm" (consistently capitalized throughout the novel), which ironically marks the site of Waldegrave's murder, as a reference to the tree at which the founding of the state was sealed in a peace treaty between Quakers, led by William Penn, and Lenni Lenape/Delaware Indians in 1782. For in-depth accounts of Brown's use of this event, see Krause, Luck, and Sivilis. Rowe discusses the Walking Purchase as a key event of the rise of U.S. imperialism, in which Brown's novels participate by providing a respective imaginary.

6   For a longer discussion on the importance of the picturesque in the visual appropriation of the North American continent, see my essay "Transatlantic Landscapes." In "Frontiers of Discourse" Wall Hinds also stresses the imaginative conquest of space thus performed, supporting Mitchell's claim that landscape can be understood as enacting the "'dreamwork' of imperialism, unfolding its own movement in time and space from a central point of origin and folding back on itself to disclose both fantasies of the perfected imperial prospect and fractured images of unresolved ambivalence and unsuppressed resistance" (10). For discussions of the picturesque in *Edgar Huntly*, see Bertold and Lueck.

either precarious or failed dwelling, turn the frontier into a *social* space—a space that becomes visible as produced by the "interlocking and articulating nets of social relations" (Massey, *Space, Place* 168) that exist among those who live in these houses and those who contest their presence in the frontier landscape. And this also means that the houses depicted in the novel turn the frontier into a place *formed* out of a particular set of social relations interacting at a specific locale, and *deformed* by the corrosive forces inscribed into the process of colonialization—a process that is problematized by letting the most lavish house degenerate, or by using the dwelling sites as a stage for recurring revenge violence.

Countering this *western* frontier is another, rarely acknowledged but no less foundational fiction of modern America: the *eastern* frontier of the Atlantic, embodied by the figure of the immigrant or "alien other," and imagined as an unstable contact zone of possible contagion.[7] Gibbons notes that, "[i]n terms of historical grievances and political trajectories, both frontiers represent very different presences on the political landscape: the Native American is territorially defined and seeks to retain—or regain—tribal land; the immigrant, by contrast, has forsaken the homeland and has chosen to reinvent himself or herself in the New World" (25). And because this is so, the two frontiers provide opposing frames for imagining potential dwelling places. In the first scenario, these places are to be gained in a territorial conflict with roots in the past that haunts all possible forms of belonging with the question of where do we come from. In the second scenario, they are to be gained in a social conflict about future mobility that haunts future forms of belonging with the question of where do we go.

In *Edgar Huntly*, the two frontiers overlap and seep into each other, with the result of complicating the possibilities of belonging imagined in the novel. Three of the dwellers at the western frontier—the drunkard in the dilapidated mansion, the nameless builder of the hut on the outer edge of the province, and the murder suspect of Edgar's friend, Clithero, who lives in this hut for a while—are Irishmen, and the Native American woman who stays behind when her tribe moves west temporarily lives in the same hut, too. I will return to the indigenous character in the final section of this chapter, but now I want to take a closer look at the mysterious Irishman who most fully embodies the uncertainties associated with the eastern frontier. When "conn[ing] over the catalogue" of his neighborhood, Edgar

---

[7] My reading is inspired by Gibbons, from whom the terms of the "eastern frontier" and the "alien other" are drawn. For further discussions of this topic, see Slotkin, Rowe, and Garner. Garner specifically elaborates on how the racializations of these multiple others (including the millions of involuntary immigrants brought from Africa as slaves) and their legal regulation through the Alien and Sedition Acts played a distinctive role in forging an American identity. Irish immigrants, whom the Alien and Sedition Act particularly targeted and who play a key role in providing mysterious, potentially evil others in Brown's novels, are employed as instrumental figures not only in forging that identity but also in threatening to destabilize it.

singles him out as "the only foreigner among us," quickly adding that, in the patriarchal scheme of his community, "this was an exception to the rule. Clithero was a stranger, whose adventures and character, previously to his coming hither, were unknown to us" (14).[8] In the paternalistic order embodied by Edgar's home community, the "alien other" without a past is an unpredictable, potentially dangerous intruder. What Edgar does not acknowledge, however, is the uncanny resemblance of Clithero's position to his own, orphaned and with no prospect of inheriting land as both of them are. But the paternalistic order is vanishing. Its mode of spatial production, which used to be the predominant mechanism of domesticating the western frontier, is doomed to fail for refusing to integrate those who—like its "native son" Edgar and the "alien other" Clithero—fall outside of the scheme of land inheritance and thus threaten the cohesion of the settler community. This is the spatial predicament of the eastern frontier. The paternalistic order fails again because it is haunted by the collective guilt of conquest and dispossession that culminates in Waldegrave's death and the course of destruction following it. This is the spatial predicament of the western frontier. Moreover, and crucially, the failing frontier paternalism does not create any nostalgic longings for its Old World predecessor. Even its modernized version, embodied by the Irish noble lady who marries the proto-Enlightenment man of reason and multiple skills (ranging from surgeon via intellectual and teacher to businessman), is doomed for failing to socially reproduce itself.

Against the vanishing "old-fashioned, even feudal" (Wood, *Radicalism* 40) economy of landownership and inheritance, the emerging order of liberal capitalism is cast. This new order is depicted as a vertically and horizontally mobile "economics of paper currency and speculation" that is run by an equally emerging entrepreneurial class (Wall Hinds, "Brown's Revenge" 52). In picking up on these issues, the novel responds to the unprecedented wealth sweeping the country at this time, substantially raising the average level of prosperity and fostering wide acceptance of the newly emerging entrepreneurial spirit—not by supporting it but by articulating the anxieties stirred by these transformations.[9] Even more so than the space of the frontier with its wild scenery in need of domestication, the space unfolding from this new order is imagined through the figures that embody it. And as these figures are strikingly mobile, the space unfolding from their relations is marked by the surprising twists and turns of individual itineraries. Weymouth

---

8   Charles Brockden Brown, *Edgar Huntly; or, Memoirs of a Sleepwalker*, ed. Krause and Reid. All further references are based on this edition and given in brackets in the main text.
9   For historical work on these developments see Appleby, *Capitalism* and *Liberalism*; Watts, *Republic and Romance*. For work on the cultural implications of this shift, see Schmidtken, *Property*. See Wall Hinds, *Private Property* for an in-depth discussion of these issues in Brown's fiction, with a special emphasis on their implications for contemporary constructions of gender.

is the figure that embodies the liberal-capitalist order to the fullest.[10] He appears out of nowhere at the Huntly farm to ask for Edgar's help in retrieving a substantial sum of money. In a heartbreaking account of his misfortunes, he tells Edgar how he had asked Waldegrave to keep his money for him while embarking on a trade adventure across the Atlantic. In fact, he had put everything he owned into this adventure to maximize his possible gain—except for the money (a fortune substantial enough to secure his existence) that he left with Edgar's friend. Hoping to return with abundant means to provide for his old father, the wife taken during his travels, and himself, he suffers a shipwreck, imprisonment, and a life-threatening illness, and ends up losing everything—including legal proof of the money transfer—but his own life.

Edgar recounts this story in a passage stretching over several chapters, in which the other is portrayed not as a cruel capitalist but as a farsighted, responsible, and trustworthy victim of a reckless system. Weymouth's misfortune and the insecure place to which it has brought him are construed as the collateral damage of the emerging liberal order, not as the outcome of false ambition or a flawed character.

Is such the lot of those who wander from their rustic homes in search of fortune? Our countrymen are prone to enterprise, and are scattered all over the sea and every land in pursuit of wealth which will not screen them from disease and infirmity, which is missed much oftener than found, and which, when gained, by no means compensates them for the hardships and vicissitudes endured in the pursuit. (154)

But Weymouth's fate is tragic not only for his own sake. The money that he gave to Waldegrave for safekeeping (and that Edgar promises to help restore) is the same money the Edgar's fiancée miraculously inherited upon her brother's death. The prospect of material security for her (and for Edgar) dissolves through the appearance of its "rightful owner" (154) just as unexpectedly as it materialized through Waldegrave's untimely death. In this ironic twist of fate, the future place envisioned by Edgar and Mary on the basis of Mary's inheritance turns out to be a chimera arising from the unlikely conjunction of two impossible spatial orders: the blood-drenched grounds of the paternalistic frontier and the unpredictably shifting grounds of the emerging liberal order. Their future relationship is not only bound up with Waldegrave's murder but also with Weymouth's financial wreckage. In fact, the second order proves to be equally as hazardous in this scenario: It "infects" the old, presumably stable prospect of securing one's place in the

---

10 In *Arthur Mervyn* (1799), Brown's skepticism concerning this newly emerging order and its representatives reaches an extreme in the figure of Welbeck. Initially coming across as generous, well-meaning and committed, behind this calculated façade hides an unscrupulous liar, manipulator, and murderer willing to do anything for his own advancement. The novel's young protagonist Arthur, who becomes a victim of the other's evil schemes, is yet another figure embodying the emerging order of liberal capitalism with irresolvable ambiguity.

world by means of inheritance with the contagious instabilities of entrepreneurial capitalism.

Epistolary Transgressions

If the world in which belonging is sought in this novel emerges from two conflicting orders and their respective modes of spatial production, both are rejected in the figure of its protagonist.[11] Edgar is excluded from the patriarchal scheme not only once but twice (first by orphanage, then by screwing up the prospect of becoming Mrs. Lorimer's heir), and he does not show any professional aspiration. His two outstanding talents—storytelling and box-making—are used for non-commercial ends only, his actions are completely devoted to leisure, and he shows no desire to change his bohemian life. Edgar's distinctive (self-)positioning *outside* of the two available orders constitutes the space of enunciation from which the story evolves. However, the yearning to belong that drives the narrative is not geared toward emplacing its teller in either one of those orders, as both of them are imagined as unsuitable for dwelling. Rather, it is geared toward asserting a sense of belonging in and through the act of narration itself.

The novel opens programmatically in this regard—by staging an allocative vertigo that generates its momentum directly from an ailing state of incoherence, so that "narration [becomes] the only viable form of 'explanation'" (Brooks, *Reading* 54).

I sit down, my friend, to comply with thy request. At length does the impetuosity of my fears, the transports of my wonder permit me to recollect my promise and perform it. At length I am somewhat

---

11 In construing the novel's central figure as an orphan with fluctuating figures of authority, Edgar's lacking position within the available social orders is tied to a resentment against patriarchal authorities that was not uncommon at the time of the novel's production. For Elliott, this crisis of authority is closely intertwined with the waning influence of religious, and particularly Puritan authorities. He sees the emergence of professional writers like Brown in direct response to this development. Fliegelman delineates how Lockean and Rousseauean ideas of authority unsettled traditional modes of parental care, romantic courtship, and family life. New pedagogical ideals, such as the cultivation of affective individualism, fostered a less authoritarian, more contractual understanding of social relations. The novel clearly resonates within these reframings, yet it preferably features social contracts that are canceled rather than ratified or productively altered, thereby stressing an atomization of social life and adding to the general trend of mobilization and the sense of instability and precariousness of existence conveyed by it. Sarsefield, for example, breaks with Edgar because the latter did not adhere to his advice; Edgar cancels his engagement to Mary as the financial circumstances on which it was founded change. Both relations are dissolved on the basis of a written exposition explaining the altered grounds legitimizing the termination of the "contract."

delivered from suspense and from tremors. At length the drama is brought to an imperfect close, and the series of events that absorbed my faculties, that hurried away my attention, has termined in repose. (5)

Yet if these opening lines assert the form of a letter, *Edgar Huntly* is not an epistolary novel (unlike Brown's later novels, *Clara Howard* and *Jane Talbot*). Rather, it uses the form of the letter in artful and intricate ways, a topic virtually untouched by the abounding scholarship on this novel. In fact, it is through the epistolary form that this novel discovers some of its most effective (and potentially abusive) strategies for the narrative pursuit of belonging. The force of these dynamics is directly tied to the epistolary novel as the first popular subgenre of the novel in the mid-eighteenth century. The immense success of Samuel Richardson's *Pamela* (1740) and *Clarissa* (1748), Johann Wolfgang von Goethe's *Die Leiden des jungen Werther* (1774), or Laclos's *Les Liaisons dangereuses* (1784) is indeed so closely tied to the rise of the novel that it makes a lot of sense think of it as evolving from the epistolary form. Approaching this genealogy of modern literary forms with an interest in the narrative productivity engendered by the need to belong makes tangible some rarely acknowledged yet crucial aspects of the creative adaptation from which the novel's rise departs. The ingenious move of epistolary novel was to fictionalize a pragmatic form of writing whose *raison d'être* was to maintain a sense of belonging in an increasingly mobilized world. This move was ingenious indeed, for it emancipated the dialogic structure inherent to actual letter writing from the needs to wait and to respond. The epistolary novel turned the self-sufficiency afforded by fiction into a main source of gratification. Readers were invited to participate in an epistolary exchange without having to create their own narrative accounts. Instead, they could fully immerse themselves in the reception—and consumption—of a *narrative* exchange. In fact, replacing a real (and in this sense demanding) form of intersubjective exchange with the imagined, non-reciprocal intersubjectivity of the fictional tale was the lure of this new kind of literature.

Edgar Huntly's use of the epistolary form stages and reenacts this artistic emancipation. From its first paragraph onward, it simultaneously borrows from and bends the conventions of epistolary storytelling. Yes, the reader is directly addressed, but the formal line of address and indications of place and time that are a staple of the genre are omitted, so that we have to wait, just like in a regular novel, for further clues about characters, place, and time. And once the epistolary form has been "out-used" for the task of initiating the act of telling and establishing a basic frame for it (the narrator has experienced something so disturbing that he can only now begin to tell about it, and needs a "real" interlocutor to be able to tell his tale), the narrative becomes epic in its desire to assume a totalizing completeness in its own right.[12] There is indeed a remarkable contraction engrained into the novel's epistolary pretensions and borrowings: It uses the epistolary form to depart from the addressee's request to stay informed about its writer's life, and ends the epic letter stemming from this request with the promise that he will visit her "as soon as [he has] seen Sarsefield" and "discuss with [her] in conversation [...] [his] schemes for the future" (282). Yet despite the epic proportions of Edgar's letter to Mary and the novelistic pose of self-sufficiency it asserts (for example, through its division into chapters), the story is far from complete without the three short letters dovetailing it. This correspondence between Edgar and Sarsefield not only introduces a new interlocutor but it also grants him a voice of his own. In fact, it leaves the novel's final pages to someone who explicitly challenges the narrative authority that has ruled sovereignly so far. Making up a total of just ten pages, the final correspondence overturns many of the most vital conclusions reached in Edgar's long letter to Mary. We learn, for example, that Clithero is not on his way to recovery, but has turned into the dangerous maniac about whom Sarsefield warned Edgar all along. And that, in his obsessive desire to relieve this man from the ill-guided belief that he has murdered his former patroness (who is now Sarsefield's wife), Edgar himself has become entangled in the other's evil schemes (murdering her to set the record straight) by telling him Mrs. Lorimer's whereabouts. Now he pleads for Sarsefield's forgiveness, but the other's response shatters any hope for reconciliation. In a strikingly matter-of-fact tone (especially when read back to back with Edgar's highly sentimentalized writing mode), Sarsefield reports only basic information: that he left his home immediately upon receiving Edgar's warning about Clithero being on his way with "mysterious intentions" (283); that while supervising the latter's deportation to a psychiatric asylum, he witnessed him drowning; and that Edgar's second letter arrived in Sarsefield's absence, was read by Mrs. Lorimer, and caused the loss of the child she was carrying. The "Farewell" concluding Sarsefield's letter leaves no doubt that their relationship will not be resumed in the future.[13]

12　This silencing has a clear gender bias: None of the female characters—Mary, Mrs. Lorimer, Clarice, Shelby's wife, Old Deb/Queen Mab—are allowed to speak for themselves, and the latter is even said to speak in unintelligible tongues. For an in-depth discussion of the silenced women in Brown's fiction, see Person.

13　Luciano (7-9) reads the final correspondence as showcasing the novel's juxtaposition of Edgar's sentimental/feminized and Sarsefield's rational/masculine way of dealing with texts (both as readers and writers). Throughout the novel, not Edgar's actions but his letters/stories have the gravest effects, but as much as he is a teller, he is also a receiver of stories. The problem is that "Edgar reads like a woman" (7), meaning that he becomes so emotionally involved with his reading that his moral judgment gets impaired (precisely in the way in which he fears that Waldegrave's heretic letters would affect his sister). Echoing an Enlightenment-inflected hierarchy of reading methods, the novel employs Sarsefield's "emphatic preference of logic" (7) as an

And yet, the twists leading up to the end produce a sense of non-closure rather than a sense of an ending (in Frank Kermode's sense), with vast implications for Edgar's future prospects of belonging. The novel's hybrid mode of epistolary and conventional storytelling—one projecting a series of present moments into an open future, the other reconstructing what has happened in the past—is generated by two conflicting yearnings.[14] The retrospective parts are driven by the desire to resume a place at and through which meaning and familiarity are at least provisionally restored, while the epistolary parts are driven by a desire to keep all questions of belonging pending. The result is a narrative that simultaneously stages a yearning for recovery and its rejection. And while the retrospective mode makes up the largest part of the narrative, the most powerful moments of asserting narrative agency are spurred by the epistolary deviations from the dominant mode. But the opening paragraphs unmistakably warn their readers that this agency is impaired. Edgar's claim of finally being calm enough to give account of what has happened is soon relativized: Full recovery may eclipse the events and experiences that need accounting. The sneaky way in which narrative agency is hence at once assumed and deferred deserves a lengthy citation:

Till now, to hold a steadfast pen was impossible; to disengage my senses from the scene that was passing or approaching; to forbear to grasp at futurity; to suffer so much thought to wander from the purpose that engrossed my fears and my hopes, could not be.

---

implicit critique of Edgar's sentimentalized listening and reading habits. In the final letter exchange this opposition is brought to a climax: Edgar's fateful "misreading" of Clithero's character does not do any harm in his first, brief letter, but does in the second, sentimental one, whose reading causes Mrs. Lorimer to lose her child. The final word of the novel is given to Sarsefield's rational didacticism that sharply contrasts with Edgar's voice. Yet despite the harmful effects Edgar's final letter had and the implicit judgment it casts upon his character, there is no conclusive celebration of "enlightened reasoning" as Sarsefield's authority is questioned by his possibly premature judgment that Clithero is dead. Has he forgotten that not long ago he was certain to have seen Edgar drown only to find out a bit later that he was alive and well? Sarsefield's position is further weakened by his being severely damaged by Edgar's storytelling. In fact, his superior rationality does not protect him where he is most vulnerable: in his desire for social reproduction. In a larger perspective, the weakness of his position can be read as a general weakness/absence of father/authority figures, to which several scholars have dedicated their attention. For work on this topic see Keitel, and Scheiding.

14 See McArthur for an in-depth discussion on the non-closural dynamics of the epistolary novel. For the closural drive of conventional novelistic storytelling, see Brooks and Miller. The retrospective narration of *Edgar Huntly*'s main letter has been read in terms of a "quest romance," an "epistemological novel" or a "novel of ideas," all traditions with a strong, yet usually disappointed longing for meaning and closure. See Schulz; Hamelman; Frank; Berthoff.

Yet am I sure that even now my perturbations are sufficiently stilled for an employment like this? That the incidents I am going to relate can be recalled and arranged without indistinctness and confusion? Time may take away these headlong energies, and give me back my ancient sobriety. But this change will only be effected by weakening my remembrance of these events. In proportion as I gain power over my words, shall I lose dominion over my sentiments; in proportion as my tale is deliberate and slow, the incidents and motives which it is designed to exhibit will be imperfectly revived and obscurely pourtrayed. (5-6)

The double movement of at once claiming narrative agency and insisting on its insurmountable limitations creates a tension that pervades the narrative both formally and structurally, drawing the reader into a thick web of ambivalences and contradictions. Moreover, and crucially, realizing the limitations of his capacity to tell his story does *not* diminish the need to tell. On the contrary, Edgar knows that he *must* tell his story, not so much because he has made a promise to his fiancée, but because he needs to separate himself from a haunting experience to resume a place in the world. Alas, our narrator is caught between two equally unappealing choices: Revisiting this experience may thrust him back into confusion, while distancing himself too far from it may forever eclipse the possibility to reconstruct what has happened.[15]

In explicating this troubling state, the novel engages a kind of narrative agency that is inherent to all acts of remembering. As the narrator sets out to tell his story, he discovers a discrepancy between the object of remembrance as it *was* and his

---

15 For Bray, the epistolary form is particularly well-attuned to exploring this troubled state since its narrative conventions evolved side by side with eighteenth century concerns about the human mind, and hence generically incorporates the tensions between past and present selves (16). This issue harks back to last chapter's discussion about the human mind, specifically to Hume's assertion that memory and imagination cannot be distinguished with certainty. Taking up Locke's basic categorization of simple and complex ideas (simple ones being the imprint of immediate sense perception, complex ones the result of further mental reflection), he writes: "When we search for the characteristic, which distinguishes memory from the imagination, we must immediately perceive, that it cannot lie in the simple ideas it presents to us; since both these faculties borrow their simple ideas from the impressions, and can never go beyond these original perceptions. These faculties are as little distinguish'd from each other by the arrangement of their complex ideas. Since therefore the memory is known, neither by the order of its complex ideas, nor the nature of its simple ones; it follows that the difference betwixt it and the imagination lies in its superior force and vivacity. A man may indulge his fancy in feigning any past scene of adventure; nor would there be any possibility of distinguishing from a remembrance of a like kind, were not the idea of the imagination fainter and more obscure. [...] We are frequently in doubt concerning the ideas of the memory, as they become very week and feeble; and are at a loss to determine whether any image proceeds from fancy or the memory, when it is not drawn in so lively colours as distinguishes that latter faculty" (85).

mental image of it now. The novel exploits this discovery—a common gap between the object and the subject of remembrance, and as such a constant site of hermeneutic inspection—as its primary narrative motor force. What makes this narrative situation so endlessly productive is the split between the experiencing self and the narrating self, one mobilizing the narrative and driving it into the future, the other contemplating this process and making sense of it through emplotment.[16] And if an essential part of creating a viable sense of belonging hinges on asserting a form of narrative agency that is able to reconcile the two selves, *Edgar Huntly*'s opening passage stages no less than a war between them. The narrator longs to tell his story, but at the same time he has the greatest difficulties to separate himself from his experience—to let the narrating self take over. The truce that is achieved between the two selves comes at the expense of drawing someone else into the conflict: the recipient of the letter. His opening words, "I sit down, my friend, to comply with thy request," draws the addressee into a binding commitment, and what she is asked to give in return is made perfectly clear: to let the narrative take possession of her.

Thou wilt catch from my story every horror and every sympathy which it paints. Thou wilt shudder with my forboding and dissolve with my tears. As the sister of my friend, and one who honors me with her affection, thou wilt share in all my tasks and all my dangers. (6)

If one thinks (with Peter Brooks) of the desire to tell as "the desire for an interlocutor, a listener, who enters into the narrative exchange" (*Reading* 216) and expects something in return, this novel does not discover this contractual nature of storytelling as it approaches its end (as it is often the case). Rather, it *departs from* this idea, establishing a contract between teller and listener in the first paragraphs. Moreover, and crucially, it creates a teller who does everything in his power to bend the terms of the contract. He expresses a yearning to have her as his sympathetic listener, yes, but there is another desire at work in this narrative. And as the novel's long first letter progresses, it becomes increasingly clear that Edgar wants to have Mary as a listener to bequeath the past while not wanting to belong to her in the future. In fact, he longs to separate himself from her once she has received his story.

---

16   The terms are drawn from Stanzel. Although not seamlessly compatible, the terms correspond to Roland Barthes's differentiation between a "proairetic code" (also called the "code of action") and the "hermeneutic code" (also called the "code of enigmas and answers"). See Barthes, *SZ*. In his discussion of these terms, Brooks point out that "Plot might then be best thought of as an 'overcoding' of the proairetic by the hermeneutic code, the latter structuring the discrete elements of the former into lager interpretative wholes, working out their play of meaning and significance" (*Reading* 18).

What he tells her to this end is certainly inconclusive and confusing. The mystery around Waldegrave's murderer is lost out of sight, then abruptly picked up again, and halfheartedly resolved by turning him into the victim of a random act of revenge violence. The story of the Nartive American Old Deb/Queen Mab, first elaborately built up, is resolved by having her arrested, without resistance, for her inflammatory actions. The narrator's own sleepwalking is never really reflected. More examples could easily be found. Against the backdrop of this maze of loose ends and incoherent plotlines, the future of Edgar and Mary's relationship—its end—is clearly projected. In a long passage of direct address, situated almost exactly halfway through the narrative, Edgar exploits his letter-writing agency to the fullest: He cancels their engagement. In the fabric of this utterly inconclusive narrative, this is a rare moment of closure. Interrupting the retrospective mode for four entire pages, it is by far the longest passage of direct address. The circumstances, rhetoric, and effects of this bold and abusive narrative act deserve closer scrutiny: Directly preceding this passage is the Weymouth episode, whose quintessential role for describing and rejecting the liberal order has been discussed in the previous section. Listening to the stranger convinces Edgar that he is the rightful owner of Mary's inheritance, and that she must return it to him. The situation is delicate, however, since neither legal proof nor private documentation exists to substantiate Weymouth's claim—which means that Mary has to base her decision on Edgar's retelling of the other's story. Despite the lack of "hard evidence" and in full awareness of the gravity of the consequences—returning the money would thrust her back into poverty, dissolve the financial basis of their marriage, and leave Edgar and his sisters homeless in the near future—Edgar urges her that returning the money is the right thing to do. And as if to authorize his bold advice with personal sacrifice, he stresses his own share of the burden before announcing his withdrawal from their engagement.

I know the precariousness of my condition and that of my sisters, that our subsistence hinges on the life of an old man. My uncle's death will transfer the property to his son, who is a stranger and an enemy to us, and the first act of whose authority will unquestionably be to turn us forth from these doors. Marriage with thee was anticipated with joyous emotions, not merely on my own account or on thine, but likewise for the sake of those beloved girls, to whom that event would enable me to furnish an asylum.

But wedlock is now more distant than ever. My heart bleeds to think of the sufferings which my beloved Mary is again fated to endure, but regrets are only aggravations of calamity. They are pernicious, and it is our duty to shake them off. (156-57)

The use of the substantive form—"precariousness"—stresses the severity of Edgar's concern. Yet although the first paragraph speaks about the future, the verbs are determined rather than speculative. Adding "unquestionably" amplifies the passage's closural force. And while Edgar's breakup is drenched in a rhetoric of sacrifice, the term "wedlock" turns the prospected marriage into a mere technicality that does not seem to have anything to do with his loving feelings for her. Pitted against an impersonal legal entity, the shared sense of duty offers a vision of unity beyond their disengagement. The decisiveness of his announcement that "wedlock is now more distant than ever" makes the concluding outlook—"[t]hese considerations [...] will be weighed when we meet" (156)—have a hollow ring to it.

The force of the narrative action undertaken here stems from it being at once veiled and direct: Edgar wants Mary to return the money even though this means the end of their planned union; he is indeed quite outspoken about his willingness to manipulate her to this end. "I will exert all my influence, it is not small, to induce her to restore [the money]" (144), he tells Weymouth—and thus also tells *her* since his promise to the stranger is part of his letter to Mary. But changing the contractual terms of their relationship also changes the terms of narrative transfer. Edgar does not tell this story in order to arrive at a point where they will belong together; he tells it to dissolve the prospect of belonging to her. The motive he gives for his actions is strictly moral: They cannot build their future on money that does not rightfully belong to her. But the epistolary form creates a narrative surface too opaque to offer any real insight into the narrator's psychic life. Had he only considered marrying her as long as she had money? Or had he begun to have doubts about marrying her prior to finding out that the money may not be rightfully hers, so that Weymouth's plea came as a handy excuse to cancel the wedding? In rendering these questions indeterminable, the epistolary mode employed in the passage lays open the limits of asserting stable meanings and predictable conduct with this narrative mode. For no matter how disturbed this letter-writing narrator may be, we must assume that what he says, and how he says it, is carefully weighed against the effects he hopes to produce in his correspondent. And hence the epistolary form both exposes and veils the narrator's psychic state: Stating how one feels and what one thinks lends a letter credibility for sure, but what one says and how one says it is always weighed against the anticipated response and judgment of one's correspondent. Everyday letter writing is (or was) subject to the same strategies and calculations, but being embedded in lived rather than fictional relations relativizes their potentially distorting effects through other forms of interaction beyond the lettered exchange.

Literary adaptation amplifies these effects by putting the recipient in a position in which both sides, both psyches have to be imagined with none of them being that of the reader. And if the epistolary borrowings and pretentions of the novel make it impossible to gain any definite insight into Edgar's "true" or "private" state of mind, the timing of his most decisive and brutal turn to narrative action is all the more striking: It happens right after his retells Weymouth's story—from which we not only learn that Mary will most likely be poor again, but also that she seems to be pregnant—and right before Edgar's mysterious awaking in the pitch-dark cave. In fact, the letter to his fiancée is plotted in a way in which Weymouth's visit *causes* Edgar's sleepwalking into the wilderness, connecting this event directly to Edgar's transformation into the fearless Indian fighter that he becomes after this "rebirth" in the cave, and with his odyssey home, where home means not a home with Mary. Placing the termination of their engagement in between these two life-changing events assigns it with a key function in the narrative design of the novel. It separates the first part, dedicated to the search for Waldegrave's murderer, from the second, dedicated to Edgar's horrifying experience of awaking in the cave and its disconcerting aftermath, while also binding the two parts together. From this fault line within the errant plot of the novel, the narrative changes radically its course, with the effect of disrupting a no-longer-desired trajectory of belonging.

Yet there is more to this abusive and self-serving assertion of narrative agency: Cancelling his engagement with Mary is the narrator's ultimate act of dismissing any prospect of belonging through material means. And if the passage of his letter that executes this breakup exposes the degree to which any prospect of belonging depends on narrative agency, from now on it is channeled to the retrospective parts of the story, to which Edgar happily dedicates himself for the remainder of his letter. Prolonging the act of telling is indeed his most vital desire.

Belonging as *Unterhaltung*

It is no surprise to find an internal drive toward narrative mobilization in a novel in which belonging is primarily sought in prolonging the act of telling: To the extent that the possibility (or desire) of restoring the narrator's unsettled senses of place and self in actual moments of arrival or return is dismissed, the promise of recovery is shifted to the realm of imaginative self-assertion—where it is most effectively realized by means of staging and asserting the act of storytelling itself. Assuming narrative agency and testing its capacity thus becomes a practical *rite de passage* in this tale, a ritual prone to lift the narrator to a more comfortable state of belonging. But since the agency employed to this end is impaired, the consolidation pursued with it cannot aspire to mastery in any conventional sense. Rather, engaging the limits of the narratable becomes the primary means and end of narrative form-giving. In fact, belonging as narrative self-assertion is sought at these limits: in the semantic grey zone where the imagination fades and falters, and where mobilizing rather than stabilizing the narrative offers itself as a viable course of action.

Throughout the novel narrative mobilization has strikingly physical qualities. All main characters are constantly on the move, delivering, spreading and, merging their stories whenever they meet. It is hardly a coincidence, then, that Edgar's adventure begins on the road, on a walk home from a rendezvous with his correspondent. As his nocturnal journey makes him melancholic, he abandons his route to revisit the site of his friend's recent murder, not minding that "[his] journey would, by these means, be considerably prolonged" (9). In the account that follows, Edgar barely rests. Driven by his quest to find his friend's murderer, he walks back and forth between his uncle's house and the site of the crime, pursues his sleepwalking suspect all over the countryside for nights on end, takes more long walks as he waits for the much desired interview, and even in those rare moments in which his movements are arrested, Edgar paces. So yes, physical movement is a narrative motor force, but this narrator is frequently dissociated from consciousness, through either reverie or sleepwalking. At once propelling and impairing narrative agency, these dissociated physical movements turn out to be the most effective vehicle to push against contemporary confines of belonging. I will return to this issue in the concluding section. For now, I want to consider it as part of a larger strategy of narrative mobilization. The sentimentalism that comes in tow with a letter-writing protagonist recovering from threat and terror is an enormous resource in this regard.[17] For only to the extent that his narrating self *feels* can he begin to reconnect with the experiencing self, and only if the connection *holds*, can the protagonist narrate himself back into having a place in the world. And because of this sentimental causality, his feelings function as the throbbing pulse of the narrative. They determine the intensity and direction of every action performed or accounted for, and they are the coercive force that holds together the meandering and inconclusive plot.[18] Edgar reports, for example, to have left the road home to revisit the site of the murder when his "recollections

---

[17] The revaluation of sentimental storytelling has been a substantial part of recent revisionism of early American literature. Jane Tomkins's *Sensational Designs* was an early landmark study in this regard. Brown is one of the authors she discusses. Most recent accounts have been particularly interested in sentimentalism's concern with the body as a primary resource of imaginative mobilization. See especially Luciano; Burgett; Dillon.

[18] Hedges notes about this narrative mode that "Few novelists of any stature have been so much of the time so unconcerned as him [Brown] with the sensuous reality of the life they were depicting. We sometimes have to wait for several paragraphs before getting hints of how his characters look or sound." Voloshin goes so far as to account Edgar Huntly (not Brown!) with an "affective narrative theory" that, "like his moral theory," is grounded in "late eighteenth-century aesthetics and ethics, owing of course a great deal to the Lockean emphasis on sensation as a source of knowledge and motive to response. [...] the coherence and indeed the very possibility of his tale are intimately associated with the coherence of consciousness" (267-68). In Locke's words: "First, *our senses*, conversant about particular sensible objects, do *convey into the mind* several distinct *perceptions* of things, according to those various ways wherein those objects do affect them. And thus we come by those *ideas* we have of *yellow, white, heat, cold, soft, hard, bitter, sweet,* and all those which we call sensible qualities; which when I say the senses convey into the mind, I mean, they from external objects convey into the mind what produced there those *perceptions*. This great source of most of the *ideas* we have, depending wholly upon our senses, and derived by them to the understanding, I call SENSATION" (33-34; emphasis in the original).

once more plunged [him] into anguish and perplexity" (7); when arriving there, the "mighty anguish" and "heart-bursting grief" of the half-naked stranger whom he finds suspiciously digging at this site moves him so profoundly that "[e]very sentiment, at length, yield[s] into sympathy" (11).

Edgar's feelings have a strikingly physical quality in this passage and elsewhere it: They plunge, they burst, they yield. Sympathy is the feeling that guides Edgar's actions in the first half of the novel, for instance, in his nocturnal pursuit of the stranger whom he finds digging at his friend's grave through the province's western wilderness, his quest for an interview, his explorations of the cave into which the other has disappeared, and his provision of food for him. In amplifying the mediating capacities of compassion as the narrator's primary form of attachment to the world, the narrative taps into contemporary beliefs about the pedagogical merits of sentimental fiction (not without warning of the "dangers" involved).[19] In doing so, it engages David Hume's idea that "passions" are an indispensable ingredient of any mental activity: They stimulate the imagination and hence make it possible to integrate new thoughts and impressions into the realm of the already familiar. Just as in Hume's model, sense can be made when feelings intermingle with the ideas that the narrator relentlessly generates in a search for meaning that is habitually acted out across space.[20] Following this basic pattern, the narrator's

---

19 Based on their reception of sensationalist models of the human mind, specifically those of Locke and Hume, progressive writers such as William Godwin, Mary Wollstonecraft, Thomas Holcroft, Robert Bage, Helen Maria Williams, Thomas Paine, and Brown had come to believe that emotions can encourage moral behavior and that imaginative literature could be used with the aim of fostering a more democratic society. For further discussion, see Clemit, and Kelly.

20 For Hume, the imagination conditions all mental activity, be it directed toward external objects or toward introspection, just as it is impossible to know with certainty whether impressions or memories derive from a supposedly external object or are produced by the creative power of the mind (84-85). In one of the many passages in the *Treatise of Human Nature* (1734) dedicated to this matter, he writes: "Let us fix our attention out of ourselves as much as possible: Let us chace [sic] our imagination to the heavens, or the utmost limits of the universe; we never really advance a step beyond ourselves, nor can conceive any kind of existence, but those perceptions, which have appear'd in that narrow compass. This is the universe of the imagination, nor have we any idea but what is there produc'd. The farthest we can go towards a conception of external objects, when supposed specifically different from our perceptions, is to form a relative idea of them, without pretending to comprehend the related objects. Generally speaking we do not suppose them specifically different; but only attribute them different relations, connections and durations" (67-68). In this at once enabling and veiling conception, the imagination could become a counterforce to Hume's skepticism: If all relations made by the imagination are incomprehensible, the laws of causality and principles of cognition (especially those still taken for granted by Locke) turn out to be "fictions of the mind." Hume uses the expression frequently, cf. *Treatise* 216, 220ff, 254, 259, 493. Iser points out that Hume did not mean this in any derogatory way. As

physical mobility generates lists of questions that add up to entire paragraphs. Wondering whether or not to revisit the site of Waldegrave's murder, Edgar asks himself:

> What could I expect to find? Had it [the site] not been a hundred times examined? Had I not extended my search to the neighboring groves and precipices? Had I not pored upon the brooks, and pryed into the pits and hollows, that were adjacent to the scene of blood? (8)

The text is full of these cascading lists of questions, and this creates an air of constant speculation and uncertainty. If in the narrator's emotional economy one sentiment leads to and enforces another, his intellectual economy thrives on one question leading to another question—never to an answer. In one of these passages, Edgar steps aside to reflect upon the nature of his quest, realizing that he is not interested in revenge or any other direct action but in knowing itself.

> For what purpose shall I prosecute this search? What benefit am I to reap from this discovery? [...] Curiosity, like virtue, is its own reward. Knowledge is of value for its own sake, and pleasure is annexed to the acquisition, without regard to anything beyond (15-16).

I read these lists of questions as an echo of Hume's skeptical epistemology, which was widely known in intellectual circles in the U.S. at the time. With no certainty about the external world, the narrator is in constant need to make hypotheses about this world.[21] And this also means that curiosity is not at all an end in itself, as Edgar seems to think. It is a vital strategy for bridging the gap between his inner and his outer world by means of constant speculation—which, in turn, becomes Edgar's only hope to restore his impaired sense of belonging. For while the intellectual quest for meaning is mainly retrospective, its larger objective lies in the future:

---

an incomprehensible premise of cognition, "fictions of the mind" became an essential concept in what Hume critiqued as misguided epistemological postulates (*The Fictive* 175). For concise discussions of Hume's model of the human mind and his notion of the imagination, see Engell; Iser, *The Fictive*.

21 See, for instance, Armin-Paul Frank, who reads *Edgar Huntly*'s open-ended, reality-testing mode of narration as a prototypical feature of the Romance. Frank locates the emergence of the genre in Hume's speculative epistemology and argues that it can be directly related to patterns of sense-making that are paradigmatic to the American experience: "Die aus Europa in die Neue Welt gekommenen mehr oder weniger intelligenten Wesen mussten erkennen, dass sich viele der mitgebrachten Erfahrungssätze (*verites*) hart mit amerikanischen Fakten stießen. Auf die alten Automatisierungen konnte man sich nicht verlassen. Neue Deutungsmuster mussten erst aufgebaut werden. Einstweilen war der Kolonist von Fall zu Fall auf eigene interpretierenden Anstrengungen angewiesen" (63). From here it is only a small step to the means and ends oriented epistemology of pragmatism that is often regarded as the only genuinely American philosophy.

Edgar seeks to recover his senses of place and self so that his life can continue. Yet the desire of self-extension driving this intellectual quest is destined to transgress continuously what has already become familiar. And it is precisely in this vein that Edgar cultivates a habit of venturing ever deeper into the western parts of the province. In fact, his excursions connect the epistemological and geographical uncertainties of his habitual state of being-in-the-world—and likewise, the intellectual and physical dynamics of narrative mobilization—in consequential ways. Earlier trips into the wilderness undertaken with Sarsefield "chiefly consisted in moralizing narratives and synthetical reasoning" and had "familiarized [him] with [the province's] outlines and the more accessible parts" (92). But after his mentor had left, Edgar kept exploring for the sole reason of expanding the realm of the familiar:

Every new excursion indeed added somewhat to my knowledge. New tracks were pursued, new prospects detected, new summits were gained. My rambles were productive of incessant novelty, though they always terminated in the prospect of limits that could not be overleaped. (93)

The last sentence is especially telling with regard to his motivation: More than providing any certainty of knowledge about the region, Edgar's excursions incessantly assure him of—familiarize him with—the limits of his known world. Novalis's saying that "[a]ll philosophy is really homesickness, an urge to be at home anywhere" (Novalis 179; my translation) addresses precisely this double bind of post-Enlightenment modes of belonging. Edgar's quest to recover his sense of place and self can be read as an early American version of this quintessentially modern feeling of homelessness—not just in the transcendental sense of falling out of the security of religion but also in the pragmatic, geographical sense of being exposed to western wilderness beyond the frontier.

Edgar's account of his awaking in the cave maps the two senses of existential uncertainty onto one another. The utter unfamiliarity of his surroundings twisted his guts, but the despair that he felt in this situation is all the more dramatic in the absence of a God with whom to reason. Edgar's atheism is indeed closely associated with his sleepwalking habit. In the first reported incident, he hides the letters that Waldegrave had written to him during a short phase in which he was an atheist. Yet while Waldegrave soon reconverted, Edgar never did. In the second, much more disturbing incident, in which Edgar finds himself in the cave, his atheism prevents him from making sense of his incomprehensible "captivity" and the life-threatening dangers caused by it in terms of a transitory stage in a longer journey home.

I had none but capricious and unseen fate to condemn. The author of my distress and the means he had taken to decoy my hither, were incomprehensible. Surely my senses were fettered or deprived by some spell. I was still asleep, and this was merely a tormenting vision, or madness had seized me, and the darkness that environed me and the hunger that afflicted me, existed only in my own imagination. (164)[22]

Edgar's response to this threat is to kill with one strike and then eat the ferocious panther that suddenly emerges from the darkness of the cave—a deed that redirects his self-devouring urge "to bite the flesh of [his] arm" (164) to an object in his environment. It has often been noted that this moment marks a fundamental transformation in the novel's protagonist: his rebirth as a savage-killing American performed, in Turner-like fashion, by the wild setting of the western frontier.[23] I agree with this interpretation. However, just as striking as this transformation of character is the shift in talking about his fate. In his efforts to make sense of what has happened, the tyrant who mysteriously took him captive becomes an incomprehensible *author* of distress—a position that Edgar, in assuming narrative agency to mediate this experience, seizes for himself just as instinctively as he slays and eats the panther.

Calling the novel Edgar's "memoirs" bears testimony to this second rebirth: that as an author who to narrates himself back into having a place in the world. In fact, what the author of this memoir yearns for more than anything else is to be sustained by his capacity of telling stories. The German term *unterhalten* (entertain) has three meanings that converge in this longing: to be pleasantly diverted, comfortably supported, and engaged in a valuable exchange. In Brown's novel, the desire to retreat into a self-absorbed and self-sustaining state of *Unterhaltung*—the narrator's longing to dwell in his story—turns out to be stronger than any longing for a place in the world. The final lines of his long and self-serving letter to Mary read like a concession in this regard: "I am surprised at the length to which my story has run. I thought that a few days would suffice to complete it, but one page has insensibly been added to another till I have consumed weeks and filled volumes.

---

22 Many critics have pointed out the resemblances between this novel and the colonial accounts of Indian captivity that were still popular at Brown's time. See for example Slotkin, Hamelman, Rowe, and Smith-Rosenberg, "Captured Subjects." Luciano takes the argument even further when suggesting that *"Edgar Huntly* is itself a captivity narrative, though of a different sort: Although Edgar is at no point in the novel imprisoned by Indians, he is captivated by the carnal body, as much as he hopes the reader will be by his narrative" (11). For reasons that will become clear as I further unfold my own reading of the text, I would modify this argument by stressing that Edgar is captivated by his "sorely wounded" (13) mind as much as by his carnal desires.

23 To quote one of the iconic passages of Turner's seminal essay: "The frontier is the line of most rapid and effective Americanization. The wilderness masters the colonist. It finds him a European in dress, industries, tools, modes of travel, and thought. It takes him from the railroad car and puts him in the birch canoe. It strips off the garments of civilization and arrays him in the hunting shirt and the moccasin" (2). For discussions of Edgar's transformation/rebirth upon awaking in the cave see, for instance, Luciano 13-15, and Garner 444-46.

Here I will draw to a close" (282), he announces in an abortive gesture before ending with the promise to visit her—a hollow destination by now.

The Power of Narrative and the Limits of the Narratable

Read along these lines, *Edgar Huntly* is a story about the efforts and perils of narrative recovery. It is a story about a young man who sets out to narrate himself back into having a place in the world, exploits his listeners, and ends up inhabiting the world of his story rather than the world beyond it. In the process of telling this story, he integrates, in minute detail and sympathetic elaboration, narratives of others into his own with the effect of expanding the boundaries of his textual and imaginary habitat. And while these other narratives enlarge and pluralize the body of the written text, producing idiosyncrasies that can be read as early experimentations with modernist techniques (such as multiple focalization and heteroglossia), they are also crucial for the evolution of the story and the dwelling places prospected by it. In fact, throughout the novel, narrative is portrayed as an immensely powerful agent in regulating social relations and the highly mobile space evolving from them. Time and again, it directly and vastly affects states of belonging: by moving characters to unforeseeable places, by transforming them in the act of listening, and by thrusting them out of seemingly stable social relations. More often than not, these effects are disruptive, working against the prospect to belong somewhere and to someone. And hence, the prospect of dwelling is moved from actual to imaginary places.

Clithero is the most extreme figure in this regard, and that he serves as Edgar's *doppelgänger* heightens his symbolic significance: Both are sleepwalkers, both are box-makers of extraordinary skill, both hide and nearly destroy their dearest treasure while sleepwalking. In fact, both break into their theft-proof boxes to steal from themselves, in both cases the hidden treasure is a written record of a beloved person, and as Edgar takes on more and more of the other's behavior, one cannot help but wonder if he may eventually become an equally dangerous psychopath.[24] But back to Clithero: After his crime has exiled him from the comfortable home

---

24 Many scholars have written on this relation, for example Luciano; Schultz; Garner; Bellis. Contrary to Luciano and Schulz, who stress the conflation of Edgar's and Clithero's identities, Garner argues that Edgar's doubling of Clithero brings out their differences. In either case, Edgar's impulse to identify with/become the "alien other" adheres to a logic of incorporating the "dangerous other" out of desire to neutralize it and with the outcome of self-transformation. The scene in which the wounded Edgar faints on top of one of the Indians he killed and thus, by implication, exchanges blood with him has regularly been interpreted as a token of this transformation. Bellis reads Edgar's increasing resemblance to Clithero psychoanalytically as a pathological/traumatized behavior of compulsive repetition.

provided by Mrs. Lorimer on her estate in Ireland, his sense of belonging hinges on his possession of her written memoir. He takes it with him—steals it—not only for its value as a talisman but also because, once abroad, this manuscript bears the only proof that he has ever had a place where he has belonged. The document—as a material object, as a mediated presence of its author, and for the narrative record that it contains—oscillates between being a (mobile) agent of (provisional) emplacement and the painful reminder of a home forever lost. Its owner's obsession with this object highlights a fundamental contradiction in the relation between property and belonging. The most treasured piece of this poor fellow's few possessions (and thus the object kept for emotional stability) is an object to which he belongs as much as it belongs to him: He is literally possessed by it. Moreover, and crucially, his final outbreak of madness is caused by a narrative interference with a barely bearable state of belonging as non-belonging. He settled on the verge of a frontier community, and for a moment he is not wallowing in his tragedy (he was forced to leave his home for having accidently killed Mrs. Lorimer's evil brother and willfully killed her to "save" her from her grief), when Edgar hunts him down and *retells* this story to him, reminding him how exclusively his livelihood is anchored in it. Clithero's fragile state of belonging hinges on his belief that he is the bearer of a metaphysical burden, and it depends on the tale that he has crafted around this belief: He is the one with the extraordinary fate of having killed the one whom he loved most, and will have to endure this fate until God relieves him. Meanwhile, he lives in an abandoned hut whose location is removed enough to deprive him of all close social bonds, and close enough to other people to constantly remind him of his lonesome destiny. His interlocking senses of place and self are defined in the ways in which he does *not* belong anywhere, to anyone, or anything *except to his story*. Telling this story in the tragic mode grants him a sense of agency—of affirmation, of choice—that is essential for his survival. What he does not know until Edgar retells his story, however, is that the second act of killing was unsuccessful; that Mrs. Lorimer lives and is well, and that she has recently moved to America. But rather than bringing relief to the tortured stranger, the revised story horrifies him by interfering with the tragic mode of emplotment and the agency gained form it. For the life of him, he cannot give the old story away! If Mrs. Lorimer is alive, this can only mean, then, that he is "reserved for the performance of a new crime. [His] evil destiny will have it so" (289). And while Edgar is not possessed by self-fulfilling prophecies, his inclination to dwell in narrative self-assertion is severely questioned by Clithero's manic precedence.

But *Edgar Huntly* is as much a novel about the limits of the narratable as it is a novel about the power of narrative. And it is a story about the ways in which these limits regulate the possibilities of belonging that its narrative operations map out. Installing a sleepwalking narrator with a tortured psyche is a consequential choice in this matter. "The incapacity of sleep denotes a mind sorely wounded" (13), Edgar remarks after finding out that the main suspect in the murder of his friend is a sleepwalker who displays great anguish when being in this state. He waits almost until the end of his epic letter to Mary to address finally his own sleepwalking, but implicitly he also speaks about himself when saying this. The formulation used here resonates with Erasmus Darwin's then contemporary notion of sleepwalking as a mental disease: a state in which "general sensation" is disconnected from a person's bodily actions that can, in turn, engage freely in an "exertion to relieve pain" (202). And it resonates with sensational psychology's core idea that perceptions can forever form—and possibly harm and distort—a person's mind.[25] With psychoanalytical models of the unconscious still more than a century away, sleepwalking—conceived as a mode of action both purpose-driven and separated from rational conduct—offered itself as a potent vessel for exploring the limits of the narratable.

There are at least two incidents from which we can assume that Edgar's mind has indeed been "sorely wounded:" His closest friend has only recently died of violent murder in Edgar's arms, and as a child he found half of his family killed by Indians upon returning home with his two younger sisters. These events have been used as touchstones for reading the novel as a tale of traumatization, giving occasion to trace the narrative mechanisms of a compulsive desire to repeat striving against an unconscious need to forget and repress, or to decipher the

---

[25] Darwin's ideas about sleepwalking were widely circulating as part of his influential study *Zoonomia*, to which Brown was exposed at the Friendly Club, the literary club of which he was a member. Darwin himself was heavily influenced by Lockean notions of sensational psychology, particularly their challenging of Cartesian notions of enlightened rationality by proposing that the human mind does not process innate ideas but begins its life as a *tabula rasa* on which sensory perceptions leave immediate and lasting imprints. Thus conceived, the psyche emerges from an initial incident of wounding; "from its first experience after birth, [it] becomes marked, scored, impressed, and indented" (Engell 18). The shift in thinking about the human mind in terms of a safely enclosed, self-contained entity imagined by Descartes to a genuinely vulnerable target of random impressions corresponds with an uncertain, irritated sense of belonging. It is important to add, however, that Locke pairs this vulnerability with a strong instinct of survival: Not only can the mind "repeat" the simple ideas derived from sense perception, but it has the capacity "to rearrange, to alter, and to fuse the separate elements it receives in 'an almost infinite variety'" (18). Among the most immediate effects of this rethinking was a declining belief in the virtues of authoritarian childrearing and its replacement by the pedagogical ideal of fostering an "affective individualism" (Fliegelman 12-29). Locke writes: "If the mind was not formed at birth and from this moment on safely installed with rationality, the little, and almost insensible Impressions on our tender Infancies have very important and lasting Consequences" (Axtell, *Educational Writings* 12). It might be added that Descartes's self-contained model of human rationality can be read as a prior reaction to an irritated sense of belonging, sheltering human rationality in a quasi-hermetic capsule to keep the world in order after the coercive epistemologies of the pre-Enlightenment era had lost their power.

trauma-typical inscriptions of a guilt-tortured psyche from which this imaginary effort of storytelling springs (see Bellis, and Cassuto). Traumatic experience and unconscious repression constitute very real limits of the narratable, and readings sensitive to psychic operations stirred by them do important work in delineating the resulting silences as well as the strategies of narrative deferral and delayed re-semantization. But their belated, non-contemporary assumptions about the human psyche are of limited use for the project of making tangible concerns about belonging that brush against the limits of the narratable from within the enunciative structure of the text. Then-current ideas about sleepwalking are a promising venue in this regard, for sleepwalking both produces and intensifies those gaps and uncertainties in the narrative that the narrator's emplotment efforts seek to smoothen out.[26] In fact, sleepwalking serves to stage a perceptual disjunction between the narrator's inner and outer worlds, as exemplified in Edgar's walk home in a state of reverie: Moving through a familiar environment with his perceptions completely absorbed by his mental activities, he suddenly finds himself in front of his uncle's house. Sleepwalking amplifies this split state of consciousness by casting the inner world into the (semi)darkness of sleep. As a narrative device, it pulls the psychic world inside out, mapping it onto the external world, which becomes a virtual stage for experiences entrapped in a person's "wounded mind" with no other outlet than this physical, absent-minded, and ultimately "mad" kind of "exertion." In other words, the narrative is so obsessively entangled with physical and affective mobilization because the narrator's efforts to remember are not only split along the usual lines of object/subject, past/present, experiencing/narrating self. They are further punctured within that split by movements and feelings from which—despite physically embodying them—he is irredeemably separated.

The actions performed in this split state of consciousness have real effects on the external world precisely because they are fully embodied. The novel's excessive concern with embodiment has often been noted.[27] From a perspective of belonging, this concern gains yet another dimension: The novel dramatizes the fact that the body, in naturally emplacing each individual, serves as the degree zero of dwelling. Moreover, in *Edgar Huntly*, this natural nucleus of dwelling is severely troubled since the narrator's body is marked by a painfully widened and ostensibly "pathologic" gap between inner and outer world, which the novel explores through the

---

26 The reader's gradual process of piecing together the scope and details of Edgar's sleepwalking is carefully laid out by the plot: Initially evoked by the novel's title, the theme is first associated with Clithero and shifted (back) to Edgar in a guilt-laden dream of Waldegrave and his discovery of the mysteriously missing letters in its immediate aftermath, dramatized in Edgar's all the more mysterious awaking in the pitch-dark cave and largely resolved in Sarsefield's counter-narrative of Edgar's adventures in the wilderness. The possibility that Edgar may have killed his friend while sleepwalking looms until the very end of Edgar's letter to Mary.

27 See, for instance Luciano, Burgett, and Dillon.

idiosyncrasies of sleepwalking. In the process of gaining awareness of this habit that his writing seeks to put into words, Edgar's body functions both as the primary site and mobile vessel of his "pain-exerting" activities and as the mute witness of all those actions performed in disjunction from the supposedly "sane" facets of his consciousness.[28] As a self-disclosing force of mobilization, Edgar's "wounded mind" and the involuntary yet willful actions "exert[ed]" by it propel, dislocate, and puncture the narrative desire to belong. The errant, deviant movements in the external world generated this way thrust the narrator's life into a continuous state of crisis, demanding to revisit the grounds traversed with a split consciousness before. But retrospective narration under the spell of sleepwalking demands repetition of an unusual kind. While technically setting out to cover the same, disturbed grounds *again* with the desire of making them meaningful, familiar, and ideally inhabitable, it actually covers some of these grounds for the first time, for they were initially traversed in the shadowy world of the sleepwalker's dreams.

Only one passage gives us insight into the narrator's dreaming psyche, and thus provides us with clues on how to read his sleepwalking actions. When telling Mary about what later becomes discernible as his first sleepwalking incident, he mentions "the image of Waldegrave [...] flitting before [him]" in a state of "inquietude and anger," reminding him of having neglected "[s]ome service or duty" (130). Upon awaking, he remembers not only his pending promise to destroy a certain correspondence between the two but also his promise to Mary of a copy of this correspondence as a souvenir of her deceased brother, well aware of her being the last person on earth whom his friend would have wanted to read the letters. When looking for the letters in their theft-proof hiding place, however, he finds them missing; and learns from his uncle that someone walked around in the attic that night. The plotline drops out of sight as Weymouth visits the Huntly farm and triggers Edgar's much more spectacular sleepwalking incident—to be picked up a good hundred pages later when Sarsefield tells Edgar about having seen him on his way into the wilderness, barely dressed, no shoes on his feet, not responding to being called by his name. Sarsefield also tells Edgar about finding the missing letters in the attic of the uncle's house, proving the earlier sleepwalking incident.

---

28 By far the most dramatic episode in this regard is Edgar's awakening in the cave after sleepwalking into the wilderness. His alleged consciousness of "nothing but existence" (159) is a state in which his sense of embodiment is detached from any other sense of place. Yet even in this crude state, his body, not his consciousness, allows him to reconnect with the external world: by stretching out his sore limbs, feeling that he is lying on his back, noticing the rugged texture of the ground underneath him, and the striking freshness of the air in his lungs. This tactile mode of reconnection gradually expands, first into assessing the immediate space around him (walking along the wall of the cave, yelling out at the top of his lungs to estimate its size), then by providing food and drink and protecting himself against threats from the wilderness, and then by trying to get home.

Edgar's dream hence not only reminded him of his duty to destroy the letters but it also must have stirred his guilty conscience. His following action acted out the resulting pain, relieving him of his duty to copy the letters for Mary; in fact, hiding them at a place where their gradual destruction would have eventually fulfilled his promise to his deceased friend. Yet how he felt when performing these actions—was he swift or reluctant, was he grieving while engaged in them?—or why he chose this particular hiding place is "beyond recovery" as no one was consciously present when these plotted grounds were traversed for the first time.

The first sleepwalking incident also reveals, piece by piece, that no viable dwelling place can be built from this narrator's hermeneutical or imaginative work alone. His longing for other stories responds to the structural limitations of the narrative agency granted him within this storyworld. Indeed, his storytelling gravitates toward other narratives to fill the gaps in his impaired consciousness, and to compensate for the instabilities immanent to his hermeneutic efforts. Sarsefield's account of witnessing Edgar's sleepwalking is the most interesting case in this regard. For a short and happy moment, the longing for an interlocutor gives way to a conjoint act of storytelling: As Edgar and Sarsefield tell and listen to each other's stories when stumbling across one another amidst great confusion, their stories become complete, where both would have remained erring without the complementing account of the other. This triumph is soon questioned, however: Sarsefield was certain to have seen Edgar drown after his fall into the river, just as he is sure that Clithero drowned after jumping off the ship that was taking him to detention. In the first case, his flawed narrative is corrected by Edgar's account; whether or not he is also wrong in the second case is uncertain. Maybe Clithero did die after going overbroad, but the previous misinterpretation lingers, destabilizing—in not surely terminating Clithero's erring state—the prospects of future dwelling.

The narrative project of creating viable dwelling grounds is severely constrained by this narrative's eclipsed mode of recovery. It can only succeed when reconciling the narrating consciousness with the hazardous fact that it has been oblivious to its external world, absorbed with interior pains and obsessions from its past, not the present. And if sleepwalking is imagined here as being connected to unacknowledged feelings of guilt, the sleepwalking witnessed by Edgar before becoming a sleepwalker himself underscores this connection. When first seeing the sleepwalking Clithero, he is deeply moved by the other's grief and despair. The story that Clithero tells Edgar to prove that he did not kill his friend leaves no doubt that he, too, sleepwalks out of guilt. The obsessive burial of a stolen manuscript belonging to the person whom he believes to have murdered is his "pain-exerting" action. He, too, breaks into his own secret hiding place, hides and nearly destroys his most valued treasure elsewhere. In both cases, sleepwalking generates actions that are potentially harmful to the one performing them, thus turning the perpetrator into a possible victim. This leveling of distinctions between victim and perpetrator is indeed of great importance for what Brooks would call the "narrative design and intent" of this tale and its implied prospects of dwelling in the world. In crafting a story in which sleepwalking springs from an ailing, inarticulable sense of guilt that is potentially hazardous for its bearer, it does *not* exploit the topic of guilt to teach a moral lesson. On the contrary, guilt serves to *suspend* moral judgment. Trapped between a haunted past and a rejected future, dwelling in this narratively created state of suspension is the desired way of belonging that drives the telling of this tale. And it is to this end that sleepwalking is not exploited as a stabilizing metaphor but as a metonymic trajectory, "the figure of contiguity and combination, the figure of syntagmatic relations" (Brooks, "Masterplot" 281). Its conjoint forces of driving, deferring, and punctuating the narrative align Edgar's yearning to dwell in his narrative with the yearning to dwell in a state of suspended guilt.

The suspension of guilt is most powerfully pursued through sleepwalking, but it is practically omnipresent as the motif and motivation of storytelling in this novel. When Edgar decides to reconnect with his fiancée, he knows that he has kept her waiting, possibly for an irresponsibly long time, and perhaps he has made up his mind about terminating their engagement when he starts writing his letter. Prone to feel guilty about these matters, creating a favorable frame for her inevitable judgment is of utmost concern. Similar dispositions are at work in Edgar's final letter to Sarsefield, which closes with the words: "I shall not escape your censure, but I shall likewise, gain your compassion. I have erred, not through sinister or malignant intentions, but from the impulse of misguided, indeed, but powerful benevolence" (290). The breakup passage is another example: Edgar urges Mary to return the money, confronts her with the resulting consequence while doing everything to make the end of their engagement seem inevitable, including portraying himself as a victim. And although this passage achieves a remarkable conclusive density (thus creating the strongest sense of an ending in the middle of the book), the final sentence counters the moment of closure that has just been reached with a resurging longing for suspension: "These considerations, however, will be weighted when we meet" (157), he announces before steering straight into that part of his adventure that will turn him into the greatest victim of his sleepwalking—the moment of his awakening in the cave.[29]

---

[29] In the same passage, guilt suspension also plays out on a very different register of speech—omission—in Edgar's silence to rumors about Mary's pregnancy. Is this true? Is it Edgar's child? Is his silence based on a mutual agreement or is he imposing it? Does he want to abandon his responsibility? As if responding to this massive silence, the opening paragraph of the following chapter features the word "pregnant" that has been so thoroughly avoided when recounting Weymouth's story in what can be read as a metonymic slippage of the term. "The following incidents are of a kind to which the most ardent invention has ever conceived a parallel. [...] The scene [awaking in the cave] was *pregnant* with astonishment and horror" (158; my emphasis). This proximate metonymic use of the term can be read as a hint towards an act of deferred, probably unwillful acknowledgement.

The desire for a suspension of guilt brackets and undergirds the entire narrative and again, this desire leads straight to Edgar's manic *doppelgänger*. Upon learning that Clithero has impulsively killed Mrs. Lorimer's evil brother and that, out of maddening regret, nearly killed her, Edgar defends him as having "acted in obedience to an impulse which he could not control, nor resist. Shall we impute guilt where there is no evil design?" (91) This judgment is indeed crucial, for it turns the other from being the bearer of Edgar's unbound sympathy into being the personification of suspended guilt—and hence into a powerful figure of imaginary kinship. As a result of identifying with this imaginary placeholder of guilt suspension, Edgar outgrows the desire to save the other that drives the first half of the plot, and begins to reenact or double the other's behavior. This new desire constitutes the narrative thrust in the second half of the novel. The narrator's transformation into a sleepwalker is its most evocative sign of this shift of gears, and his passionate defense of Clithero turns *him* into a major suspect in the case of his best friend's murder.[30] This suspicion is officially proven wrong at the end of his letter to Mary. The deceased, it turns out, was the random victim of a revenge-seeking Indian determined to kill "the first human being whom he should meet" (281), with Edgar crediting himself for being the likely killer of that Indian.

Even so, our narrator is not quite rehabilitated from the suspicions of having played an active role in his friend's violent death. Does the desire to destroy Waldegrave's letters acted out in his first instance of sleepwalking not hint at an even deeper desire to destroy the one who wrote them? Could this desire have something to do with the latter's return to faith while Edgar stayed an atheist, a topic passionately discussed in these letters? Had Edgar secretly wished for his friend's death because he knew about Weymouth's money, started a relation with Mary out of sheer calculation about the inheritance, and now feels so guilty that he sleepwalks into the wilderness? And what about his odd friendship with the old Delaware woman known to the region's settlers as Old Deb/Queen Mab (both, obviously, non-indigenous names given to her by her colonizers), who turns out to be the mastermind behind the outburst of revenge violence that killed both Waldegrave and Edgar's uncle? Does this relation not strongly suggest a secret complicity of the narrator with death and destruction? Once again, sleepwalking offers itself as the most productive figure of contiguity and combination to plot evidence for this looming suspicion. In this case, it connects with the second name of the old Delaware woman, Queen Mab, a famous fairy character in English folklore, in highly suggestive ways. The name stems from a Celtic legend in which its bearer

---

30 Having the sleepwalker turn out as the murderer was presumably the idea of an earlier work, "Somnambulism," which Brown never finished. *Edgar Huntly* toys with this suspicion, for example in the final chapter, shortly before the murderer is revealed, when Edgar ponders over his and Clithero's sleepwalking, and concludes: "How little cognizance men have over the actions and motives of each other!" (278).

is a warrior queen. Frequently evoked by poets such as Herrick, Spencer, and Shelly, the best-known version of the character goes back to Shakespeare's *Romeo and Juliet*, where it brings the dreams to sleepers and presides over childbirth.[31] Edgar is closely connected to the native woman known by this name: Inspired by her "pretentions to royalty" (209) and the strangeness of her appearance, it was he who gave it to her.

In Edgar's meandering tale, this act of name-giving creates the occasion to tell her story. And in telling this story, Edgar's tale absorbs an uncanny reminder of the expulsion and dispossession imposed upon the native population that reads like a token of an emerging sense of discomfort (possibly even guilt) on the side of the settler colonialists from whose position Edgar speaks. Queen Mab's tribe, he reports, once lived on the grounds now occupied by his uncle's farm. When repeated harassments drove her people away, she refused to go along with them, burnt the wigwams, and moved to a hut deep in the woods where she "conceived that by remaining behind her countrymen she succeeded in government, and retained the possession of all this region" (208). In the narrative pursuit of belonging that becomes tangible here, "[t]he English were aliens and sojourners, who occupied the land only by her connivance and permission, and who she allows to remain on no other terms but those of supplying her wants" (208-9). When retelling Queen Mab's story, Edgar spends an entire paragraph describing the constant conversation with her three wild dogs, granting her (as the only woman and the only indigenous character of the novel) a voice of her own. And yet, she does not speak directly. Refusing the language of the colonizer, her long isolation has rendered her unintelligible even in her native language. Only Edgar has studied a little of her jargon, and, as a result, she is favorably inclined to him. For Myra Jehlen, her incessant, unintelligible speech addressing wild beasts, her control over these beasts, and their strange loyalty to her "parody the rituals of domestication," making her "a creature of romance and of Romanticism, conceivably a heroine, if a perverse one" (165). Edgar directly participates in creating this heroine: by associating her with the power of fomenting weird dreams that turns her—at least in Edgar's fancy—into a possible midwife in the dream material of his own (and by extension also his community's) worst nightmares, some of which he might have already acted out while sleepwalking. But "midway through the paragraph in which this possibility suggests itself, Brown pulls back" (165), having his protagonist concede that he has gone too far in seeing "some rude analogy between this personage and her whom the poets of old-time have delighted to celebrate: thou wilt perhaps discover nothing but incongruities between them, but, be that is it may, Old Deb and

---

31 In *Romeo and Juliet*, the character is evoked in Mercutio's speech, Act I, scene 4. A comprehensive genealogy of this reference is given in Barnard and Shapiro's annotated edition of Brown's novel (138-39).

Queen Mab soon came indiscriminate to general use" (*Edgar Huntly* 209, quoted in Jehlen 165).

Edgar's lack of insistence in the rightness of this name strips its bearer of the magic powers she has barely seized. Does this mean (as Jehlen argues) that the novel's only potentially transgressive character falters, that history wins over romance? That it was doomed to falter since its subversive potential was too weak to be fully realized by the narrative? Not necessarily. I prefer another reading (forwarded by Paul Witherington) in which romance and history are two distinct voices, both speaking from the novel in poetically sound ways (166-69). Oscillating between these two voices, the narrative is less an expression of the narrator's personal guilt (and not a product of a tension between conscious and unconscious levels of his storytelling). Rather, it makes tangible a tension between romantic aspiration and historic qualification that the text articulates in idiosyncratic yet exemplary ways. But whether one sides with Jehlen or Witherington, the double-voicedness of the narrative that both address exposes yet another limit of the narratable, and with it, another trajectory of suspending guilt. The romantic imagination emerging at this time is not yet fully hatched, which is why it cannot assume the role of a transformative force in its own right. But historical guilt cannot be aptly expressed as long as narrative agency and narrating consciousness remain disconnected. In the absence of an artistic vision (and the respective narrative techniques) that would suture the gap between a troubling experience and its redemptive mediation, guilt is exploited for the purpose of dwelling in a state of extended suspension, in which past injustice deadlocks with future anxiety.

The novel leaves no doubt that this state corrodes the foundations of the community imagined here. It tells the story of an attempted homecoming that is structurally and morally perverted: Instead of offering closure, it embarks on a process of narrative recovery whose outcome is selfish, provisional and uncertain. I read this courting of the contingent as a poetic response to a shared sense of social unrest and uncertainty that becomes bottomless in conjunction with the faltering faith in the adequacy of both reason and religion to soothe existential doubt. In tune with the emerging romantic spirit, the yearning for a place in the world turns to the imagination, the body, and the senses. Yet in distrusting their healing powers, this mode of emplacement dwells in a haunted and self-serving state of suspension.

3 The Art of Attachment
Sarah Orne Jewett's *The Country of the Pointed Firs*

Sarah Orne Jewett's regionalist masterpiece *The Country of the Pointed Firs* (1896) begins with an instance of return: A summer visitor comes back to the fictional town of Dunnet Landing on the rugged coast of Maine for a writing retreat after having fallen in love with the place several summers prior on a yachting cruise. A vacationer's return is temporary by nature, and as closely as this one gets acquainted with the place and its shrewd old inhabitants during the months of her stay, she does not become a true member of Dunnet's community. The position of the well-versed outsider is a staple of regionalism's investment in matters of belonging, and it is crucial for this book in particular. The mix of proximity and distance on which it thrives allows for an ethnographic view of a place whose remoteness offers more than a spatial sanctuary for the troubled modern soul. It grants access—return— to a different time, an imaginary past in which life is imbued with a powerful sense of stability and rootedness.

It has often been noted that the backwardness of costal Maine has a nostalgic appeal for Jewett's privileged visitor. And if the will to capitalize on the respective yearnings of an elitist audience counts as a hallmark of regionalist fiction, I do not want to contest this view here.[1] The charm of Dunnet Landing is indeed inseparably tied to a peaceful rural life for which the conflicted realities of a society grappling with the rise of urban industrialism serves as a tacit backdrop.[2] But *Pointed Firs* exploits the figure of the intimate outsider not only, and to my mind

---

1 Raymond Williams was instrumental in establishing this view. Two influential positions in the context of American letters are those of Brodhead and Kaplan.
2 For a long time, the nostalgic renderings of regionalist places were explained in terms of impoverishment: When New England's population and economic growth went elsewhere, political and cultural status vanished, and the region itself seemed to have been feminized: Regionalist writers, themselves predominantly female, were telling their stories to compensate for an actual state of lack or loss. See, for example, Westbrook; Douglas; Cox. With its focus on attachment, this chapter seeks to contest notions of the interplay of, narrative and nostalgia as a spiteful conundrum. This view, which is widely shared in our field, finds poignant expression in Stewart's *On Longing*. For Stewart, nostalgia is not only a thoroughly narrative phenomenon, transforming

not even primarily, to stage longings for a lost home. Rather, its nameless visitor is the narrating agent in an exercise in attachment that, in making porous the boundaries of her self through the love of place, is more than merely regressive. A treatment of place-as-friend provides the affective foundations for this feat, and the tale consummates it through the art of the sketch.

Jewett liked to think of *Pointed Firs* as a collection of "sketches," only rarely referring to it as a novel.[3] But her endorsement of the sketch does not mean that she was writing in its conventions (the literary genre was strictly confined to a historically-minded study of character at the time).[4] She used the description-based narrative mode that it affords to cross boundaries between sketch, story and novel in ways that were "pushing the envelope of conventional fiction," perhaps even probing a kind of "experimental fiction" *avant la lettre* (Goheen 30-34; here: 32). What makes Jewett's sketches so intriguing from the perspective of this study is their tenuous mode of engagement with the physical world; their tactile translation of sensory data into artistic form. The sketch's reputation of being a minor art form hinges on this basic makeup, and it is thus no surprise that associations with it were persistently used to diminish rather than valorize Jewett's work.[5] In what follows, I want to reverse this line of judgment and recalibrate *Pointed Firs*'s accomplishment in terms of the tenuous exercise in attachment conducted through the "minor" art of the sketch. My point of departure is simple: A sketch is always a sketch of some concrete thing in the world, and never a sketch of a mental object or image. Whether sketching is a precursory stage of a larger work or an artistic

---

the past into an imaginary shelter—which I agree with—but also a "social disease" (23)— which I find an unproductive generalization that this chapter seeks to complicate.

3   In a letter to her publisher Jewett even suggests advertising *Pointed Firs* as a sketch rather than a novel. Letter to Mr. Garrison on 22 April, partially dated, most likely written in 1880 (quoted in Goheen 32).

4   In the world of American letters, the sketch gained a high profile through Hawthorne's biographical treatment, to which Jewett was clearly not restricting herself.

5   A first reference to the sketch occurs in a letter by Horace Scudder after publishing one of Jewett's early stories. He writes: "Your story disappoints me, now that I read it in print. There seem to be good characters for a story and good scenery but no incident, no story. In other words that here is a sketch and not a picture" (Scudder to Jewett, 2 July 1870; quoted in Goheen 41). Henry James's ambiguous endorsement of Jewett's writing as "a beautiful little quantum of achievement" ("Fields" 30) resonates with these same issues. And while *Pointed Firs* was favorably reviewed, its most dissatisfied reviewer (writing for *Bookman*) ties his disappointment with the book directly to its endorsement of the sketch: "[…] the little volume comes to its quiet ending, leaving the impression that, suggestive and delightful as such books are, they cannot, save in rare instances, leave any deep impression. […] These delicate sketches of life hold the same place in literature as do their counterpart in painting, but no artist can rest an enduring popularity on such trifles light as air" (Anonymous; quoted in Howard, "Traffic" 2).

expression in its own right, it is always an act of familiarization (for the photo-realist painter Robert Bechtel even an act of "taking possession"). But familiarization is never complete, and hence the artist is inclined to move on to the next striking view, person, object, detail or scene before her work has reached a state of consummation.

Stressing the artistic thrust of this inherently unfinished practice is important, however, for art is always double-coded; it *does* something while also staging and reflecting its own doing. Approached this way, the tactile mode of engagement with an immediate "place world" that is key to Jewett's endorsement of the sketch makes tangible a longing to not only be familiar with this world but *attached* to it.[6] Reading *Pointed Firs* with an interest in its art of attachment is inspired by Rita Felski, who, invoking the Latourian notion that "[t]ies […] are not limits to action but a fundamental condition for action," and that emancipation "does not mean 'freed from bonds', but *well*-attached" (Latour, *Reassembling* 218), argues that "attachment is an ontological fact, an inescapable condition of existence" ("Latour" 738; 740).[7] Belonging, conceived here as an existential need for a place in the world, depends on and works through attachment; in fact, one could say that attachment is its basic emotional currency. But how are attachments formed and maintained, what does narrative have to do with it, and how does *Pointed Firs* exploit this relation?

In a most basic sense, attachment is an affective relation with the physical world: to places, people, and things about which and for whom we care because they are familiar to us. We have seen, felt, smelled, heard, or touched them many times, and storing these vast amounts of sensory data in our memory, let alone making sense of and creating connections between its countless bits and pieces across space and time, requires narrative mediation. But recording and storing impressions and memories is neither voluntary nor controllable. On the contrary, the fact that we have very little control over what we record and remember and what we omit, misplace or forget enhances our wish to safekeep and narrativize what we hold dear. It is indeed one of the puzzling paradoxes of using narrative for the purpose of safekeeping that, in demanding selection and combination, narrative creates its own modes of actualizing that to which it wants to attach itself. And if one of the endeavors of this study is to solicit an understanding of narrative as the mediating structure to which we turn to feel and direct our yearning for a place in the world, this chapter zeroes in on one of its most hands-on, and yet most capacious features: the capacity to create, regulate and maintain those attachments to the physical world that it takes to build a place and dwell in it.

---

6   The term is drawn from Edward Casey.
7   As I was writing this chapter Felski had just started working on her book with this topic, which bears the working title *Hooked: Art and Attachment*.

Regionalist fiction is paradigmatically invested in this operation. It tells stories about remote and backward places because it cares for them, and it is this topophilic disposition that defines its place in the context of late nineteenth-century American literature. Turning away from the urban or international scene that was realism's preferred environment (as a training ground for sensible judgment), regionalism explored the fringes of a rapidly changing society and recorded the quaint and exotic life-forms flourishing there. In terms of form, it favored shortness over length, description or dramatic exposition over dramatic development and consummation, all of which is highly conducive to Jewett's narrative art of attachment. As one of its foremost practitioners, Jewett, whose work has been favorably received throughout her own lifetime and beyond, has been substantial in defining our understanding of the genre. *Pointed Firs*, after *Deephaven* (1877) and *A Country Doctor* (1884), her third and most accomplished book, is of particular interest for conjoining matters of place and form in ways that exemplify narrative's intimate involvement with the physical world. Historically, this was a remarkable move. The need to belong that drives Jewett's tale finds relief in a radically intersubjective, reception-based model of narrative exchange that revolves around matters of familiarization and attachment at a time when its polar opposites, defamiliarization and detachment, were on the rise. These new aesthetic parameters stood in the service of an art that wanted to see the world with fresh eyes in order to overcome modern self-alienation. But these eyes were strikingly disembodied; in fact, the alleged freshness and rigor of their gaze depended on a systematic dissociation from its bearer's affective and visceral corporeality. Cognitive insight thus became a matter of cool introspection, which often went hand in hand with a twofold retreat: into the depth of one's mind and into the sheltered rooms of the private sphere. Henry James's Isabel Archer fully embodies this artistic agenda. In the pivotal moment, she sees Gilbert Osmond and Madame Merle's betrayal in front of her, framed by the doorway like a picture on the wall, yet it is only upon withdrawing to her room and spending the night reflecting on what she has seen that she is able to understand it and redirect her life accordingly.[8] Narrative

---

8 See James, *The Portrait of a Lady*, chapters XL and XLII. The instance of incomplete recognition, to be completed in Isabel's nocturnal reflection, is described as follows: "Just beyond the threshold to the drawing room she stopped short, the reason for her doing so being that she had received an impression. The impression had, in strictness, nothing unprecedented; but she felt it as something new, and the soundlessness of her step gave her time to take in the scene before she interrupted it. Madame Merle was in her bonnet, and Gilbert Osmond was talking to her; for a minute they were unaware she had come in. Isabel had often seen that before, certainly; but what she had not seen, or at least not noticed, was that their colloquy had for a moment converted itself into a sort of familiar silence, from which she instantly perceived that her entrance would startle them. [...] There was nothing to shock in this; they were old friends in fact. But the thing made an image, lasting only a moment, lie a sudden flicker of light. Their relative positions their

agency, when derived from this basic pattern, aims for the power of irritation, for self-transformation as the result of feeling unfamiliar and detached. Modernist art amplifies these dynamics while also casting doubt on the possibilities both of gaining true insight into an individual's inner core and of achieving reintegration into the social world. Yet despite their diverging aesthetic responses, both modernism and realism share the basic assumption that an improved state of belonging (if it can be attained at all) is the result of detachment.

Against the backdrop of this allegedly sketchy scenario, the present chapter wants to bring into view how Jewett's artistic practice both complements and challenges the dominant path of narrative art at her time. Doing so involves pondering over what kind of activity attachment is, and what forms of (narrative) agency it affords. Moreover, in assigning attachment rather than its opposite the role of a prerequisite of belonging, *Pointed Firs* gives occasion to reevaluate some of our most solid assumptions about narrative (and) agency. For when attachment becomes an explicit end of narration, acts of listening, retelling, mending, and caring—all of which are commonly received as passive, derivative, *female*—assume a proactive role. In telling a story that foregrounds these presumably minor components of narrative exchange, *Pointed Firs* exposes their gendered valences while rejecting supposedly "male" ends of narrative agency (such as transformation or self-realization) as superior means to dwell in the world.[9] It would be shortsighted to think of this agenda can as merely regressive, not least because a narrative agency that is geared toward attachment must forge ties to the physical world—to objects, places, people. It is this tactile, non-self-centered dimension of *Pointed Firs*'s narrative art in which I am interested here as a practical means of dwelling in the world.

Coinciding, furthermore, with the rise of realism and the professionalization of the literary field that dovetailed this development, Jewett's book raises far-reaching questions about the interstices of narrative art and the literary market—and hence, about belonging as a cultural commodity. In fact, *Pointed Firs* was conceived for, and to a viable extent even *by* this market, and the "object life" of *Pointed Firs* unleashed by this market in a series of material incarnations—a magazine and a

---

absorbed mutual gaze, struck her as something detected" (457-58). The very similar instance, reflected in strikingly similar terms—"The glimpse made a picture; it lasted only a moment, but that moment was experience" (35)—can be found in the programmatic essay "The Art of Fiction," in which James develops his visual theory of recognition and literature's guiding role in it.

9   It is no coincidence that most of regionalism's best-known authors are women—in addition to Jewett, one may think of Kate Chopin, Mary Wilkins Freeman, Mary Austin, and later Willa Cather—who turned the genre into the fertile ground for a female tradition and a hotbed of feminist ideas. Regionalism hence carved out a distinct place for women writers and for female concerns, and this in turn generated a rich body of scholarship. See, for instance, Bell, "Gender and American Realism;" Ammons, "Going in Circles;" Zagarell, "Narrative of Community;" Foote, *Regionalist Fictions*; Fetterley and Pryse, *Writing Out of Place*.

book publication as well as several posthumous editions, the most famous of them by Willa Cather—challenges the fixed and closural form of the book and the novel. New chapters were added and existing chapters rearranged in each of these publications, and many of these changes were unauthorized. And if this "object life" cannot be divorced from the printed matter in which it resides it makes palpable the process in which the book, as a cultural object and consumer good, emerges as a viable site of topophilic investment that this chapter seeks to explore.

Topophilic Dispositions

Pointed Firs tells a story of growing attachment to a place that stands out not because it is the most beautiful stretch of land on the coast of Maine but because it is already familiar. Narration set in with this personal bias—"[p]erhaps it was the simple fact of acquaintance with that neighborhood which made it so attaching"— and from the get-go the relation to this place is rendered in terms of friendship, the freest, most malleable form of interpersonal affection.

> When one really knows a village like this and its surroundings, it is like becoming acquainted with a single person. The process of falling in love at first sight is as final as it is swift in such a case, but the growth of true friendship may be a lifelong affair. (377)

Taking my cue from these opening lines, my guiding question in this section is: How and to what ends does the narrative stage and exploit the topophilic disposition on which it thrives? More specifically, I want to explore the interplay of affect(ion) and narrative mobilized for the purpose of dwelling in the world through *Pointed Firs*'s treatment of place as a friend. With this focus I am less concerned with deciphering what this place *means* and more with finding out what it *does*, especially what kind of (narrative) agency it yields.[10]

---

10 The meaning of regionalist places is an issue for heated debate, and it revolves around the basic opposition of it being ideologically coopted or resistant. Brodhead and Kaplan stress the reductive regress of tourist retreat and its conservative implications; Foote, Fetterley and Pryse insist on it being heterogeneous and different. *Pointed Firs* is an especially contested case in point. Some of the critics who praised the book for fathoming a quasi-utopian place of a female solidarity and care in the 1980s found it nativist and imperialist a decade later. See, for instance, Ammons and Zaragell. Yet no matter how original and diverse these accounts are, they all zero in on a particular ideological mechanism (nation, class, empire, race, ethnicity, sex, gender) to trace its implications for social formation and subject positioning within the fictional world of the text. The readings thus produced are mostly plausible, consistent, and even insightful when disagreeing with them, but there is a certain predictability about the ways in which they mirror

It is striking how readily the erotic force of an instant crush is dismissed for a presumably truer kind of affection. The primary measure of difference invoked here (through the organic metaphor of "growth" and its "lifelong" prospect) is temporal. The prospect for enduring friendship charges the remote coastal town not only with human virtues (trust, reliability) but also with existential vulnerabilities (growing old and frail). The place-as-friend allegory thus works toward invoking a relation of mutual, self-relativizing devotion and care. So if it has been argued that the subject of *Pointed Firs* "is less Dunnet Landing, its citizens, or even its regional interest as such, and more friendly comportment and its spiritual meaning" (Shannon 241), I almost agree. Jewett's narrative art of attachment programmatically draws these subjects together, materially reinforcing them in its treatment of place as friend.

Jewett's high regard of friendship was subtended by Swedenborgian doctrine, from which she adopted the notion that a special form of love for one's neighbor leads to salvation. Ideas of the Swedish mystic circulated widely in American literary circles at the time, so much so that it has been called his "age."[11] Their impact on Jewett was momentous for helping her overcome a spiritual crisis early on in her adult life, which involved her conflicted feelings for a close female friend.[12] Quite possibly, the mode of affective engagement endorsed in *Pointed Firs* echoes its author's personal struggles, which she came to resolve in intimate same-sex friendships, particularly with her long-term companion Annie Fields. Jewett and Fields lived in a marriage-like relationship for many years after Annie's husband,

---

the shifting ideological grounds of the field—thus making palpable that scholarly narratives, too, are engaged in matters of belonging and place-making.

11   For example by F .O. Matthiessen in his preface to *The American Renaissance* (viii). According to religion historian Sydney Ahlstrom, "Swedenborg's influence was seen everywhere [in America at this time]; in Transcendentalism and at Brook Farm, in spiritualism and the free labor movement, in the craze for communitarian experiment, in faith healing, in mesmerism, and half a dozen medical cults; among great intellectuals [for example William James, about whom I will have more to say], crude charlatans, and innumerable frontier quacks" (quoted in Hart 518).

12   Jewett was introduced to Swedenborgian ideas in the 1870s by Theophilus Parsons Jr., a Harvard law professor and one of their main disseminators in the U.S. The two met when Parsons vacationed in Maine. Donovan thinks that Jewett's feelings for her close friend Kate Birckard in the early 1870s were a crucial factor in the crisis that Jewett underwent at this time, and which led her to embrace Swedenborgianism. Be that as it may, the character Kate Lancester in her first novel *Deephaven* is not only named after Jewett's close friend, she also makes the most outspoken Swedenborgian comments in the book. See Donovan, "Jewett and Swedenborg" 732-34. Tempting as it may be to think of Jewett as a lesbian writer, it is important to bear in mind she never overtly addressed sexuality in its post-sexological sense. In Howard's apt words, Jewett "has a place among writers who portray intimacies and devotions that do not follow heterosexual scripts" ("Traffic" 8).

the influential publisher James Fields, had passed away. Such relationships between two women were so common in New England at the time that scholars have invented a name for them, "Boston marriages," and often, as in the case of Jewett and Fields, they consolidated in response to one of them becoming a widow.[13] Yet whereas Swedenborg saw heterosexual marriage as the ultimate expression of divine love in human terms, Jewett replaces the neighbor with the friend, and along with this move she sacralizes the affective domain of friendship (Shannon 236-37). Moreover, and crucially, this sacalization gives friendship a placial quality. Just as a place unfolds from a network of relations and not from a bilateral conjunction, friendship is a mode of affective attachment that is decidedly less exclusive, less normative, less private than marriage while not necessarily being shorter lived. And it is in precisely this vein that *Pointed Firs* features friendship as a place-making agent: Its topophilic disposition both grounds and mobilizes the sacred dimension of friendship in and through the love of place. So if, in "[y]oking together the realms of spiritual and material life, friendship forms the soul's 'country'" that, in turn, "translates, transports and transfigures the self" (Shannon 228), it is through the allegorical treatment of place as friend that *Pointed Firs*'s concerns with dwelling in the world are brought to converge in an overarching concern with attachment to a spiritually enhanced place world.

Clearly, the strongest friendship bond in the book is that between the nameless narrator and her landlady, the wondrous, widowed Mrs. Todd. And while the rapidly growing affection between the two women is enforced by the fact that they live under the same roof, their shared site is not merely domestic. Mrs. Todd is the local herbalist who runs her business from home, and it does not take long until her tenant helps out in dealing with the frequently calling customers. From this house the place-making power of friendship branches all the way out to the remote channel island where Mrs. Todd's mother and brother live. In fact, the island gains its fabulous appeal through friendship as place (a local constellation of people who are affectively disposed to the narrator and display their affection at particular sites) and form (shared observations, memories, meals, songs).[14] The

---

13 See Faderman 90; Donovan, "Love Poems" 101. Faderman defines a "Boston marriage" as a monogamous relation based on female values, in which one woman's life was spent primarily with another woman, each giving to the other the bulk of affection and energy (109). The relation between Jewett and Fields lasted for almost three decades, during which they lived together for part of the year, travelled together, corresponded daily, shared interests in books and people, and gave each other a sense of belonging. See Roman and Fryer for an emphatic endorsement of their relationship. Love thinks that this line of work too readily dismisses the loneliness and isolation that homosexual women must have experienced at the time, and that reverberates so strongly and coherently from Jewett's writing that, for her, it emblemizes a "spinster aesthetic" (310-13).

14 "The Bowden Reunion" chapter, in which the visitor gets as close as she will to belonging to Dunnet Landing, and which has recently been predominantly read in terms of a nativist and

place-making power of friendship is also directed inward, where it complicates the intimacy within Mrs. Todd's "quaint little house with as much comfort and unconsciousness as if it were a larger body, or a double shell" (421). These are curious metaphors for a dwelling place, animating it both in human and in non-human terms as a magical equilibrium between separation and unity. And if this nearly perfect state is threatened by the arrival of another visitor, this long-term acquaintance of Mrs. Todd's becomes a "sincere friend" (421) of the narrator within hours of being exposed to her company. It is through recurring instances of this kind that friendship gains a placial quality throughout the narrative: by exploiting the topophilic disposition at its core for the purpose of fostering multilateral acquaintance, and by giving shape to the setting through the caring bonds among female friends (the anxiously awaited houseguest is, of course, yet another elderly woman).

Moreover, and crucially, finding herself in a local web of female affection is essential to the growing state of attachment that motivates the narrator's act of telling. These bonds are especially strong since Dunnet's women are neither bound up in heteronormative commitments nor confined to the domestic sphere. These women make up the thrust of *Pointed Firs*'s narrative-generating love of place, while the men (old and frail as most of them are) are consigned to the margins of a gendered topography that invokes an alternative "female world of love and ritual" (Smith-Rosenberg, "Female World").[15] The fictionality of *Pointed Firs*'s setting might be a tribute to this tacit utopianism, and when wondering what bestows the place with its utopian air, the matrifocal community immediately comes to mind. Like in Charlotte Perkins Gilman's *Herland*, written a few decades later and possibly inspired by Jewett's novel, this utopia is spatial rather than temporal; no magical time travel is involved in getting there since traveling (back) in time is rendered as a function of traveling across space.[16] In stark difference to *Herland*, however,

---

elitist exclusionism performed by a local clan, can also be read along these lines. Against claims that the reunion is both a "celebratory mythologization of a rural martifocal community" and a "protofascist" endorsement of "racial purity and white cultural dominance" (Ammons, "Material Culture" 91-92, 96), or of the Bowden family as "one of the many fraternal [sic] organizations— among them the Knights of Columbus and the KKK—that flourished during this period" (Gilman 113), Shannon makes a compelling case for reading it as "a ritual of affiliation, specifically the relationships it suggests between friendship and family," not least since the Bowden clan comprises "almost everyone within a sphere of contact" (Shannon 250-51).

15 Most of the men in *Pointed Firs* have died long ago, and those who are still around are aptly represented by the shrewd Captain Littlepage whose name alone carries a humorous gesture of diminishment. For an inventory of the marginalized male characters in *Pointed Firs* see Bell 67-71.
16 I owe this insight to Katharina Metz, who writes about Gilman's utopian novel in her dissertation *The Language of Altruism*. Female and feminist utopian fiction was a flourishing genre at the time. For an overview see Lewes, *Gynotopia*. *Pointed Firs* is not among her list of over 50 volumes published between 1836 and 1900. Levy, in her study on feminist utopian visions of the home place,

which solves the problem of social reproduction on its all-female world-island through virgin birth, there are no children in the self-contained "land of the pointed firs," not even on the horizon. All of the women whom we encounter are past childbearing (with the exception of maybe the narrator, who seems to be in her forties but does not come across as an aspiring mother).

Pointed Firs's dismissal of procreation is crucial for at least two reasons: It rejects the heteronormative alliance of motherhood and domesticity that was the overpowering ideal of femininity at the time. Even more pertinently, however, it forecloses the future for its community. The enchanted place unfolding from Dunnet's network of loving and caring relations is *dying*, and this creates a powerful paradox. For what do we make of a utopia of old and dying people even if they are as radiant as Mrs. Todd's eighty-something-year-old mother, "a delightful little person herself with bright eyes and an affectionate air of expectation like a child on a holiday" (406), who might be the secret queen of Dunnet Landing but by sheer biological fact is facing the end "of her summers and their happy toils" (408), with children who are themselves old and childless remnants of an earlier age? What ends, we may ask, are served by conjoining elegiac mood and utopian air in and through the love of place as friend? In grappling with this paradox, a crucial distinction is in order: Regardless of the actual place that inspired the narrative (had it already ceased to exist when writing about it, or had it never existed as remembered here in the first place?), the beloved place in the world of the text is not dead; it is dying. The difference is crucial because anticipating death has its own temporality—a heterochronic hyperpresence that absorbs the past in the absence of a knowable future. This extraordinary, "artificial" time creates its own topographic realities in the world of *Pointed Firs*—"waiting place[s] between this world an' the next" (397), one of them being the mythical "country 'way up north beyond the ice" (395) populated by zombie-like, "fog-shaped men" (396), another the small inaccessible channel island ("a bad place to get to, unless the wind an' tide were just right") that served Joanna Bowden for her lifelong hermitage after being "crossed in love" (429).[17] These two sad places find a viable counter-site in Green Island, with its youthful old people, shared meals and song, an abundant growth of rare herbs and affective bonds. It is a place of hospitality and enchantment rather than exile and despair.

Even so, with the queen of Green Island being over eighty years old (which was ancient at the time), Green Island is a waiting place nevertheless. Bestowed with mythic perfection in the narrator's emphatic account—"one could not help wishing to be a citizen of such a complete and tiny continent and home of fisherfolk" (407)—the remote island resembles a heaven on earth. The reason for this is that

---

uses *Herland* to set the stage for discussing the works of Jewett (with a special focus on *Pointed Firs*), Willa Cather, Ellen Glasgow, Katherine Anne Porter, Eudora Welty, and Gloria Naylor.

17 The term "heterochronic" is, of course, drawn from Foucault.

it materializes friendship as "a consecrated way of life" (Shannon 241). Rife with Swedenborgian ideas about an afterlife in which "old friends renewed their love and brought it to greater intensity" (Donovan 732), it is a place that can dismiss the future because it embodies an extraterrestrial state. Dunnet Landing's difference from its heterotopian otherworldliness is marked by the narrator calling it "large and noisy and oppressive" (420) upon returning there. But the contrast dissolves at night, when "the village was so still that I could hear the shy whippoorwills singing as I lay awake in my downstairs bedroom, and the scent of Mrs. Todd's herb garden under the window blew in again and again with every gentle rising of the sea breeze" (420). That Dunnet Landing resumes this hyperpresence of caressing sounds and smells as the nameless visitor anticipates the "small death" of sleep exposes the degree to which it, too, is a mythical waiting place—possibly of the Green Island variety.

The Sketch and the Journey

Except for the first short chapter, *Pointed Firs* is the first-person narrative of our nameless summer vacationer, and hence the place that we encounter is quintessentially *her* place—filled with her longings, mediated through her senses, put forth in her language and imagery, rendered by her selective taste and compositional skill. Jewett opted for this most subjective of all narrative voices, and yet she gave it neither a name nor much of a life story. In fact, the nameless narrator tells a story that dwells in close contact with the physical world while leaving introspective reflections of temporal matters largely aside. With Edward Casey, I want to think of the point of view endowed here as *placial*: Rather than prompting an immersion in the unfolding of time, which is always closely tied to consciousness and the mind, it engages "an alliance between an outlook into place and our existence as bodily beings. Adopting such a viewpoint [...] precipitates us [...] into bodily comportment: how we move, where we stand" (452). Jewett's nameless visitor fully inhabits this point of view. Nowhere in her narrative does she delve inward to contemplate the course of her life; introspection—the narrative scheme in which troubled states of belonging are so often reflected and potentially resolved—does not play a role in this book. Instead, narration revolves around the "experience of living through [her] corporeal intentionality as it engages with the places of [her] near sphere— and as they in turn nestle within the containing horizon of [her] immediate place world" (Casey 452). In doing so, the act of telling performed in *Pointed Firs* is always within touching distance (*in Tuchfühlung*) of its subject matter.

The sketch is the perfect form for this kind of narrative, for no other artistic practice is so genuinely directed toward the immediate place world of the person engaged in it. Where one stands, and how one moves vis-à-vis one's subject matter affects the outcome immediately. And while the translation of sensory data into artistic form is never unmediated (simply because there is no such thing as unmediated experience), sketching stands out in its relatively direct engagement with the physical world. And this brings me back to my earlier claim that the most basic impulse behind the art of the sketch is familiarization. It is both literal—for the promise of unobstructed encounter—and serial—because acquaintance is never complete. A new angle on the same object, a slight change of light, a rivaling site of interest in the vicinity will start the familiarization process anew. How seamlessly compatible this potentially open-ended type of artistic production is for the purpose of catering to an audience craving for a tangible, familiar world as a commodity will concern us later on. For now, I want to focus on the affordances of the sketch as a narrative mode. Stemming from the repertoire of the visual arts, the sketch brings to mind techniques such as pencil drawing or water coloring, both of which capture the nook of the world in front of the artist in a few precise gestures. Some playful lines on paper are enough to evoke the object or scene at hand (along with the body of the artist).[18] In the world of letters much of the discrete physicality of the sketch is lost; what remains—and is masterfully put to use in *Pointed Firs*—is the translation of select physical details into evocative signs. Selection can be as random as putting two juvenile chickens into the domestic setting of Mrs. Todd's upbringing on Green Island, arguably the sacred core of the entire fictional place world. Approaching the "small white house" from the landing, the narrator registers "the bright eyes and brainless little heads of two half-grown chickens who were snugged down among the mallows as if they had been chased away from the door more than once, and expected to be again" (408). The image evoked here is uncannily precise and suggestive. Placing the chickens at Mrs. Blackett's doorstep, tucked in with the mallows (just like the house itself is tucked "iceberg"-like into the landscape "as if [it was] two-thirds below the surface" [408]) gives the domestic scene an air of wholesomeness. Dumb and ordinary as they are, the juvenile birds have a place in this perfect little world.

Jewett's sketches thrive on being descriptive for sure, but this is not to say they are transparent or neutral. Finding chickens—not one but two—important enough to put in the "Green Island" sketch, combining them with further details (the tender mallows, the doorstep to Mrs. Blackett's house), describing them affectionately (the birds are "snugged" to the ground by the door), all of these choices attune our perception of the place world made visible here with the caressing gaze of the narrator. And if description is always geared toward making something visible, how this is done modulates our perception of and relation to its subject matter. But Jewett does not engage vision as the disembodied master sense of truthful

---

18 For Byerly, the sketch in visual art is "a rapidly drawn picture that sacrifices aesthetic finish for a sense of spontaneity." This idea, when appropriated into literature, displays a certain disdain for *techne* and removes the layer of artifice so distrusted by displaying the kind of honesty gleaned from spontaneity.

perception which classical realism (especially of the Henry Jamesian kind mentioned above) values as a primary tool of self-assertion.[19] Her sketches take us close, so close that the visual sense is pushed back on behalf of the less assertive senses—especially sound and smell, which make us feel at their mercy rather than in control. Without a shutting mechanism, their default *modus operandi* is pure exposure: They break down distance and bring the world up close, and Jewett's narrator exploits them to this very end. Mrs. Todd's "queer little garden," for instance, is described through the "fragrant presence" of the herbs flourishing there. The "bushy bit of green" gains discernible contours when the breeze comes in from the sea, "laden with not only sweetbrier and sweet-mary, but balm and sage and borage and mint, wormwood and southernwood," and after a short while the narrator knows "in exactly which corner of the garden [Mrs. Todd] might be" (378) based on the smells set free by the stroke of her skirts and the weight of her feet. Likewise, the soundscape around Shellheap Island—"gay voices and laughter from a pleasure-boat" (444)—deepens the narrator's understanding of Joanna Bowden's hermitage. More examples could easily be found, and in all of them the placial point of view endorsed in *Pointed Firs* is crucial for their synesthetic renderings of proximity. In fact, it is through this technique that familiarization is fathomed in terms of attachment—as a fully embodied, multi-sensual form of close contact in which reception and description are seamlessly intertwined.

A brief comparison of Jewett's style with that of another regionalist writer, Kate Chopin, is instructive here: Chopin's writing is equally sensuous for sure, yet whereas her impressionistic style resorts to a semantic field of bodily and emotive— erotic—stimulus with the aim of engendering an aching desire for change, Jewett's descriptive mode stresses the sensuous materiality of the physical world with the aim of engendering attachment. And while Chopin mobilizes Edna, her heroine in *The Awakening*, to the degree that she realizes that social norms and expectations make it impossible to build a viable dwelling place, turning temporal relief (death) into the ultimate resort of self-realization, Jewett lets her nameless narrator record her near sphere in ways that make building and dwelling seem feasible. But are there not pitfalls to such a descriptive mode, and if yes, how do they play out in *Pointed Firs*? For Susan Stewart, "all description is a matter of mapping the unknown unto the known" (26); doing so involves a hierarchization of information, and hierarchization means imposing significance and value.[20] The chicken detail,

---

19 For matters of vision and visuality in Henry James see especially Brosch, Schneck, and Seltzer; for a counter-agenda of regionalist writers such as Jewett and Freeman see Bader, "Dissolving Vision."
20 Again, Stewart's stance on the matter is highly representative of our field. This is how she further elaborates her point: "Descriptions must rely upon an economy of significance which is present in all of culture's representational forms, an economy which is shaped by generic conventions and not by aspects of the material world itself. While our awe of nature may be born in the face of her infinite and perfect detail, our awe of culture relies upon a hierarchical organization of

for instance, values ordinariness, creatureliness, togetherness, organic belonging to a domestic cosmos, and the list could easily be continued. But the sketch makes this detail suggestive rather than definitive; the reality that it helps construe is tentative rather than solid. And while detail is certainly used realistically in *Pointed Firs*, it does not so much mime reality as *authenticate* it. Jewett's use of detail neither adheres to the logic of abundance employed in realism's signature style of verisimilitude nor does it seek to create a mental image that is believable because it is accurate. Rather, the "reality effect" of the sketch aims for credibility by using just a few spontaneously selected details that are prone to capturing our interest but require further affective and hermeneutic investment.[21]

This kind of realism—Jewett herself referred to it as "imaginative realism" (Cary, *Jewett Letters* 122)—is typical of the art of the sketch as a whole. Its mode of description is thin rather than thick, its valorizations are tentative rather than thorough; hence the air of the fleeting and the provisional that always surrounds the sketch. As an ephemeral art it asks not only for a high degree of participation but also for our care. Moreover, and crucially, in exposing a generic dependency on the physical world, the sketch also displays—and in *Pointed Firs* empathically—the yearning for material intimacy that drives it. And this is where Jewett's description diverts from Stewart's assessment in ways that trouble Stewart's analytical grid. In embracing the new, object-based epistemology that came to fruition in the 1890s and in which "physical things attach people to place" (Brown 197), significance becomes determined by generic conventions *and* by aspects of the material world.[22] The details that make up the storyworld of *Pointed Firs*—rocks, trees,

---

information, an organization which is shared by social members and which differs cross-culturally and historically. Not our choice of subject, but our choice of aspect and the hierarchical organization of detail, will be emergent in and will reciprocally effect the prevailing social construction of reality. As genres approach 'realism,' their organization of information must clearly resemble the organization of information in everyday life. Realistic genres do not mirror everyday life; they mirror its hierarchization of information. They are mimetic of values, not of the material world. Literature cannot mime the world; it must mime the social" (26). Of course, I agree that description (like any representation) is social and thus laden with value. But the mimetic understanding of realistic genres suggested here fails to do justice to the dialogical dimension inherent to it. They do not so much mirror or mime social reality as proactively participate in their construction, which also means that they negotiate rather than simply perpetuate values. In fact, the selective use of detail serves precisely this end.

21 The term is drawn from Barthes, "L'Effet de Réel." See also *S/Z*. For a lucid discussion of realism's inherently dialogical form that counters received notions of realism as a straightforward mimetic extension of ideology see Ickstadt, "Concepts of Society."

22 Recent scholarship has given a heightened attention to object and material culture in *Pointed Firs*. See especially Bill Brown's chapter on Jewett in his landmark study on the interstices of material culture and literature, *A Sense of Things*, which was published separately as "Regional Artifacts"

houses, herbs, tools, pieces of furniture, animals, items of food and drink—are molded straight from the environment about which Jewett writes, and how she writes about them oscillates between fiction and ethnography.

Such writing calls for a special use of details, one that exceeds the aim of producing a resemblance of reality in the reader's imagination, that uses details not as mere signs or referents but as facts, or rather: as *data*. In close correspondence to the sketch as a literal record of sensory imprints, Jewett's details function as material inscriptions of reality into the storyworld.[23] Charged with a discrete physicality and inscribed with a history of long-term exposure (to seasons and weather, work routines and daily chores), they saturate bodily life and gain corporeality in and through Jewett's characters. Or, as Willa Cather puts it in her preface to *Pointed Firs*: "Miss Jewett wrote people that grew out of the soil" ("Preface" 8). And while *Pointed Firs* is, at the end of the day, clearly a work of fiction with invented places and characters and a made-up course of events, the factual gravity of its naturalistic use of detail-as-data is crucial to its persuasiveness as a literary text. Mrs. Todd's brother William, for instance, is described as "an elderly man, bent in the shoulders as fisherman often are" (411), and Captain Littlepage has "the same 'cant to leeward' as the wind-bent trees on the height above." With his "thin, bending figure," his "narrow, long-tailed coat" and walking stick he looks, to the narrator, "like an aged grasshopper of some strange human variety" (384-85). It is through descriptions like these that Jewett evokes an acute intimacy between the place and its people, a sense of human bodies being molded into shape by the routines and conditions that physically define the place world to which they belong. Couched in her narrator's casual rendering, the old sea captain's peculiar shape is the "natural" course of things in a world in which nature and culture are continuous, interlocking forces.

Perhaps William Dean Howells's grasshopper varieties have prompted this image of Littlepage: "the ideal grasshopper, the heroic grasshopper, the impassioned grasshopper, the self-devoted, adventureful, good old romantic card-board grasshopper," all of which "must die out before the simple, honest, and natural grasshopper can have a fair field" (*Fiction and Criticism* 13). Featured in one of Howells's influential *Harper's* editorials that he used to flesh out and promote the new literature that he found apt for his age, these grasshoppers make up the satirical thrust of an attack against the "culturally constructed type"—and against a narrative art in the service of cultivating the ideal rather than being "simple, natural, and honest [...] like a real grasshopper" (12-13).[24] Jewett's grasshopper is

---

in *Critical Inquiry*. Ammons, in "Material Culture," reads Jewett's object world as manifesting the author's ideas about nativism and imperialism.

23   This understanding of detail in naturalism draws from Howard, *Naturalism* 147.
24   Howells wrote his monthly statements "From the Editor's Study," which were later published as *Criticism and Fiction* between 1886 and 1892. Patchworked as they are, his editorials are the most

also humorous (in an endearing rather than a disseminating kind of way), but it is certainly not "real" in Howells's sense of referring to no more than the living creature itself. Indeed, Jewett's realism does something quite different than what her former mentor had in mind.[25] Naturalistically inclined as her details are, they invoke a material history of the metonymic trace. Describing the old sea captain as an aged grasshopper not only makes present physical force as it equally affects man and animal, flora and fauna, live and dead matter. It invokes a narrative trajectory in which the shape of a human figure embodies a state of rootedness. Doing so also hints at the alternative lives that did not or could not materialize for this human figure in the given circumstance. But rather than further dwelling on this unrealized matter, Jewett lets her narrator proceed instantaneously, with the effect of turning a detail that so clearly stands for more than the literal meaning lingering on the descriptive surface into a viable echo chamber.

"Don't write a 'story' but just *tell the thing*" was a piece of advice that Jewett liked to give to younger writers (Cary, *Jewett Letters* 120; emphasis in the original). And if storytelling thrives on the dramatic art of emplotment—of which Jewett thought herself as incapable—*thing-telling* thrives on the tactile, descriptive art of the sketch.[26] So yes, Jewett's advice clearly harks back to the object-orientation of her narrative art. But the idea of transmitting the physical world as faithfully as possible is not materialistic *per se*. It is charged with a symbolism that is steeped in Swedenborgian doctrine.[27] Besides being taken with the Swedenborgian notion of "use" (which Jewett was able to translate into a professional and artistic sense of purpose), it was the idea of the spiritual permeating the material world that profoundly impressed her. And because she thought of her writing as striving to express this relation, she found herself at odds with "Mr. Howells [who] thinks [...] that it is no use to write romance anymore"—marveling instead "how much of it there is left in every-day life after all" (*Letters of Jewett*, ed. Fields 59). But while the residual symbolism stemming from this belief was didactic and overt in her earlier work (especially in her first book *Deephaven*), it becomes a tacit feature of everyday

---

comprehensive account of Howells's understanding of realism, and publication with *Harper's* saw to their wide circulation. The grasshopper passage is part of the December editorial of 1887.

25   Howells was an avid supporter of Jewett's early work. He published some of her first stories during his time as the editor of *The Atlantic Monthly* and was pivotal in encouraging the production of her first novel, *Deephaven*, published by Osgood and Co. (later Houghton Mifflin) in 1877.

26   In an often quoted letter to Scudder, Jewett writes: "[...] I don't believe I could write a long story [...] In the first place I have no dramatic talent. The story would have no plot. I should have to fill this out with descriptions of characters and meditations. It seems to me I can furnish a theatre, and show you the actors and the scenery, and the audience, but there is never any play!" (*Jewett Letters* 29)

27   In my account of Swedenborg's influence on Jewett's artistic practice I am substantially drawing on Donovan, "Jewett and Swedenborg."

life and its object world in *Pointed Firs*, where naturalistic details are allegories for something unstated. Jewett had distanced herself from the direct, didactic allegory promoted by Swedenborg, and yet she remained invested in his idea that language is founded upon correspondence. In fact, her notion of "telling things" places *things* in a context of unstated correspondence (both in the relational and the communicative sense) in which they become part of a larger whole precisely because they are *told*.

Pointed Firs exploits this dynamic as its form-giving principle: Cosmic unity becomes tangible in metonymic traces, and what these traces reveal under the careful scrutiny of the narrator's caressing gaze are lives devoted to daily routines and chores (and an act of living resembling the act of writing a narrative script). The narrator's visit to Mrs. Blackett's bedroom is a case in point. The intimate space that she enters here revolves around a mundane everyday object, Mrs. Blackett's rocking chair. The adjectives used to describe it (old, quilted) as well as the activities conducted when sitting in it (resting, reading) value the object through a material intimacy with the human body. The object becomes *legible*, and what we read is a story of human attachment through touch. And as the narrator grasps that the old chair is part of an assemblage of other things she beings to elicit the following narrative: The "worn bible on the lightstand," the "heavy, silver-bowed glasses," the "thimble [...] on the narrow wood-ledge," the "thick striped-cotton shirt that she was making for her son" and that now lay "folded carefully on the table"—every little detail in this passage is part of an everyday routine that ties the old lady, through the modest possessions gathered here, to an object world of used and useful things. But it is the needlework the captures her attention most acutely. The imaginative act inspired by it turns a tedious chore into a labor of love and the object world gathered by it into a virtual shrine of belonging. "Those dear old fingers and their loving stitches, that heart which made most of everything that needed love! Here was the real home, the heart of the old house on Green Island!" (420)[28]

The shirt that the old mother is sowing for her elderly son brings to mind all the shirts she has ever made for him (and for other members of her family) when sitting in this very spot. In the legible, object-based presence of repetitive routines and domestic rituals description veers into narrative, and what we are told is a mythical tale about the true meaning of this nuclear place. And if no belonging (and no narrative) is possible without repetition and ritual, in Jewett's descriptive

---

28 The narrator's visit to Mrs. Blackett's bedroom is one of several instances in which Jewett uses of needlework as a metaphor for female bonding and intergenerational collectivity, as well as for psychic and somatic integration. And if the old quilted rocking chair in which the work is routinely performed is the "heart" of the home, the "little brown bedroom" is both a literal room and an allegory of a peaceful psychic state. Tropes of quilting, sewing, weaving, or knitting, even though they are rallying points of feminist scholarship, have to my knowledge not been explored with regard to Jewett's work. For general scholarly work on the topic see Hedges; Torsney and Elsley.

style repetition and ritual are agents of topophilic stability and enchantment. The move from tactile description to emphatic meditation that is a defining feat of this style is conducted via a heightened intensity (the two final sentences of the rocking chair passage have exclamation marks). Shifts like these occur throughout the text, and often the move beyond the domain of the literal is indexed by imagistic or fictional markers ("like," "as if"). In moments like these, the metonymic trace on the surface of an object is prone to eliciting not only narrative but also attachment. The operative principle of Jewett's descriptive mode becomes tangible here: The yearning for attachment that drives narration from sketch to sketch is told *intermittently*, in the recurring shifts from tactile description to emphatic meditation.

Thematically, the episodic instances of familiarization strung together this way may best be described as a series of reduced and yet highly evocative expositions of different states of belonging. There is the wondrous Mrs. Todd, a longtime widow to a seafaring husband, who leads her admirably self-determined life as the village's eminent herbalist. There is Captain Littlepage whose deep-seated fear of death entraps him in the story of the mysterious "waiting place" between this world and the next way up in the Arctic Sea. There is Mrs. Blackett's perfect homestead on Green Island, which magically keeps her young. There is her son William's shrewd withdrawal from other people, ended in a later Dunnet Landing story with his marriage to a shepherdess. There is the long-anticipated visit of a friend equipped with the skills to make a whole way of life out of visiting (and one should, of course, bear in mind that "visiting" was a social institution at the time that meant taking someone into one's home for weeks and months on end). There is Joanna Bowden's self-imposed exile after disappointed love. There is the yearly reunion of the Bowden family, a social event of unmatched grandeur in which the narrator gets to participate. And there is the poor fisherman Elijah Tilley and his inconsolable grief about his long-deceased wife. The states of belonging invoked here alternate between isolation and embeddedness, lack and abundance. It has been argued that this pattern creates a unified whole in the end (Berthoff, "Pointed Firs;" Waggoner); in terms of belonging, this New Critical sense of unity might translate into a state of aesthetic transcendence that resides in an artfully crafted story and has the power to redeem alienation.

The stronger and more obvious force holding the sketches together, however, is the travel motif that is so typical of longer narrative forms. And while travel depends on narrative to grapple with the unfamiliar that it always encounters, "[t]he different stages of travel—departure, voyage, encounters on the road, and return—provide any story with a temporal structure that raises certain expectations for things to happen" (Mikkonen 2007, 286). Thinking of narrative in terms of travel is indeed so pervasive that "we have come to understand personal life and mental development as a voyage" (286). The travel motif in *Pointed Firs* exploits this tacit conundrum. The trip to the remote coastal town ignites a process of spiritual transformation that is broadened and deepened in the manifold travel activities conducted over the course of the summer; the tale that we read is an account of both journeys.[29] For a scarcely plotted story like *Pointed Firs* the travel motif provides a temporal baseline that follows the logic of the itinerary: The narrative moves from place to place, and it is at these places—which are always particular, and always interrelational—that events happen, one after another. In the narrator's account of her summer, the consecutive relation between places and events is at times more explicit than at others. It is accentuated, for instance, when, right after Captain Littlepage's dreadful story about the mysterious "waiting place" in the Arctic Sea, the magical illumination of Green Island by the evening sun inspires the voyage to this place that is the theme of the following sketches. But when Mrs. Fosdick comes for a visit after the narrator's return from Green Island it is not clear at all; in fact, we do not even get a sense of how much time passes between the separate events in this latter case. In this episodic structure, acts of familiarization and attachment are amplified, while a more forceful plot would have diminished their emotive force.

Moreover, and no less importantly, the implied chronology in the order of the sketches that needs to be *in place* to grasp that the narrator's spiritual journey diverts from the travel narrative's usual scheme: It does not move from departure to return but proceeds the other way around. The result is a narrative in which the sense of belonging yearned for by the narrating agent and found in Dunnet Landing is not a safe haven to be reached at the end of her journey. It is a thoroughly transient, cyclical state, in which belonging is gained, lost—and possibly regained again, here or elsewhere.

Receptive Agency

The plot of *Pointed Firs* is quickly recounted: A nameless visitor from the city, probably Boston, spends her summer in Dunnet Landing as the lodger of Mrs. Todd's after having fallen in love with the place at an earlier occasion, grows attached to it during her stay, and leaves again. What happens in the episodic narrative filling this simple timeline is strikingly eventless and devoid of drama. And while the narrator seems to suffer from a spiritual crisis when arriving to Dunnet Landing, her troubles are merely hinted at; at no point do they take on a questing or desiring kind of urgency that could become a driving force in this first-person narrative. To

---

29   Pennell reads *Pointed Firs*, somewhat along these lines, as a "transformation of a literary form long familiar to New Englanders, the spiritual biography. [...] In Jewett's fiction, sorority, the bonding together of women in an acknowledged sisterhood, becomes a manifestation of spiritual union and fulfillment, and it allows Jewett to shift the means of establishing the identity of women away from the relationships with men and patriarchal institutions and center it instead in ties to other women and to a female heritage and tradition" (193-94).

reiterate an earlier point, the narrator assumes her role decidedly not (and entirely unlike the letter-writing narrator of *Edgar Huntly*) by dwelling on herself. In fact, it is because she abstains from herself that she comfortably dwells in her surroundings. And if the placial point of view and the sketch, with their tactile directedness toward an immediate place world are a perfect match in terms of giving form to this narrative, what kind of narrative agency is at work in *Pointed Firs*? Immediately striking in this regard is the attention that is given to the narrator reading her surroundings and listening to the people whom she gets to know over the course of her summer. In one of the numerous examples that could illustrate this point she strolls along the shore where she meets one of the shrewder fishermen of Dunnet Landing. He "was carrying a small haddock in one hand, and presently shifted it to the other hand lest it might touch my skirt" (474), from which she concludes that her company is accepted, and the short walk that they take together leads to a visit to the fisherman's modest home later that day.

It is by virtue of the persistent and careful directedness toward the world in which the narrator finds herself that narration is guided, first and foremost, by a willingness to take this world *in*. In this basic makeup, it is neither active nor passive but both. The affective engagement with the world on which it thrives depends upon a sensory openness that is at once an active endeavor (an opening up) and a passive state (a being open); the German term *einlassen* perfectly captures this mix. In the resulting narrative act, emphatic contemplation of what is observed marks the highest degree of narratorial self-assertion. These moments are powerful because they are short and suggestive. Afterwards, the narrative gravitates toward attaching itself to the physical world once again. The first thing to be noted about the agency put to work in this kind of narrative, then, is the tactile degree to which it endorses reception and receptiveness. In the recurring shifts from tactile description to emphatic meditation discussed above, the narrative operation performed by the text weaves moments of acute, multi-sensual perception and receptive exchange into sketches, and sketches into a communal texture that reads like—evokes, creates—a viable dwelling place.

The resulting narrative is meandering rather than linear. The narrator tells us about returning to Dunnet Landing and settling in at Mrs. Todd's; renting the Schoolhouse for the solitary work of the writer, yet soon abandoning it again to be more immersed in the everyday life of Dunnet's community; taking trips to some islands and walks along the shore; cherishing the twosome intimacy within Mrs. Todd's house until "some wandering hermit crab of a visitor marked the little spare room for her own" (421); participating in the Bowden family reunion and leaving shortly thereafter. The gallivanting movements performed by the narrative exploit the temporal impulse of emplotment for the purpose of building a place without getting stuck in it. At the center of the weblike structure thus created stand Mrs. Blackett's house on Green Island and the close-by grove where Mrs. Todd's favorite herb, pennyroyal, grows in lavish abundance; it is here that real friendship between her and her lodger, our narrator, starts to emerge. The farthest and bleakest outpost in this imaginary geography is the mystical "waiting place" in the Arctic Sea, construed as a thoroughly male fantasy and told by one old sea captain to another in a life-threatening deadlock. Mrs. Todd calls it one of Littlepage's "great narratives" and thinks it might be the product of the excessive reading that he did during "his seafarin' days" (400). The old sea captain's name mocks his bookishness (he recites Milton and brags about his knowledge of Shakespeare on an earlier occasion), and hence it is no surprise that the antidote to this harmful, "male" circulation of narratives is located in the structures of oral storytelling that, in the world of *Pointed Firs*, are predominantly maintained by women.

The combination of a gyratory and emphatic style and a plot that prioritizes communal care over individual advancement has been praised as prototypically female.[30] The world of *Pointed Firs* is devoid of conflict and the progressive development ignited from trying to solve it. One can read the disposition toward harmony and sense of stasis that it invokes as specters of nostalgic retreat; I prefer reading them as a willful rejection of the future-bound implications of narrative that serve the purpose of dwelling in the present. Mrs. Todd's favorite herb symbolizes this latter implication. It bears strong associations to childbirth, but with procreation not being an issue in the world of *Pointed Firs*, it does not work toward procuring tomorrow's community; rather, it deepens the bonds among its childless, aging women *in the present*.[31] And if neither the place nor its shrewd old people change over the course of the narrative other than in terms of increasing attachment, this is precisely the point. As a paradigm for the productive conjunction of narrative and belonging *Pointed Firs* is of interest, then, for staging an affectionate process of place-making by means of engaging in an unusual kind of storytelling. Instead of being driven by an individual quest or bundled desire (and thus generative of a narrative agency geared toward the pursuit of that quest or desire), the story is almost entirely devoid of self-determination. In fact, in the world of *Pointed Firs* individual action, be it narrative or other, tends to meander while (narrative) agency dissolves into intersubjective exchange and communal interdependency—a utopia, possibly female, that not only dismisses the romantic ideal of liberating the individual from social constraints but also steps back from the realist formula of "self-assertion through painful experience plus conversation," which remains stubbornly centered on the self—fixed on transforming individuals at the expense of fostering communal ties in comparison.

---

30 See, for instance, Ammons, "Going in Circles;" Zagarell, "Narrative of Community;" Folsom; Pennell.
31 As Ammons points out, pennyroyal is a strong and potentially dangerous herb, and as such, a perfect symbol of Mrs. Todd, Jewett's "midwife of the spirit." The herb's stimulus of menstrual flow and uterine contractions is used in childbirth, where it helps to expel the placenta and is thus involved in the healthy delivery of new life. But it is, for the same effects, also associated with miscarriage and abortion, and thus the end of new life. Ammons, "Jewett's Witches" 175.

Telling and reading or listening procedures are intertwined so closely in *Pointed Firs* that reception and receptiveness become a major theme, motif and driving force of the narrative. And this also means that narrative agency becomes receptive agency to a substantive degree. The merger is endorsed early on in the story, when the narrator wakes up to hearing Mrs. Todd outside her window. "By the unusual loudness of her remarks to a passer-by, and the notes of a familiar hymn which she sang as she worked among the herbs [...] I knew that she wished I would wake up and come and speak with her;" indeed, the commotion outside of her window feels "as if directed purposely to the sleepy ears of my consciousness" (402). Just a few moments later the two women converse through the blinds of the narrator's room (which is, in this passage, decidedly not rendered as an interior space of enclosure but as a space that is permeable even in its delicate early-morning privacy).

"I expect you are going up to your schoolhouse to pass all this pleasant day; yes, I expect you're going to be dreadful busy," she said despairingly.
"Perhaps not," I said. "Why, what's going to be the matter with you Mrs. Todd." For I supposed that she was tempted by the fine weather to take one of her favorite expeditions along the shore pastures to gather herbs and simples, and would like to have me keep the house. (402)

Note how the last sentence is unvoiced. And yet, Mrs. Todd's eager reply can only mean that she has heard it.

"No, I don't want to go nowhere by land," she answered gayly,—"no not by land; but I don't know's we shall have a better day of the summer to go out to Green Island and see mother. I waked up early thinkin' of her. And the wind's light northeast,—'twill take is right straight out, an' this time o' year it's liable to change round southwest an' fetch us home pretty, 'long late in the afternoon. Yes, it's going to be a good day." (402)

The two women, it seems, have settled into a permeable state of consciousness in which an extrasensory communication is a casual routine. Mrs. Todd and her mother are able to communicate long distance in this same fashion, and again, the semi-consciousness of arousing from sleep is rendered conducive to it. Moreover, the reading and listening skills put to work here and elsewhere display an acute intimacy with the environment. Increasing smoke from Mrs. Todd's mother's hearth is a gesture of welcome—"Look at the chimney, now: she has gone right in and brightened up the fire" (405)—, her backward potatoes speak of a lack of rain, and the weedy potato patch gives away William's preoccupation with catching herring. This also means that the narrator does not monopolize the receptiveness on which the narrative thrives; on the contrary, it is a shared sensibility. That, after the narrator and Mrs. Blackett had known each other for just a few hours, they "understood each other without speaking" (420) testifies to her increasing participation in this conducive state. But it is Mrs. Todd who is most keenly attuned to it. She brings the onion that her mother needs for their stew, catches a perfectly-sized haddock for their shared meal, adds a special blend of herbs to her usual spruce beer brew to calm the narrator's nerves on the day of Mrs. Begg's funeral, and once she even talks to a tree. Having found it "drooping and discouraged" on an earlier occasion, she hails with "that quick reassuring nod of her head which was usually made to answer for a bow" (454) when seeing it next.

So yes, extrasensory communication includes non-human life-forms and inanimate matter (on the way home from Green Island the wind picks up as if being called upon). And when the narrator—toward the end of her stay and thus at the height of being part of Dunnet Landing's panpsychic consciousness—visits a local fisherman who is trapped in grief for his long-deceased wife, her receptiveness even reaches the dead. As she reads the old man's house (a shrine of his mourning, unchanged since his wife passed away) and listens to his litanic lament the dead person becomes present at her former dwelling site—"I began to see her myself in her home" (478). In a later, posthumously published Dunnet Landing story, "The Foreigner," the theme of bringing back the dead is amplified (the deceased person is evoked so powerfully in the story told by Mrs. Todd to the narrator that she returns as a ghost that both women can see) and more explicitly tied to the occult (the ghost is the mother of a woman of Caribbean descent from whom Mrs. Todd learned many of her special powers). Yet, the most puzzling thing about these extrasensory powers is how utterly ordinary they are in the world of *Pointed Firs*. They are nothing that deserves further notice, and the utter casualness with which they occur throughout the tale has the effect of amplifying their capacity to perforate the boundaries between self and other, here and there, now and then in emphatic acts of attachment to a concrete, beloved, and densely storied place world. Hence a psychic disposition toward permeability subtends the general openness toward the world on which the topophilic disposition of the narrative thrives. Contrary to Brown's erring letter writer, whose narrative act sutured a gasping rift between forcefully disjointed worlds, the receptive agency at work in *Pointed Firs* makes inner and outer worlds seamlessly continuous. And if Edgar Huntly's psyche was fathomed (with Darwin, Locke and Hume) as wounded by a violent exterior with which it could reconnect only in the absent-minded state of sleepwalking, the spiritistic ideas undergirding the psychic imaginary of *Pointed Firs* invoke a mystic state of interconnectedness, not only with the material world but also with the afterlife.

Such mystic ideas were taken quite seriously at the time; they were a feasible part of making sense of a world caught in transition from metaphysical to secular, scientific ways of construing one's place in it, and as such, they have a persistent place in Jewett's work.[32] A fellow thinker in this regard was William James, whom

---

[32] An impressive historical record of Spiritualism in mid-Nineteenth century America is *Emma Harding's Modern American Spiritualism: A Twenty Year Record of the Communication Between the*

Jewett read and admired, possibly because of their striking like-mindedness (he, too, was strongly influenced by Swedenborgian ideas, being exposed to them at home and through some of his most important interlocutors).[33] Throughout his career, James was keenly interested in questioning the confines of an individual's psyche, an interest that led him to reconsider the significance of religious, spiritual, and mystic experience in his late work, especially in his monumental *Varieties of Religious Experience: A Study in Human Nature*.[34] At the core of religious experience, according to James, lies an acceptance of something "more," which is beyond the individual's grasp. To further define this "more," which connects the material with a spiritual world, James put forth his central hypothesis about the subliminal constitution of consciousness: "whatever it may be on its farther side, the 'more' with which in religious experience we feel ourselves connected is on its

---

Earth and the World of Spirits, first published in 1870. Harding, herself a famous medium, gave lectures that were instrumental in circulating the ideas of Spiritualism at the time. For more recent accounts, with a special focus on the interrelations of Spitirualism and woman's rights in Nineteenth century America, see Nelson, *Spiritualism and Society*; Ann Baude, *Radical Spirits*. Ammons traces Jewett's lasting concern with the occult and its manifestation in a series of female characters with mystical powers in "Jewett's Witches."

33 James's *Varieties of Religious Experience* came out six years after the publication of *Pointed Firs*; Jewett writes enthusiastically about it in a letter to Annie Fields (*Jewett Letters*, ed. Fields 90). The letter is dated 1892 in Fields, but as Ammons rightly points out, this must be a mistake, for *Varieties* was not published until a decade later ("Jewett's Witches" n33). James's interest in the occult dates back to at least 1882, when he was introduced to the work of the Society of Psychical Research while visiting his brother Henry in London; his father died that same year, making him feel "as [he] never began to do before, the tremendousness of the idea of immortality" (James in a letter to his wife; quoted in Blum 78). James's father, Henry Sr., was also responsible for his exposure to Swedenborgian ideas; in fact, he was to one of their most influential disseminators in America, bringing such intellectuals as his close friend (and William's Godfather) Ralph Waldo Emerson and Charles Sanders Peirce into their orbit. For a concise discussion of James's high-powered social milieu see E. Taylor, "Spiritual Roots."

34 A foremost figure in establishing psychology as a scholarly discipline, James was also involved in empirical research of spiritistic and occult phenomena; in fact, he set up an American branch of the London-based *Society for Psychical Research* that was at the forefront of conducting this research, and served as its president for a term. Only recently, Deborah Blum has delivered a book-length study, *Ghost Hunters*, about James's obsession with finding scientific proof for life after death. The group of researchers under scrutiny in this fascinating account includes Alfred Russel Wallace, Henry Sidgwick, Fredric Myers, William Crookes, and Edmund Gurney. That James's fellow "ghost hunters" were among the most renowned scholars of their time underscores the degree to which spiritism was indeed a serious scientific concern.

hither side the subconscious continuation of our conscious life" (556-57).[35] With its endorsement of receptive agency and permeable boundaries between inner and outer worlds, here and there, now and then, *Pointed Firs* reaches out to this "more." Against the suspicion that this agenda marks its author as shrewd, esoteric, and backward, association with James makes tangible that Jewett, too, was a bridge figure between the intellectual culture of the mid-nineteenth century and the modernist movements to come.

But her path lay not in exploring the literary tenets of "stream of consciousness" interweaving discrete instances of experience into a continuous sense of flow, as was done by James's brother Henry and so many modernist writers thereafter (William was, of course, the one who had developed the idea in the "Stream of Thoughts" chapter of his monumental *Principles of Psychology*). Counteracting concerns with mapping internal procedures, Jewett turned toward the physical place world to dwell on what would become a foremost implication of James's doctrine of "pure experience": that "our fields of experience have no more definite boundaries than our fields of view. Both are fringed forever by a 'more' that continuously supersedes them as life proceeds" ("Pure Experience" 35). Her haptic mode of description, her tacit symbolism of unstated facts, and the receptive agency drawn from their midst are the outcome of this experimental agenda.

CONSECUTIVE ENDINGS, EDITORIAL CARE, AND THE BOOK AS DWELLING SITE

Pointed Firs endorses the receptive agency on which it thrives tacitly. The narrator's initial obligation to get on with a joyless writing job wears thin as she finds herself spending more and more time fostering her sprawling attachments. What we are reading may very well be what she wrote during or after her summer instead of the commissioned work that she seems to abandon early on. Even so, the narrator's deepening bonds do *not* mean that she is becoming a full member of Dunnet's community; they mean—demand—that she, being a writer who has to leave again at the end of her summer, must tell about it. This need to tell mobilizes both her narrative and her attachments. But ironically, it also sets her apart from

---

35 Concerns with the "fringe of consciousness" run through James's work. Developed originally in *The Principles of Psychology*, subliminal consciousness assumes a key role in *Varieties*, where it becomes the medium that makes religious experience possible and in which religious experience in all its varieties takes place. Acting as an embodied relay between the material and the spiritual world, it concretizes individual notions of the absolute. As the cornerstone of James's "science of religion," the subliminal (or transmarginal) consciousness also mediates between the domains of religion and science whose antagonistic relation James seeks to resolve with his late work. See Albers, *Spiritismus*.

the predominantly oral mode of narrative exchange and communal belonging that reverberates through her tale (just as none of Dunnet's storytellers will ever become a professional writer). Her need thus sparks an act of telling that consecrates *their* stories in and through the written text. The difference is crucial, for it marks narration as acting upon a need to tell that is both circular and self-serving. Through the solitary act of writing and the literary products that are its results, narrative proceedings seize the place of the community, with the result of both compensating for and distancing it. At the risk of stating the obvious, this pattern (memorably described in Walter Benjamin's "The Storyteller" four decades later) repeats itself on the side of consumption: Jewett's readers are engaged with printed matter, not with a place and its people. Her tale may have inspired travel and vacationing, but the formative experience was that of a literary text.

Conceived at the historical juncture when narrative consumption of belonging coincides with the consolidation of print capitalism, the act of telling that becomes manifest in *Pointed Firs* partakes in erecting this constellation. In doing so, it replicates and reinforces a logic that turns cultural artifacts into commodified (and socially stratified) sites of topophilic investment.[36] Approached this way, *Pointed Firs*'s object-life in a series of material incarnations emerges as a busy trajectory with immediate impact on its narrative form. Like many literary works at the time, *Pointed Firs* was first published serially in a magazine, the prestigious *Atlantic Monthly*, which featured it in four installments over the course of the year of 1896.[37] That these installments were spread out to appear in the January, March, July, and September issues signals a reorientation in the business of publishing magazine fiction: away from the monthly installments of the serialized novel, which had been its staple for decades, and toward the short story and short serial that was Jewett's preferred métier. *Atlantic* editor Horace Scudder, who also happened to be editor-in-chief at Houghton Mifflin, the renowned publishing house where Jewett's collection of sketches was scheduled for book publication later that year, had not only solicited the tale that was to become *Pointed Firs*. He had encouraged Jewett to submit a short serial rather than a singular piece, which led her

---

36 That the consolidation of the literary field at the time contained well-defined "regions" of distinction and taste is another manifestation of the shifting, highly mobilized parameters of emplacement at the time. The genre of regionalist fiction was clearly not regarded to be "high" literature, but relative proximity to this consecrated sphere (through the same publishing venues and promoters) made it suitable for the needs of an audience inclined to believe that a comfortable dwelling place was a matter of making the right investments. Perhaps it is rooted in this constellation that investment could become such common form of attachment in our own time. My understanding of the consolidation of the field of American letters is indebted to Florian Sedlmeier, *Field Imagination*.

37 My account of *Pointed Firs*'s intricate publication history closely follows Sedgwick and Goheen.

to expand her initial idea for a story about old sea captains into a more general tale about a place and its people.

The internal units that so clearly stand out even from *Pointed Firs*'s loosely plotted narrative bear the mark of the serial: The four "Green Island" chapters appeared in the March issue, the four "Poor Joanna" chapters in the July issue, and the four "Bowden Reunion" chapters in the September issue. In fact, the gentle, almost leisurely alternation between states of communal embeddedness and lack thereof that subtends the narrator's journey gains its tact from a publication mode in which the story will eventually be continued, with a need to go on that is casual rather than throbbing. Following the story in its various installments over the course of the year made the reader subscribe to a sense of belonging with an amiable ebb and flow—and subscribe not just in the metaphorical sense: The first installment appeared in the January issue that was instrumental to committing the magazine's readers for the year. Thematically less unified and formally more piecemealed than latter installments (it uses four short sketches to introduce the setting and the main characters, and another three to tell Captain Littlepage's story), the first installment ends not with an interim conclusion but pilot-like: with making plans to visit the remote channel island "struck" by "a gleam of golden sunshine" where Mrs. Todd's mother lives. "The sunburst upon that outermost island made it seem like a sudden revelation of the world beyond which some believe to be so near" (400). Subscribing to the magazine for the year meant subscribing to dwelling in this world.

In the fall, with the book publication drawing close and Scudder feeling "that his readers would not greatly miss a narrative conclusion to the serial" (Sedgwick 84), the end of the Bowden feast came to serve—incidentally—as the end of the narrative's first incarnation. That *Pointed Firs* assumed a second material form was a pleasant surprise to its author. "How little I thought of the 'Pointed Firs' […] turning into a book of parts when I began," Jewett wrote to her sister Mary in August (quoted in Sedgwick 84). The book that came out in October was indeed to a substantial degree the making of a keen and persuasive editor acting under the pressures of the literary market on two intersecting fronts (book and magazine publishing). Jewett only slightly revised the existing sketches for the book publication, but she added two more chapters at the end. Considerably shorter than they would have been as the serial's final installment, these new chapters alter the narrative decisively. The first of them, "Along the Shore," about Elijah Tilley's endless mourning, elevates the receptive agency endorsed by the tale to an unprecedented level of permeability. Even acuter, however, is the impact of the book's final chapter, "A Backward View," which postpones and revises the former ending. Whereas the magazine publication had left things with the Bowden reunion—suggesting, through the performative power of the ending, the narrator's initiation into Dunnet's community—the new ending turns this happy moment into a transient, cyclical state. With the narrator's departure spelled out rather than merely pending, belonging can only be consummated in textual form—ideally as the unified literary object, a souvenir of the reader's journey to be kept on her shelf, which *Pointed Firs* had become in its second incarnation as a book.

Later, posthumous publications, the most famous of them an edition by Willa Cather, added even more chapters, again with the effect of producing substantial change but this time without consent from the author. The version of *Pointed Firs* that has been consecrated through Cather's reputation as a writer extends the tale both into the past and the future, bringing the narrator back to Dunnet Landing to celebrate William's wedding, and introducing the wondrous shepherdess who will become his bride in a chapter set prior to the narrator's blissful summer. None of the posthumous publications made palpable to its readers that it was diverting from the authorized text (Jewett's endorsement of *Pointed Firs* as a collection of sketches may have invited this peculiar editorial practice). Since 1924, additions have included a third chapter about a visit to an alleged twin of Queen Victoria, residing in the Dunnet area. All of these changes were made prior to Cather's edition, and yet it is puzzling that she, who must have been fully aware of their weight, stuck with the unauthorized twenty-four-chapter version. She must have even felt the need to "improve" it by rearranging the new chapters. Placing "The Queen's Twin" in between "A Dunnet Shepherdess" and "William's Wedding" is the most elegant solution in terms of narrative flow (the future wife is introduced, and the interim between this event and the marriage is bridged by another chapter, which is also set at the end of the summer). For Goheen, Cather's rearrangement epitomizes, for precisely this reason, not only an illegitimate seizure of authorship but also the "unmaking" of a story that was "perfect" in striving against the dictates of plot that her editorial work enforces retroactively (37-40).[38]

In terms of respecting the integrity of Jewett's work, Cather's actions are a definite violation, a seizure of authorship on behalf of an editor who was, furthermore, a disciple and a close friend. But what happens when these actions become part of our understanding of Jewett's art of attachments? It is well documented in their

---

38 If there is a structural logic at work here, it may best be described as a gradual movement from adding on further Dunnet stories to merging them with the authorized body of the text. The first edition, coming out with Houghton Mifflin in 1910, the year right after Jewett's death, featured two additions at the end of the authorized text. "A Dunnet Shepherdess" had appeared in the *Atlantic* in December 1899, "William's Wedding" (though most likely still unfinished when Jewett died) was published there July 1910. "The Queen's Twin," first published in the *Atlantic* in February 1899, made its first appearance in the 1919 edition, where it was, just like the earlier additions, placed at the end. The 1924 edition changed this order insofar as it reinstalled "The Backward View" chapter, which concludes the authorized text at the end. Goheen also points out that the added sketches/stories/chapters, all of which are divided into numerous subsections, bear a greater resemblance to the collection of sketches as a whole than to its individual chapters, which are consistently made up of one single section.

Willa Cather wearing a necklace from Sarah Orne Jewett.
Studio portrait by Aimé Dupont, c1912.
Kaufman, Anne L. and Richard H. Millington (Eds.). *Willa Cather and the Nineteenth Century.* Lincoln and London: U of Nebraska P, 2015. Frontispiece.

lettered correspondence that Cather's editorial work was steeped in a relationship fervid with friendly affection, professional mentoring, artistic kinship, and personal grief (when Jewett died unexpectedly in 1909, the two women had been acquainted for sixteen short yet intense months).[39] Can the multiple, partially violent

---

39 The relationship between Jewett and Cather is a much-studied subject, both in terms of literary influence and in terms of the question of open or closed lesbianism. For the latter, see especially Homestead and Love. Scholars concerned with their literary relationship take issue with the massive influence that Jewett allegedly had on Cather, who was much younger and the less established writer at the time of their friendship. See Cary, "The Scuptor and the Spinister" for an early effort to relativize the impact of Jewett's mentorship. For an extremely nuanced reading of Cather's changing relationship to her deceased mentor and friend, see Carlin.

and transgressive outcomes of Cather's editorial work—commemoration, canonization, re-authorization, and self-assertion among them—be detached from the printed matter in which they reside? And does the possessive exegesis of editorial care not also expose a desire for the narrator's return to the place, for the friend to which she had grown so attached? A desire that may cut across these various outcomes while amounting, first and foremost, to producing yet another book?[40] Perhaps Cather even toys with slipping into the role of *Pointed Firs*'s narrator in this charade. In a well-known studio photograph taken in 1910, the year after Jewett's premature death, she wears a jade necklace given to her by Jewett as a token of their friendship (see previous page)—just as the narrator receives a coral pin from Mrs. Todd when it is time to say farewell.[41]

In the space opened up by the trail of objects and writings left behind by the Jewett-Cather relationship (the necklace, the photograph displaying it, the letters written back and forth, the edited volumes thereof, Cather's essay "Miss Jewett," and its revised version prefacing her edition of Jewett's work), the Cather edition emerges as a remarkably durable site. When it first came out in 1925 (Cather had just been awarded the Pulitzer Prize), many libraries acquired this book for its prestigious editor, and to this day it is this version of the text that is most easily available for purchase. With the Cather edition as a firmly established presence, critical awareness of the limits of Jewett's authorized text—a text whose form engendered by multiple, "serial" agencies including narrative genres, literary objects, editors, readers, writers—begs special importance.[42] Reconstructing these limits, which had been buried in and through the proliferating posthumous editions, has been an important critical task, and like most of those engaged in this task, I, too, prefer the authorized text to its later editions. Yet to assess the full scope of Jewett's art of attachment, a rigid "border patrol" of the original text is just as unsuited as being oblivious of the violation of borders—not least because fostering affective bonds always entails the possibility of possessive transgression. And has not the

---

40 These questions bring to mind Winters's lucid discussion of possession as a pervasive issue in Cather's work. All her novels are concerned with it, with each of them presenting a different take on the questions what can be possessed, and who possesses it. Explorations range from the posessives carried in the titles of *My Antonia*, *One of Ours*, and *My Mortal Enemy* that ask who owns a person's story, to the question who owns a place and its memory in *O Pioneers* and *Death Comes to the Archbishop*, to the possession of houses, of one's family's happiness, of the artifacts of bygone civilizations in *The Professor's House* (38-40).

41 Mrs. Todd's gift is clearly double-coded: The coral pin used to belong to Joanna Bowden; passing it on to the narrator is both a token of their lasting friendship and a tacit acknowledgement of the narrator's loneliness—and by extension possibly also an emblem of the loneliness of lesbian women at the time.

42 The term "serial agencies" is drawn from Kelleter's actor-network-theory inspired study with the same title.

most vital incarnation of *Pointed Firs* been conceived from the consecutive labor of two affectionately connected "mothers"? With a bit of good will, one can read the Cather edition as an empowering gesture of collective female authorship, whose violation of the historically fixed body of the work transports regionalism transhistorically into literary modernism. In short-circuiting authorial desire and editorial care, it invigorated Jewett's tale, prolonging the literary life of its enchanted place world while producing yet another, inherently progressive and remarkably durable site of topophilic investment.

4 Dwelling in What is Found
Henry Roth's *Call It Sleep*

In our modern world migration recurrently raises concerns with belonging on a massive scale. Who stays and who leaves, where to go, and how those who leave their home in search for a better future are received, all of these things depend on narrative, be it in word-of-mouth accounts, storied images, or elaborate tales. The vast archive of literature speaking from these experiences gives voice and form to concerns with belonging across geographic, linguistic, and cultural fault lines, with the effect of both exposing and soothing displacement in its attempts to fathom new modes of dwelling. Henry Roth's *Call It Sleep* does so in an unusual combination of ethnographic documentation and modernist experimentation. An immigration novel that resists easy categorization, it has a history of falling through the cracks of academic reception that reenacts its thematic concern with lacking a proper place. Set at the peak time of "new" immigration (1.28 million people arrived at Ellis Island in the novel's opening year 1907 alone) and published in 1934, the low point of the Great Depression, Roth's novel takes concerns with belonging to the urban ghetto of the early twentieth century, recording with striking eloquence and sensitivity the modes of dwelling that emerged from this prototypically modern environment.[1]

Inspired by Mike Gold's groundbreaking "slum novel" *Jews Without Money* (1929), *Call It Sleep* was part of what Alfred Kazin called "age of the plebs—of writers from the working class, the lower class, the immigrant class, the non-literate class,

---

1 The family at the center of the novel is part of the "new" immigration of increasingly poor, unskilled, non-WASP people from Southern and Eastern Europe in the late nineteenth century that was met with nativist hostility and led to the ratification of the National Origins (or Johnson-Reed) Act of 1924, a milestone in the "repression of America's ethnic past" (Singh et al. 5). Yet while Roth's novel speaks from this particular moment in the history of immigration, mass migration is a persistent reality in the modern world: From the 1830s to World War II over 40 million people left their homes to find a new and better place to live (Bodnar xv)—a staggering number that, nevertheless, pales in comparison to the 60 million people on the move today. The global spread of "narrativized" migration experience via digital communication technology is a powerful mobilizing factor.

from Western farms and mills—those whose struggle was to survive" (*Starting Out* 12). What these writers wanted, Kazin (who was one of them) goes on to argue, "was to prove the literary value of our experience, to recognize the possibility of art in our lives, to feel that we had moved the streets, the stockyards, the hiring halls into literature" (15).[2] The demographic upheaval of the literary field occurring at this time had lasting impact on the shape and form of concerns with belonging in narrative art: first and foremost by expanding the range of lived experience to include the (promisingly "authentic") struggles and concerns of less privileged writers. Entering the field in the aftermath of modernism, however, these writers had to position themselves with regard to its daunting heritage, which for Kazin as for Roth was a matter of demonstrating "that our radical strength could carry on the experimental impulse of modern literature" (*Starting Out* 15).[3]

Call It Sleep endorses this agenda like no other novel of its time. Reading *Ulysses*, Roth said, had "opened my eyes to the fact that the material for literature was all around me. [...] That life was a junkyard [...] and that you just pick up the pieces of junk. That language and art was the way you transmuted it" (Roth in Lyons 53). His novel embraces the Joycean celebration of the ordinary stuff that makes up modern urban life in a remarkable experiment of dwelling in what is felt and found. In doing so, it disappointed those who had expected a "truly proletarian novel." For them, it was an untimely infatuation with childish introspection flawed by an unfortunate lack of social realism and political will. The first review, published anonymously in the communist magazine *New Masses* in February 1935, brims with resentment: *Call it Sleep* degenerates into "impression on a rampage," is too long, contains "vile spelling of dialects," and bores its readers with "the sex phobias of this six-year-old Proust. [...] It is a pity that so many writers drawn from the proletariat can make no better use of their working class experience than as material for introspective and febrile novels" (quoted in Wirth-Nesher, "Introduction" 12). Still, many of the established critics liked the novel, and even commercially it was a modest success.[4] Then its publisher went out of business, and the

---

2   Kazin's autobiographical *Starting Out in the Thirties* is still a most valuable read for anyone interested in the troubled decade.
3   Noted as early as in the first reviews, the Joycean influence on *Call It Sleep* has been of persistent scholarly interest. The best account of it is McHale's "Roth in Nighttown." Besides Joyce, Roth's modernism was influenced by Eliot and O'Neill. He was introduced to all of them by Eda Lou Walton Roth, with whom Roth (twenty-four at the time and twelve years younger than her) was living when writing the novel. Walton opened the literary world to him: She was a professor at NYU, a practicing poet, and an established promoter of modernism with a circle of friends who were formative of the contemporary cultural moment (among them Hart Crane, Margaret Mead, Ruth Benedict, and Constance Rourke). *Call It Sleep* is dedicated to her.
4   John Chamberlain of *The New York Times* wrote: "Mr. Roth has done for the East Side what James T. Farrell is doing for the Chicago Irish. [...] The final chapters have been compared to the Nighttown

book plunged into oblivion, staying out of print for nearly twenty-five years with a few treasured copies passed around in select circles of rare-book lovers. Its revival has by now become legendary: Endorsed simultaneously in Walter Rideout's widely noticed *The Radical Novel* (1956) and by both Alfred Kazin and Leslie Fiedler in *The American Scholar* special issue "The Most Neglected Books of the Past 25 Years" of the same year, *Call It Sleep* was reissued, sold a million copies, and became the first paperback ever to be reviewed on the front page of *The New York Times Book Review*, where Irving Howe celebrated it as "one of the few genuinely distinguished novels written by a 20th-century American" ("Life" 60-61). (It took some serious effort to track its author down when this happened: Roth was working on a turkey farm in Maine, had dropped all ties to the literary world, and was suffering from a writer's block that lasted for almost sixty years.)

The novel's notorious resurgence went hand in hand with a critical shift in perception. Still valued as a powerful evocation of turn-of-the-century slum life in either the tradition of experimental modernism (Joyce, Eliot, Frazer) or of American naturalism (Dreiser, Farrell), now its alleged Jewishness was enthusiastically praised.[5] But as much as the novel's belated recognition benefitted from the burgeoning interest in ethnic literature at the time, its place in the annals of U.S. literature remained uncertain. When choices had to be made on which texts to

---

episodes of Joyce's *Ulysses*; the comparison is apt." Kenneth Burke defended it in a letter to the *New Masses* by comparing it to Frazer's *Golden Bough* and locating its "great virtue" in "the fluent and civilized way in which he found, on our city streets, the new equivalents to the ancient jungle." Alfred Hayes wrote that there "has appeared in America no novel to rival the veracity of this childhood. It is as honest as Dreiser's *Dawn*, but far more sensitive. [...] It is as brilliant as Joyce's *Portrait of an Artist*, but with a wider scope, a richer emotion, a deeper realism." Edwin Seaver of the *New York Sun* accused the *New Masses'* anonymous reviewer of suffering from the "infantile disorder of leftism" and calling Roth "a brilliant disciple of James Joyce," and Fred Marsh for the *New York Herald Tribune* found it "the most compelling and moving, the most accurate and profound study of an American slum childhood that has yet appeared in this day. Henry Roth has achieved the detachment of universality of the artist." All quotes are drawn from Wirth-Nesher's "Introduction," which gives a comprehensive overview of the novel's turbulent history of reception.

5 Howe wrote that although the novel "is structured according to the narrative strategies of modernism [...] [it] draws its substance, the whole unfolding of socioethnic detail, from the Jewish immigrant experience" (*World of our Fathers* 588); for Kazin it was "the most profound novel of Jewish life [...] by an American" ("Introduction" ix); and Fiedler praised it as a "*specifically* Jewish book, the best single book by a Jew about Jewishness written by an American certainly through the thirties perhaps ever" (*The Jew* 38). It is no coincidence that the three critics most instrumental to its revival were children of immigrants, moved by it as a powerful transcript of the kind of "ethnic passage"—"out of immigrant confines into the larger world of letters" (Ferraro, *Ethnic Passages* 8)—which they had undergone, and could now critically and professionally affirm in their sophisticated praise for Roth's novel.

include in the new canon, the "ethnic realism" of Cahan, Gold or Yezierka would routinely trump over the "ethnic modernism" that is the artistic trademark of Roth's novel. By the mid-90s *Call It Sleep* was once again among the "most forgotten book of the past 25 years" (Ferraro, *Ethnic Passages* 90). For the study at hand, Roth's novel is intriguing precisely for the unusual combination of modernist experimentation with language and perception with an unabashed saturation in Jewish folk life that interfered with its canonization. Are the formal tensions responsible for foreclosing a proper place for this striking novel not by definition laden with contradicting assumptions about dwelling in the world? If the need to belong yields a narrative drive that both spurs and draws from narrative art, how does Roth's novel give voice and form to this need by drawing from two notoriously conflicted traditions?

Both its high modernism and its ethnic realism respond to basic troubles with belonging—alienation and displacement—but with substantial stylistic differences, and with vast implications for the practice of narrative art and its investment in matters of dwelling in the world. The high modernism of Joyce and Eliot enlisted by Roth calls for an art that, in the alleged service of a humanist ethics, aims at dissembling mimetic conventions and social entanglements to arrive at a more viable state of being. To riff on Viktor Shklovsky's famous definition, the purpose of this kind of art is to convey a perception of things that make us really see rather than merely recognize them (18). The "ethnocultural authenticity" aspired by ethnic realism also calls for an art that is true to life, but here it asks to cultivate marginal experience—and hence a hands-on truth about being in the world, residing in the concrete particularities of unprivileged life at the margin—as a bulwark against the corrosive forces of modern life, and as an imaginary repository for mainstream needs to belong. Ethnic and modernist realism are indeed closely related in this regard, separated mainly by the partisan perspective of the critics. The measure of difference is the value ascribed to the literary, a value openly negotiated in Roth's novel at a time when the pressure on literature to be politically engaged was omnipresent. *Call it Sleep* engages the conflict about literary value as its form-giving principle. In doing so, it troubles modernist yearnings for "aesthetic transcendence" as a universal remedy with practical needs for a familiar, predictable life-world while confronting yearnings for "ethnocultural authenticity" with a deromanticized depiction of life at the margin.

Childhood as Immigration

The novel's congenial move in this regard is its choice of mediating the converging displacements of modernization and immigration almost entirely through the consciousness of a child: a young boy named David Schearl, who is almost six years old when the main narrative sets in and eight when it ends.[6] This focalization allows Roth to interweave the commonly told immigration story of losing and regaining a familiar world with the tacit depiction of a world emerging from displacement as an experience of inherited, secondary, rather than immediate, loss of one's home. Having arrived in the New World as an infant too young to remember the place of his birth, a *stetl* in Polish Galicia (then part of Austria-Hungary), David cannot make sense of their transplanted lives on the basis of his own experience of displacement. And yet he grows up firmly knowing that he has come from a "world somewhere, somewhere else" (23), a mysterious, dreamlike place powerfully present all around him—in the children's songs that he hears in the street, in the magical glow of the stories told by the elders at home, in the linguistic boundaries drawn around their domestic space by the Yiddish spoken there, in his mother's beloved picture of a corn field, and his father's enigmatic cow horns on a plate.[7]

David's quest to belong is confronted with the challenges of the protomodern environment in which he grows up *and* with the ghost of the displaced world of his family's past. The narrative process of mapping the world emerging from this fault line is driven by the boy's maturing desire for an *own* place in the world. Focalization through his consciousness wires the narrative to an innocent and deeply immature need to belong.[8] That this narrative is existentially inclined heightens

---

6   Though clearly a work of fiction, David's story is closely modeled after its author's own immigration experience. Roth's family first lived in Brownsville, moved to the Lower East Side when Roth was seven, and moved again to Harlem when Roth was nine (and with that, past the protagonist's age at the novel's end). Roth also used the basic coordinates of his family's arrival in the novel's Prologue: he and his mother came through Ellis Island in 1907, and were picked up by his father who had left their home in Polish Galicia a few years earlier. Just like David, Roth was seventeen months old when he arrived.

7   Triggered by a song about a boy named Walter Wildflower (in the vernacular of the street "Waltuh Wiuhflowuh") that some girls sing along with their game, David imagines knowing this boy back in Austria with "warm, nostalgic mournfulness," and as he shuts his eyes, "[f]ragments of forgotten rivers floated under the lids, dusty roads, fathomless curve of trees, a branch in a window under flawless light. A world somewhere, somewhere else." Roth, *Call It Sleep* (New York: Picador, 1991), 23. All references to the novel are from this edition and will from now on be cited parenthetically in the text. For Sollors, this passage is a paradigmatic articulation of "the second (or the first *American*) generation's difficulty with nostalgia" for a place only known through second hand accounts ("A World" 142).

8   Due to the dominant focalization through a child protagonist and the at times quixotic quest to make sense of the world, the novel can be compared to Mark Twain's *The Adventures of Huckleberry Finn*, but its dependence on significant others as a main site of struggle also makes it akin to Henry James's *What Maisie Knew*. In terms of narrative modes, *Call It Sleep* takes a middle position between the two: more distanced than *Huck Finn*'s first-person narration and more immediate and introspective than *Maisie*'s auctorial narration.

the sense of urgency on which it thrives: In the world of the novel, children are not safely contained in the loving care of those who raise them but thrust into a world in which they are forced to start out as strangers. The trope of childhood as archetypal immigration is introduced early on.[9] The Prologue, set at Ellis Island five years prior to the main narrative and written last, presents us with a family that is unhappy and divided. A rift runs through its members that seems to go deeper than the tensions caused by the chaos of arrival, splitting it—in strikingly Oedipal fashion, about which I will have more to say—into the lonely figure of an angry father, and the symbiotic unity of a well-meaning mother and frightened child. Resonating with Freud's saying that "[e]very new arrival on this planet is faced by the task of the Oedipus complex; anyone who fails [...] falls a victim of Neurosis" ("Three Essays" 226n, quoted in Altenbernd 682), the task of immigration fathomed in here is twofold, with a definite stress on the domestic side of the matter.

After the conflicted family triangle is established, narration plunges into the consciousness of the child and into the throbbing world of New York's tenement quarters where he grows up. Focalization through the boy turns *his* longing for a place in the world into the dominant narrative drive; in fact, it is his desire for a drink of water (one cannot survive for too long without it) that sparks narration. As he closely eyes "the bright brass faucets that gleamed so far away, each"—teasingly, it seems—"with a bead of water at its nose," we learn that he "*again* became aware that this world had been created without a thought of him." Cast against the disinterested reality of the towering sink, whose "iron hip rested on legs almost as tall as his own body," feeling out of place is presented as the boy's uncomfortable, yet most familiar state of being. There is an aching corporeality to this state: "by no stretch of arm, no leap, could he ever reach the distant tap" (17; emphasis mine). In

---

9   Approaching the novel this way draws from Wisse, who writes: "Every child hopes to arrive in a friendly new land, a golden land that will treat him with dignity and warmth. Happy families may be alike at least in this respect, that the fortunate pairing of the parents is retroactively confirmed by their desired, beloved children. Children of happy families are made to feel that their arrival benefits the existing settlement. But children born into less than perfect unions can never do anything to alter the condition that produced them. Because they loom for their parents as reminders of rejection and lovelessness, they must look out for harm from the very person who should be protecting them. [...] Child and immigrant both are required to learn a new language and adapt to new surroundings. The burden on each is to adapt to a world already complete without him. Children may appear to be the most adaptable of immigrants because they are anyway engaged in the process of adjusting to their surroundings, and are already exercising the required skills of observation, emulation, intellection. In addition, the child has the greatest incentive to learn because he is the most disparate immigrant, lacking the advantages of maturity and mastery in other areas that sometimes help to compensate for physical or social disadvantage. Immigration is humiliating to adults because they are forced back into the position of children, and required to relearn what took so much effort the first time" (61-62).

the move from perception to intellection performed here, David's displacement is channeled into a strikingly poetic mode (or even hermeneutics) of world-making: The faucet gains a nose, the sink has hips and legs, and so on. A "child's magical thinking" (Allen 446) mobilizes the search for a place in the world in this novel.[10] But the transformative power of creative enchantment is not without hazard. As David's desire shifts from wanting a drink to taking imaginative measure of the world around him, the latter assumes a life of its own. "Where did the water come from that lurked so secretly in the curve of the brass? Where did it go, gurgling in the drain? What a strange world must be hidden behind the walls of a house!" With every question the boy's imagination expands—until the game becomes so exhilarating that he has to actively divorce himself from it. "But he needed a drink" (17).

Wired to the ravishing receptivity of an emerging consciousness, dwelling in narrative may take on a self-absorbing, potentially totalizing drive in this novel. Brown's letter-writing sleepwalker fell prey to a similar danger. But where *Edgar Huntly* gave the force of the imagination a pathological spin (sleepwalking was conceived as a form of madness at the time, and in the world of the novel it was interlinked with the imagination in ways that corroded all viable prospects of dwelling), *Call It Sleep* ties it to the inquisitive mind of an innocent child. As in *Edgar Huntly* and *The Country of the Pointed Firs*, a specific narrative space creates a specific need to tell. Yet if spatial imagination and narrative design will once again serve as the two main trajectories for my reading in this chapter, focalizing the story through the consciousness of a child conjoins them more thoroughly than in the other stories: As David gets older, the external world expands and social relations multiply. Corresponding with this dynamic, processual rendering of the external world is the child's inner growth, which climaxes in a narrativistic attempt of self- and place-making. Born from an extremely vulnerable and erring need to belong, the narrative drive of this novel is at once universalized by the fact that everyone was a child once, and amplified with the particular challenges of this immigrant child's young life.

---

10 About the transformative work of the imagination employed by the text Freedman writes: "The imagination does not literally create, it transforms, and what it transforms are the very materials which Roth has transfigured in *Call It Sleep*—the fears, the anguish, the ugliness of life—here a young boy's life on the Lower East Side" ("Redemptive Imagination" 114). Allen, who has credited the novel with being "the most powerful evocation of the terrors of childhood ever written" (444), stresses that David's world is not a world of "simple fantasy or make-believe but one he creates with the desperate, compulsive imagination of the poet" (446).

SPACE AS FELT, STORIED, AND SCRIPTED

The opening image of a small white steamer approaching Ellis Island unmistakably situates the novel in the world of immigrant fiction. On the threshold to this world we find the following striking inscription: "(I pray thee ask no questions/ this is that Golden Land)" (9). The deictic "this" of the novel's motto places us at the gates of a longed-for destination, the aspired end of a strenuous journey. But the "that" following suit displaces both the spatial marker and the affirmative investment, creating a suspicious perceptual dissonance between outer and inner world, reality and expectation. Hence we become attuned to a narrative operation that takes us onto unstable, problematic grounds. Bearing not even the slightest resemblance to the mythical idyll evoked in the motto, arrival comes in the shape of a hungry, people-eating machine. A harsh, naturalistic language underscores its life-conditioning force: Endless numbers of immigrants, "natives from almost every land in the world," are "delivered," like goods, "from the stench and throb of the steerage to the stench and throb of New York tenements" (9).

The urban environment that serves as the story's nourishing ground is thoroughly mobilized (how can the available space contain them all?) and intensified (what will become of this heterogeneous mix once they have been "delivered" to those tenements?) under the impact of this mechanical procedure. It is tempting to think of the naturalistic force inscribed into this setting as turning its inhabitants into "a force among forces" and ask "whether the idea of agency—of the self as independent actor—makes sense in a world where people come to consciousness by becoming aware of the myriad of forces impacting them" (Minter 228-29). But *Call It Sleep* is decidedly not a novel in which character is a mere effect of the environment; the alienating forces of modern life at work in it may be daunting, but they are not overpowering *per se*. Rather, the space produced from these forces calls for specific—imaginative and narrative—strategies of survival. In fact, the naturalistic air of the setting is not geared toward dramatizing the futility of these strategies; it serves as a force field to explore and refine them.[11]

---

11 That the main characters exposed to this setting are Jewish is crucial to this balancing act: "Jews are generally so conscious of the pressure of history that it was a notable achievement for Henry Roth [...] to put character ahead of environment" (Kazin, "Introduction" xiii). As a prototypical urban dweller, the Jew is fathomed as the quintessential "modern Everyman." In fact, twentieth-century Jewish fiction was at the vanguard of creating "myths of urban alienation and terror," turning the Jew into a virtual model of what "Western man in general [was] becoming" (Fiedler, *Love and Death* 493-94). Their immigration could become a metaphor for a collective transition from agrarian/rural to an industrial/urban society and the alienation that comes with/from it, because most Jews came from rural environments and were exposed and fundamentally shocked by the foreignness of city life as well as having been torn from belonging to a safe religious community and work structure.

Perhaps the most striking thing about the space imagined by the novel is how packed it is. At the time, New York's immigrant quarters may very well have been "the most densely populated place on earth" (Wirth-Nesher, "City" 95). This is how Irving Howe remembers them:

> In 1890, within the small space bounded by the Bowery on the west, the river and its warehouses on the east, Houston on the north and Monroe on the south, there were some dozen Christian churches, a dozen synagogues (most Jewish congregations were storefronts or in tenements), about fifty factories and shops (exclusive of garment establishments, most of which were west of the Bowery or hidden away in cellars and flats), ten large public buildings, twenty public and parochial schools—and one tiny park, on Grant and East Broadway. Gangs of German boys pressed down from the north, Irish from the south. A dominant impression of the Jewish quarter, shared by immigrants and visitors alike, was of fierce congestion, a place in which the bodily pressures of other people, their motions and smells and noises seemed always assaulting one. Of spaces for privacy and solitude, there was none. (quoted in Wirth-Nesher, "City" 95)

And this is how haptic and noisy the place becomes in Roth's rendering. The passage describes the corner of the Lower East Side to which the Schearls move from the less populated slum of Brownsville:[12]

> Here in 9th Street it wasn't the sun that swamped one as one left the doorway, it was sound—an avalanche of sound. There were countless children, there were countless baby carriages, there were countless mothers. And to the screams, rebukes and bickering of these, a seemingly endless file of hucksters joined their bawling cries. On Avenue D horse-cars clattered and banged. Avenue D was thronged with beer wagons, garbage carts and coal trucks. There were many automobiles, some blunt and rangy, some with straw poops, honking. Beyond Avenue D, at the end of a stunted, ruined block that began with shacks and smithies and seltzer bottling works and ended in a junk heap, was the East River on which many boat horns sounded. On 10th Street, and 8th Street Crosstown car ground its way toward the switch. (143)

Orientation is an obvious challenge in such a high-strung environment. Quick judgments and decisions are crucial to getting around—which means, in turn, that appearance becomes a matter of utmost concern. Thanks to the "American" clothes that the father provided to the mother and the child, they blend in upon arriving at Ellis Island (a typical theme in immigrant fiction). But the child's "odd, outlandish, blue straw hat" (10), a farewell gift from a friend back home, gives them away as foreigners. Albert Schearl loathes the attention that this hat attracts: "Can't

---

12 Taking his cue from Allen's remark that *Call It Sleep* may be "the noisiest novel ever written", Adams dedicated an entire article to the urban soundscape of Roth's novel, arguing that the many sounds filling and often disrupting David's familiar environment are the key to evoking the effect of immediacy that is such a strong and compelling feature of the novel.

you see that those idiots are watching us already? They're mocking us!" (15), he snaps before tearing it off the child's head, terrifying the little boy, and driving his wife to silent tears.[13] Already tainted by the cloud of unhappiness under which the reunion is cast, the desired effect of blending in is now damaged beyond repair.

Fueled by the feeling of constantly being watched and judged, Albert's violent temper is a permanent threat to his environment. "They look at me crookedly, with mockery in their eyes! How much can a man endure?" (22). Losing job after job as a printer due to his unpredictable rage, he becomes a milkman, working alone when others are sleeping. (Ironically, the new line of work bears a remote resemblance to his former, rural job as a cowherd while the need to be close to the stables demands that the Schearls move to the hyperurban Lower East Side.) David's father is an insanely proud man, degraded by the conditions of survival in the New World, and profoundly alienated from everyone including his family. Once he tries to articulate what ails him: "I *think* when you come out of a house and step on bare earth among the fields you're the same man who you were when you were inside the house. But when you step out on pavements you're someone else. You can feel your face change" (31-32, emphasis in the original). Brief as it is, his account impressively captures the compound displacements of modernization and migration. The aching disjunction between place and self expressed here harks back to what Ernst Bloch (right around this time) called *Ungleichzeitigkeit* [non-contemporaneity]: "Not all people exist in the same Now. They do so only externally, through the fact that they can be seen today. But they are there by not yet living at the same time with the others. They rather carry an earlier element with them; this interferes" (quoted in Kaes 185). Bloch does not mention migration, but his concern about the dangers of this tension-ridden simultaneity of the urban and the rural find a powerful echo in Albert's unpredictable rage.

There is a strikingly physical dimension to Albert's sense of displacement—a change of the part of his body most exposed to the gaze of others, his face—which creates an irritation so profound that it destabilizes the spatial moorings of his entire family. The somatics of spatial production at work here persist throughout *Call It Sleep*; space emerges directly from the bodily experiences of its characters. David's desire for a drink that he is too small to get gives this process a distinctly phenomenal quality early on. Wherever the boy goes, he takes in the environment with all of his senses; instant by instant, his world is molded from his perceptions. "How could you hear the sound of your own feet in the dark if a carpet muffled every step you took?" he wonders when traversing the dark hallway of their tenement building. "But if you couldn't hear the sound of your own feet and couldn't see anything either, how could you be sure that you were actually there

---

13   The fact that he mockingly calls it a "crown" (14) has been read as pointing towards David's symbolic role as a potential savior, being brought to the New World in the arms of a Madonna-like mother figure. For further elaboration of this theme, see Altenbernd.

and not dreaming?" (20) Living in a world that is inherently troubled by displacement spurs an especially urgent need for narrative mediation, and in the world of the novel this need is geared toward affirming social ties. Albert's brief account addresses Luter, the only person in the New World whom he longs to befriend. The self-imposing "I *think*" gives voice to a desire to be heard and received by this man. Genya's many stories, told to her son or to the few adults in her small world, serve a similar function: They either affirm another's or her own place in this foreign, unstable environment. In all of these cases, narrative acts are instruments of asserting and emplacing the speaker in the unfamiliar world from which the tale evolves.

But these narrative acts of self-assertion and emplacement are acutely charged with matters of language. Different languages reign in different spaces, and the boundaries between them tend to become effective (and at times unbridgeable) as linguistic boundaries.[14] The domestic space of the Schearls unfolds from the Yiddish spoken there, transposed by Roth into "splendid, almost too splendid, King James English" (Kazin, "Introduction" xv). "Shudder when I speak to you," Albert furiously demands of his son. But as Kazin rightly points out, "The English does not convey the routine, insignificant weight of the word 'shudder' in Yiddish," veiling the fact that "The people speaking Yiddish in this book are not cultivated, careful in choosing their words" but "hard-pressed, charged up, deeply emotional" (xv). They are also less religious than their language makes it seem. Roth sets this graceful, exalted language against the crude (and possibly exaggerated) vernacular used among the children when playing in the street—here with a dissembled alarm clock: "'So what makes id?" he asked. In the street David spoke English. 'Kencha see? Id's coz id's a machine.' 'Oh!' 'It wakes op mine fodder in the mawning.' 'It wakes up mine fodder too'" (21). How different he sounds when talking to his friends! Speaking English gives him access to a world more or less closed to his mother, while her secret spaces of the "old county" gain imaginative substance when David overhears a conversation between her and her sister, in which the two accidentally switch back and forth between the—for David unintelligible— Polish that guards these spaces and their habitual Yiddish. The Hebrew David learns at his *cheder* promises to open the gates to a mystical space of salvation, gradually turning the school itself (through this very prospect and despite the abusive authority of the rabbi) into a viable shelter away from his troubled home.

In depicting space as a heterogeneous entity that is socially activated through different, often "storied," forms of language use, Roth spells out the extent to which access and orientation depend on them. "I know that I myself live on one hundred and twenty-six Boddeth Stritt" (33), Genya once set out to describe her shrunken world, but before she can go on with her story, Albert impatiently corrects her:

---

14 A substantial body of scholarship has been dedicated to the novel's striking use of language and its significance for negotiating matters of belonging. See in particular Wirth-Nesher, "Between Mother Tongues;" Fiedler, "Many Myths; " Diamant; Buelens; Baumgarten; Aarons.

"Bahday Street!" Repeating the mispronounced name with gentle self-mockery, she seamlessly weaves the disruption into her melancholic tale:

"It is such a strange name—bath street in German. But here I am. I know there is a church on a certain street to my left, the vegetable market is to my right, behind me are the railroad tracks and the broken rocks, and before me, a few blocks away is a certain store window that has a kind of whitewash on it—and faces in the white-wash, the children draw. Within this pale is my America, and if I ventured further I should be lost. In fact," she laughed, "were they even to wash that window, I might never find my way home again." (33)[15]

But Genya shows little desire to challenge either the close boundaries of this world, or its aching absence of meaning and attachment. And hence, it is not the mother but the son who cannot find his way home one day. In his emerging world, the questions of who he is, where and how he belongs have exponential gravity, culminating once, early on in the book, in a situation in which walking away from his home presents itself as the only viable option. Enthusiastic about his adventure at first, he soon finds himself "losted," and in growing despair when realizing that the address he readily gives to the friendly strangers trying to help—"a hunnder 'n' twenty six Boddeth Stritt" (101)—does not exist on their map. It refers to a place only a few blocks away but displaced to a no-man's-land by the boy's vernacular bending of his mother's foreign pronunciation. To reiterate the nodal points of this discussion, then, *Call It Sleep* treats space as conjointly produced through perceptual and narrative investment. In doing so, it charts the incentive to make it/to make a home through a socially binding, communal use of language in ways that make tangible both its power to organize space, and its power to dissect, compartmentalize, and separate. And as David's life is sustained by a patchwork of languages, stories, and social ties *more* diverse than that of his parents, his place among them becomes increasingly troubled.

The issue of David's discomfort within his family touches upon another crucial feature of spatial production at work here. Undergirding the perceptual and linguistic malleability of place(-in-the)-making is an organization of space that is strikingly psychological—or rather psychoanalytical. In fact, the family triangle of an angry, isolated father, a loving mother, and a fearful child that is nestled into the tenement setting as the smallest spatial unit from which the narrative evolves

---

15   Genya's disorientation is also infused with the phenomenon of *Ungleichzeitigkeit*. In the conversation that leads to the sad account of "her America," she mentions that "nothing ever came to [her] hamlet except the snow and the rain," and that prior to her departure, the most modern experience of her life had been to listen to an even then outdated gramophone. She inhabits a "displaced corner of the Old World" (Samet 571), a description that aptly captures the peculiar distance between her and her environment. Her remoteness is further enhanced by her frequent indulgence in nostalgic stories about the "old country."

has a powerful Oedipal script.[16] But *Call It Sleep* not merely gives its spatial order a Freudian spin; it exploits this feature (which is based on a mythical tale about the human condition) as the very means to push beyond the conventionality of the immigrant's tale. In daring to suggest that David's troubled sense of belonging has a source other (or at least more complicated) than the difficulties of living in the disorienting, transitory space between different languages and cultures, it deromanticizes the nurturing ideal of the Jewish family.[17] With his father's unpredictable temper as a constant source of terror and threat, David's home is anything but a safe haven from the hostile world. The boy is haunted by recurring dreams of "his father's footsteps booming on the stairs, of the glistening doorknob turning, and of himself clutching at knifes he couldn't lift from the table" (22). In his emerging world, the fear of his father is a major structuring force, which thrives on a basic distinction: There are "black days" (the good days when his father is away at work and David has his mother and the family's domestic space all to himself), and there are "red days" (the dreadful days when his father is at home). Naming them so is the secret code that David uses to gain control over a space threatened by his father's open dislike of him. Yet intermingling with the ever-looming fear of being abused by his father are feelings of envy and adoration. When seeing him dress, David is awed by his muscular physique. "How long would it be [...] before those knots appeared above his own elbow and those tough, taut braids at his forearm. He wished it were soon, wished it were today, this minute. Strong, how strong his father was, stronger than he'd ever be" (177).

In the light of such fancies, David's habit of collecting the old calendar leafs becomes tangible as the desire to create a material record of time progressing toward him finally being "big enough" (18). "You peel off the year as one might a cabbage," (19) his mother once teases him; that David's father made the calendar at one of his many jobs as a printer turns the boy's ritual into a symbolic routine of dismembering his awful power—a process in which the mother, in providing him with the daily leafs, is an accomplice. David's symbiosis with his mother (who is also rejected by the father and has no other object for her love but her son) is the bulwark raised against a menacing world. "Darkness was different without his mother near. People were different too" (37). The thought of her listening until he has traversed the threatening hallway is of existential reassurance for him. But as the story progresses, the codependence of mother and son becomes suffocating, further troubling David's already tainted comfort in the family's domestic space. The

---

16   A substantial body of work is dedicated to the Freudian subplot of the novel. See for example Altenbernd; Ferraro, "Oedipus in Brownsville;" Fein; Samet; Freywald.
17   Yezierka's *The Breadwinners* is an earlier portrayal of a problematic immigrant family, yet while both novels share the figure of the threatening father, *Call It Sleep* goes much further in deconstructing the ideal of the Jewish family, and adds psychological depth to the conflicts among its members.

symbiosis between mother and son eventually cracks under the weight of the boy's jealousy—his obsession with "erotic images of her naked flesh, which he compulsively fantasizes being stared at by strangers and ravished in his father's planned absence by a boarder who pretends to be his friend" (Fiedler, "Many Myths" 25).

Roth downplayed the Freudian influence on his novel that so clearly becomes tangible here. "I don't know much about Freud and never did. [...] If I had known about things like Oedipus complexes I probably would have never written the book at all" (Howard 76), he stated in an interview, conceding soon thereafter: "Of course, I knew about Freud, but I only had a smattering of it. I only knew what everyone else knew of Freud, and that wasn't a great deal" (Freedman, "Conversation" 155). Deliberately exploited or not, what he knew was forceful enough to earn *Call It Sleep* the reputation of being "the most Freudian of the American great novels" (Guttman 50). Roth's intense engagement with Joyce, Eliot, and O'Neill are likely sources of an "osmotic" reception. Yet what interests me about the novel's investment in Freud's ideas are not so much possible sources or routes of transmission. Rather, I am intrigued by how readily these ideas were absorbed in contemporary efforts of giving voice and form to concerns with belonging. When Roth began writing his novel in the summer of 1930, psychoanalysis had undergone a short and steep history of success in America. Launched by the series of lectures Freud had given at Clark University in 1909 (the occasion of his only visit to the United States), psychoanalysis was rapidly institutionalized as a medical discipline, and widely received in writing (mostly through the published lectures themselves, and the translations of Freud's other major works of the time: *Introduction to Psychoanalysis, Interpretation of Dreams,* and *Psychopathology of Everyday Life*).[18] *Call it Sleep* can indeed be read as a showcase of the ways in which a popularized set of Freudian ideas began to form a more or less coherent repository of narrative frames and storylines about modern individuals and their place in the world. Three components of the emerging psychoanalytical imagination are pertinent to

---

18 Opening his monumental study on Freud's reception in America, noting that 1909 was the last year an American President rode to his inauguration in a carriage, Hale aligns the arrival of psychoanalysis in the U.S. with modernization. There is wide agreement among Freud scholars that the shared sense of transition pervading U.S. society during the early decades of the twentieth century was a decisive factor in propelling the favorable reception of psychoanalysis, and the quick and thorough spread of its main ideas (in Europe, they were met with suspicion until reimported from the U.S.). While it must be assumed that these feelings of instability and change were unevenly distributed and subjectively experienced throughout the social field, experiences of immigration and of the disintegrating forces of modern life had a measurable impact in turning "analytic absorption in [...] individual histories" (Roazen 273) and the "search for meaning in [...] dreams, wishes, fears and confusions" (Turkle 31) into welcome venues for emotional stabilization and intellectual reorientation. For further reading about Freud in America, see Illouz, *Saving*; Zaretsky; Hale; Borchers.

rendering concerns with belonging in Roth's novel: the key roles assigned to the nuclear family and to sexual desire, which are closely related through the Oedipus complex; the turn to the sphere of the ordinary and the everyday, prototypically embodied in the "Freudian mistake" that is significant precisely because of its randomness; and the secular revision of former frames of self-narration, most significantly the biblical salvation story with its clear-cut patterns of dealing with existential doubt (Illouz, *Saving* 45-68).

While the latter two aspects feature prominently in the novel's narrative design to be discussed in the following section, the Oedipal nexus of nuclear family and sexual desire has a decisive impact on the novel's spatial organization—with two important effects. First, it amplifies a use of symbolism in which related pairs of opposites (light and dark, good and evil, inside and outside, cellar and roof) gain meaning in close relation to space. The Oedipal script of the family thus interlinks with a thoroughly spatialized symbolism, connecting darkness (the dominant symbol of fear) to the space of the cellar *and* to the father, just as light (the symbol of salvation) is associated with the roof and the rail *and* with the desired escape from male authorities (the father, the rabbi). That the symbolic couplets thrive on an inside-outside opposition, which is firmly grounded in the novel's imaginary geography, amplifies their signifying power (the problematic interior spaces of the Schearls' home, the cellar, the *cheder* versus the promising openness of the urban wasteland by the river and the rails).[19] Such a highly charged environment is riddled with boundaries that are both geographic and symbolic, which makes movements across especially effective in spurring narrative action. Second and closely related, the psychological dimension brought into play by the Oedipal rendering of the family has the effect of mobilizing the space imagined by the novel from within the storytelling process. Contrary to Freud's "geographical" model of the psyche, with its fixed realms of the ego, the superego, and the id, the Oedipal family follows a progressive and predictable script. Out of sheer psychic need, the relation between its members *has* to change, with the effect of altering

---

19 This pattern can be further extended in the sense that the cellar resembles the unconscious and the roof resembles the super ego. On the symbolism of light vs. dark, good vs. evil, see Lyons, *Henry Roth* 40-42; Freedman "Mystic Initiation" 27. For the psychoanalytical enhancement of this symbolism, see Fein. For psychoanalytical cellar and roof symbolism, see Freywald 445-48. Furthermore, all the headings for the individual books into which the novel is divided—"The Cellar," "The Picture," "The Cheder," "The Rail"—have not only significant symbolic meanings but also these symbols are attached to and substantially gain their meanings in relation to the novel's imaginary geography. See Lyons, "Symbolic Structure." With regard to Books I, III, and IV, these references have already been mentioned. Book II, entitled "The Picture," is associated with the cornfield in which David's mother lived out her affair with the Christian organist of her village.

the space they share among themselves and with others.[20] Such an implicit mobilization of space resonates with Freud's conception of the family as a biographical event. In stark difference to the genealogical mechanism of emplacing an individual within a fixed and given social order that we saw at work as a socio-economical determinant in *Edgar Huntly*, construing the family as a biographical event goes hand in hand with a mode of symbolic production that molds and expresses one's individuality in a unique and subjective way. *Call it Sleep*'s spatial imagination is indeed deeply invested in this kind of eventfulness. The Schearl kitchen as its epicenter mirrors Freud's insistence (in opposing Marx) that the domestic rather than the work sphere is most formative for a person's life, with the family constituting the very entity from which individuals have to separate themselves to become a mature being.[21] The eventfulness inscribed into the Schearl family through the Oedipal script climaxes when David throws a dipper onto the streetcar's electric rail in a desperate attempt of self-creation, and act of near self-electrocution. He seizes the tool—symbolizing the (sexual organ of the) father (the cowherd, the milkman, the one allowed to touch his mother's breasts)—from a milk can in the street when escaping from home after the final showdown with his father, and takes it to the open space by the river on his erring flight. Yet all too soon, he finds himself back in the family kitchen, injured and in need of his parents' care. It is not in the vision of an urban, democratic community taking shape in the public space out there by the river, but in the Schearls' domestic space—in the flicker of the softening fatherly hatred upon David's return—that a new form of belonging becomes tangible in this novel.

I will resume this train of thought in the following section. For now, we need to stay tuned with the space evolving from the family as a biographical event, more precisely, with the ways in which the Oedipal constellation between its members *prescribes* its mobilization. In providing a progressive script with predictable phases such as "arousal of sexual desire for the mother" or "increasing conflict with the father," it encodes the space imagined by the novel with a specific semantics of action (from powerlessness to self-assertion). The Oedipal subplot of the family hence plants narrative "seeds" that generate events and direct the course

---

20 The rise of Freud's ideas coincided with a transformation of the notion of the family. A decreasing birthrate led to conceiving it as a close, triangular relation between father, mother and child, while the increasing emphasis of the generational divide had the effect of juxtaposing the functional unit of the parents against their child. Within this basic structure, the growing specialization of gender roles resulted in an intensification of emotional bonds between mother and child, structurally prefiguring a conflict between father and son that became the touchstone of the Oedipus complex. See Illouz *Saving* 69-72.

21 Ironically, this revaluation happened when the traditional foundations of the family began to falter, making it return as a "story" in which the self was placed rather than having an institution regulating it. See Illouz, *Salvation* 67.

of the action while the narrative space of the novel unfolds. Yoking spatial organization and narrative action in this way directly affects the novel's investment in matters of dwelling. It choreographs a search for meaning-as-form that takes us on a journey in which "return" is never an option (neither can David go back to an earlier, more innocent state of his evolving world nor can he return to a more comfortable place called home in the Old World). The journey on which the narrative takes us along with its maturing child protagonist is geared toward self-assertion and empowerment, and this turns travelling down the plotted path into a narrative ritual in more than one way. Plot—in its capacity of laying out the grounds to be traversed in order to make the boy's world more suitable for dwelling in it—reigns over the prospect of mastering the rite of passage thus imposed on and through the boy, and the journey undertaken with this aim leads across the compound grounds of plotting as place-making and plotting as storytelling. Intertwining these two operations in the Oedipal script of the family (the smallest spatial unit from which the narrative is structurally destined to evolve) gives the journey a psychoanalytical spin. And with psychoanalysis being "a primarily narrative art" (Brooks, *Reading* xiv), redeeming the child's lack of belonging is bound to take narrative form. The desire for this narrative—to craft and to tell it—is the primary form-giving drive in Roth's novel.

Yet while *Call It Sleep* is deeply invested in the productive nexus of belonging and narrative, it was written at a time of rising suspicion against plot. *Ulysses*, for instance, the novel that had such a profound impact on Roth, has more than 500 pages but hardly any plot. Its meandering narrative is not unconcerned with belonging; in fact, one of the most compelling features of Joyce's novel is the degree to which its main protagonist Leopold Bloom is not an alienated modern individual but one that (despite the unfaithfulness of his wife that drives him from his home and makes him roam the streets of Dublin for an entire day) firmly and joyously belongs. For a displaced and fearful immigrant boy, however, aimless drifting through inner and outer worlds is not a source of comfort. His conjoint states of immaturity and displacement create a different need to tell—one that is plot-driven in strikingly modernist, erratic ways.

Found Stuff as Narrative Foundation

David has a habit that perfectly captures the novel's erratic mode of emplotment. He gathers (in what can be read as a *mise en abyme* of the novel's plotting operation) random objects from his environment and stores them in an old shoebox, to which he turns for comfort. There are two orders of things in his "treasure chest" (19): calendar leafs and "striking odds and ends he found in the street" (35). He treasures the calendar leafs for their capacity to map the contours of his emerging world by keeping a material record of time progressing toward outgrowing (the fear of) his father. The "things [...] old and worn" or "gems" (35), as his mother lovingly calls them, provide the imaginary stuff to fill this map. The link of a broken chain, the thread on a bolt of a castor wheel, the overstretched spring of a window shade are precious to him because they bear "obscurely aching" (36) marks of the places where they used to belong, and thus inspire him to assign them with new ones.

> If one had one of these [springs] on one's feet instead of shoes, one might bounce instead of walk. High as a roof; far away at once. Like Puss in Boots. But if the mouse changed into an ogre inside the puss—right before it died—I am a mouse—an ogre!—Then poor Puss would have swelled and swelled and— (36)

Following this basic pattern, stuff randomly picked up from David's environment—objects like those mentioned above but also people, mental images, pieces of conversations, anecdotes—are employed to fill his emerging world with elaborate, self-empowering stories. Using what is found as the organizing principle of emplotment—and thus as the narrative foundation of dwelling in the world—is closely aligned with the emerging psychoanalytical imagination, especially with Freud's endorsement of the random and the everyday. As spheres of the ordinary and the uneventful they become primary sites of creating and destroying the self, turning the insignificant, the trivial, and the common aspects of life into primary resources of sense-production, identity formation, and belonging (Cavell, "The Ordinary"). *Call It Sleep* embraces this logic both in being relatively uneventful (we follow a fearful Jewish boy through his daily routines and timid transgressions), and in the sense that random or minor mistakes and events essentially drive the plot. After dropping a spoon into a bowl of soup his father erupts, curtailing a series of dramatic events: the boy earns a severe beating for kicking a friend in the nose, knocks one of his playmates to the ground (is he dead?), flees the scene of his "crime," and gets lost. The rosary, a gift from a Christian friend, exposes him as a traitor, propelling the story toward its end.

This kind of stuff assumes an avalanching force over the course of the narrative. And if David's "gem" collection mimics the plotting operation of assembling random, ordinary occurrences and things, one can think of it as *found* in at least two different ways. Echoing Roth's conviction that art can be made "out of junk" (Lyons, "Interview" 53), it draws on an artistic procedure employed by Kurt Schwitters, Marcel Duchamp, Pablo Picasso (in his sculptures), and a bit later by Robert Rauschenberg, in which everyday objects (often pieces of junk) are creatively recontextualized, and hence turned into art. Roth's novel embraces this procedure to the degree that it becomes an overall practice of form-giving, applied to the protagonist's self- and place-making efforts, and to the narrative project of the novel as a whole. But one can also think of David's stuff as found in the sense of "gifts from the world." These gifts capture the boy's imagination because their displacement makes them ache with a mysterious promise of belonging, fitting, being useful somewhere again. What David "learns" from the sex games imposed on him by the neighbor's physically challenged daughter, or from being cowed to throw a metal sword onto the streetcar's electric rail by a gang of Christian boys on Passover Day, quivers with meaning in similar ways. Seemingly useless, disposable occurrences—the "junk" of his everyday life—become valuable through creative recontextualization. "Playing bad" with Annie, devastating as it may have been when it happened, provides him with the key to decode the sexual tension between Luter and his mother, just as producing "lightning" from the rail inspires his redemptive attempt at self-creation.

Moreover, and crucially, both incidents have a profound impact on the further course of the narrative. In the first case, David loses interest in the game he is playing with his friends when he sees Luter approach his house, suspecting him of wanting to "play bad" with his mother—which makes him embark on his adventure of running away after knocking down his playmate (with Luter at his home he cannot go there). In the second case, he breaks into the *cheder* and is caught by the rabbi, who ridicules him for believing to have found "God's light" (257) in the urban wasteland by the car-tracks, thus making him receptive to the Christian faith about which he learns from his new friend Leo. The latter event makes him stumble across yet another gift from the world with vast implications for the further course of the story: his friend's rosary. But this gift comes with a price. To receive it, David must help his friend "play bad" with his cousin. And when the rosary falls out of his pocket during the final showdown with his father (the most "Freudian" of his many mistakes, fueling his father's suspicions that David is the illegitimate child of a *goy*), it pushes the conflict between father and son to a point of no return. Even the rosary's previous owner, David's friend Leo, can be viewed a found object with vast impact on the plotting operation. David makes his acquaintance when, feeling betrayed and lonely, he retreats to the roof of his house, where the older, gorgeous boy is flying a kite (a powerful symbol of freedom, recalling Benjamin Franklin and his famous kite-flying experiment). Leo is lean and blond, and besides his kite, he owns a pair of skates that grant him a mobility that David envies. Leo goes where he pleases, eats what he likes, and in all of this, he is intriguingly "other" to David (Polish, Christian, American). That Leo just happens to be passing through the neighborhood when David finds him on the roof underscores the random nature of an encounter that profoundly alters David's desire to belong, with the effect of stimulating imagination and narration right away. Before even talking to the other, David fantasizes about a "bond of kinship growing up between them, [...] both inhabitants of the same realm" (300). He, who has never wanted to be anyone's friend, spends one of the "most blissful" hours of his life in the company of the other boy. "The longer he heard him speak, the longer he watched him, the more he became convinced that Leo belonged to a rarer, bolder, carefree world" (305)—a world of which he yearned to be a part.

There are numerous echoes in this yearning: his father's wish to befriend the treacherous Mr. Luter; his mother's premarital affair with the *goy* organist of her village; her husband's doubt that David is his son. Acutely charged with this family history, becoming Leo's friend is the ultimate act of digression. Indeed, once the imaginary kinship with the other boy takes shape as the shaky outpost for a new way of belonging, challenging his feeble position within the family is only a matter of time.[22] Exploiting what is found as the organizing principle of emplotment thrives on a promise of (narrative) agency and self-empowerment to be gained from creative recontextualization. The novel's plotting operation follows a pattern in which things happen to David with unsettling force, to which he responds by emplotting them. The frequent interior monologues explicate his relentless attempts to make random things fit with the effect of dramatizing his prospect of emplacement as hinging on a ceaseless narrativizing process. Once he returns home frightened and breathless, telling his mother that he "saw a man who was in a box" (63). After a lengthy interrogation about darkness, death and dying, she tells him about her grandmother's death, ending with this highly poetic image:

She died the winter of that same year, before the snow fell. [...] She looked so frail in death, in her shroud—how shall I tell you my son? Like early winter snow: And I thought to myself even then, let me look deeply in her face for surely she will melt before my eyes. (68)

Comfortably immersed in the story, David drifts into a dreamy state in which the grandmother's melting face blurs with his mother's features dissolving in the grainy light of dawn in ways that remind him of the swirling confetti he once saw at a wedding. Plunging deeper into his reverie, it occurs to him that the happy couple at the center of his randomly found mental image left in a carriage just like the one in the funeral. "It was solved now. He saw it clearly. Everything belonged to the same dark. Confetti and coffins" (70).

The boy's frantic search for meaning quietens when, in creatively connecting his found mental images with the concluding image of his mother's story, narrativizing the disturbing event of the funeral reaches a tacit moment of closure. And hence, the young protagonist learns not only to *read* (or decode) but also to *write* (or encode) his environment. The narrative-structuring process thus performed (and modeled quite consciously after Joyce) "occurs simultaneously in the character and in the reader; as motifs accumulate, we together with David gradually invest them with symbolic and emotional attributes" (Adams 45). The fusion of the reader's experience with that of the maturing child is grounded in a narrative situation in which a (more sophisticated) "narrating self" orders the impressions of a (less developed)

---

22 The implicit "Americanization" of this itinerary of belonging has led Cappell to read *Call It Sleep* as an anti-Jewish novel.

"experiencing self."[23] The result is a kind of storytelling that stages the endless process of negotiation between experience and narration across the cognitive gap inherent to all narrative activity. Similarly to *Edgar Huntly* (and quite differently form *Pointed Firs*, in which the "experiencing self" is voiceless in comparison), *Call It Sleep* aligns its form-giving drive with the internal negotiation between these two narrating agents. In fact, it enhances the form-giving process with an air of urgency by routinely assessing it from the disorderly, immature side of *experience* with the effect of structurally implementing an explicit *demand* for narrative mediation. And this means that the subsequent passage through the plotted middle ground is inherently challenged by a narrative operation that simultaneously propels and disperses the creation of order. In fact, in a narrative world founded in the perpetual operation of finding and recontextualizing the very stuff that feeds the story, the narrative drive of making the world known and familiar, which preconditions any possibility to belong, is simultaneously embraced and deterred.

In terms of narrative agency (conceived in this study as the capacity to make choices about the telling of one's story and impose them on the world) encoding the external world with meaning thus becomes especially crucial. However, encoding is not merely a complementary process to the semiotic activity of decoding, the latter being grounded in *actuality* in the sense of departing from something that exists in the protagonist's external world. Rather, encoding is an activity through which David's "imagination reorganizes reality into its own […] pattern of symbol and meaning," and in doing so, it exerts "its own pull on reality" (Diamant 346-47). Encoding is indeed absolutely indispensable to the protagonist's task of fathoming—narrating—a world with a place for him, for it can mold a given reality according to its practitioner's particular needs. But encoding becomes precarious if the imaginary reorganization of the world performed by it loses touch with the actuality of the world; if the invented patterns and narratives are hermetic, employed to ward off reality rather than engage with it. David's final response to the funeral epitomizes this drift toward hermetic closure. "Confetti" is associated with marriage, "coffins" with death, both are linked by the carriage, and the threatening darkness is effectively blocked out. In fact, his entire operation of encoding the world has this tendency. If one reads the novel as a "semiotic *Bildungsroman*" in which cognitive activity progresses toward a more refined state, the rite of passage takes shape as a movement "from flight via hermetic [storytelling] toward a more balanced […] poetic activity, which will enable the protagonist to establish a positive reciprocity with his environment" (Diamant 355). And this also means: to assert a place for himself the boy must become a different storyteller.

The funeral passage is illuminating for yet another reason: It makes tangible how the "odds and ends" of other stories, absorbed into the narrative operations

---

23 Again, the terms are drawn from Stanzel 59-91. For a superb discussion of this cognitive operation in *Call It Sleep*, see Diamant 338-40.

of a maturing consciousness, assume a key role in advancing the rite of passage engrained into the narrative design of this novel.[24] Two of David's most powerful findings in this regard are fragments of salvation stories: the story of Isaiah who sees God surrounded by the brightest light, and is cleansed of his sin when the angels touch his lips with a holy piece of coal, an aborted version of which he hears at his *cheder;* and Leo's cryptic account of "Christ, our Savior" (304) who died on a cross and possesses a holy light "way bigger [...] den Jew light" (322). Both stories capture David's imagination with their redemptive plots, and they do so with particular force since they are mystical and incomplete. Yet even more importantly, they connect themselves to David's desire for an own story. In offering models of emplotment that enhance his sense and widen his scope of agency, they can be effectively recycled to sooth or redeem his aching lack of belonging. It is thus no coincidence that David's final act of self-assertion builds on these religious narratives to envision—in an idiosyncratic mix of borrowing from Judaic and Christian faith—a viable place in the world. From the first story David adopts the idea that he, like Isaiah, can be cleansed of his sins if he finds the equivalent to God's "angel-coal" (231), a storyline most welcome to a boy tormented by the treacherous dangers of sinning. In fact, it lends itself extremely well to creative recontextualization; with almost no effort, David exploits it to indulge in the fantasy that the terrifying light produced from the rail has the same cleansing power as God's magic coal. Another random finding supports this crude story. Right before the older boys force him to throw a sword onto the rail, he sits on the docks where he sees in the sun's bright reflections on the surface of the river "God's holy light" burning the water. Connected through the Isaiah story, these two events turn the urban wasteland by the river into a space of possible healing and transcendence.

If the practical use of the Judaic salvation myth is to help the boy imagine himself cleansed of what he believes to be his sins, thus promising to create a degree (and ground) zero for a new way of belonging, his creative recycling of the Christian salvation myth is more diffuse. It is indeed as cryptic as the bits and pieces gathered from Leo's account of it. This is hardly a problem, however, for the practical use of this story is inseparable from David's fascination with its teller. His friendship assures him that he can fully and fearlessly inhabit the grounds purged from sin to become part of a new and freer world; it also cannot be separated from his desire to possess the rosary that is the token of this possible future.[25] Yoked together by

---

24 The narrative drive of the boy's consciousness anticipates a major theme in Richard Powers's *The Echo Maker* discussed in the following chapter. Inspired by recent neuro-scientific research on the human brain, consciousness is once referred to—and throughout the novel explored as—a "storytelling machine" whose entire end is "self-continuation."

25 Using religious salvation stories for therapeutic purposes is another manifestation of the psychoanalytical imagination consolidating at this time. Drawing on Kirschner's *The Religious and Romantic Origins of Psychoanalysis,* Illouz argues that the basic structure of salvation narratives

the boy's longing to escape the terrible reign of his father, these findings fuel the plotting operation like gasoline poured on fire. With a total of a hundred and twenty-two pages, the fateful day following the visit at his new friend's home covers more than a quarter of the book. Up to this point, the narrative loosely strings together events that are stretched out over more than two years. But now it shifts to closely following its protagonist through a day in which one odd and random coincidence chases another with ever-rising levels of anxiety, thrill, and exhaustion.

Toying with his new friend's faith brings him closer to becoming a member of that other, freer tribe, but to realize this fancy, his existing kinship bonds must first be resolved. His mother's story of her affair with the organist of her home village provides the "odds and ends" that David needs for this purpose. Again, it is a highly fragmented story, secretly overheard by the boy when his mother tells it to her sister Bertha, a character who, "like the sweat that pours from her body," brings all the silenced trouble "to the surface" (Wisse 66), and whose function in the evolution of the narrative is precisely that. In abiding by a now-familiar pattern, the story exchanged between the two sisters is odd and inconclusive to the eavesdropping child. Genya tells much of it in Polish, the old country's tongue that David never learned, and only accidently slips into her habitual Yiddish, giving away just enough to piece together the main thrust of the story while leaving precious gaps for her son's creative adaptation.

What had happened? She liked somebody. Who? Lud—Ludwig, she said. A goy. An organeest. Father didn't like him, her father. And his, too, maybe. Didn't want him to know! Gee! He knew more than his father. So she married a Jew. What did she say before? What did she say before? Benkart, yes, benkart in belly, her father said. What did it mean? He almost knew. (205)

And then he knows: His mother could have been pregnant from this other man— which means that he could be *this* man's son, not his father's. Transposed (at least in his hungry imagination) from possibility to actuality, this fractured storyline becomes the trajectory of the disaster tale that he tells the rabbi during the long final day. Born from the horrifying consequences of getting caught, David's panic-driven act of narrative self-assertion not only gives him a Christian father, it also denies his parents altogether. His mother is dead, he wails tearfully, the woman raising him is really his aunt. The basic plot of this tale bears striking similarity to Freud's "family romance," according to which part of gaining a mature psyche is to create, often around David's age, an account of oneself with parents other than

---

recurs in the story of the developmental-psychological self: Both are linear, closure-driven, eschatological, geared towards the future (away from a present that is incomplete and full of faults); Freud's ideas could only become so influential because their ways of self-narration were highly compatible with the salvation myth deeply engrained in Western cultures through protestant conceptions of the self and romantic adoptions of biblical narratives (*Saving* 71-80).

one's actual ones.[26] Again, this incidence can be read as a token of the "psychoanalytical imagination" taking hold at the time of the novel's production, fusing the expectation of permanent self-analysis with self-help culture that became the most powerful resource of the popular reception of psychoanalysis in America (Illouz, *Saving* 79-84, 253-65). David's self-invention is inflected with the fantasy at the very core of the American self-help myth: You can proactively turn—narrate—yourself into the person you long to be, the person better equipped to belong. [27]

David's frantic act of self-narration stands out in force and consequence because it is one of the rare moments in which his narrativizing efforts are not confined to his psyche but acted out and imposed on the world—when narrative activity (a basic mode of engagement with the world) becomes narrative agency (the capacity of making choices about the telling of one's story and impose them on the world). In terms of content, however, this narrative act is yet another incident of hermetic storytelling, performed by a terrified boy to hold the world at bay. It is indeed consequential because once uttered, there is no easy way of integrating his speech act into the world from which it was meant to create a safe distance. But the catastrophic failure of David's madly fabricated story has a productive side as well. It challenges the hermeticism of the boy's habitual mode of storytelling by exposing it to the world; in doing so, it creates a practical need for the boy to narrativize his life in ways that engage with his surroundings rather than withdrawing from them into the sheltered sphere of his imagination. If and to what extent the new need that is triggered by David's frantic confession is redeemable depends on the outcome of the densely plotted final day, and the stakes are rising in a avalanching chain of events: The rabbi calls on David's parents, and when he gives away Genya's secret recounting David's story, Albert voices his darkest suspicions: that his wife married him and then sent him ahead on a ticket purchased by her impoverished family to cover up her illegitimate pregnancy; and that she did so knowing about the parricide that left him with no other choice but to leave his home. While the parents still fight over this long-suppressed matter, Bertha and her husband arrive. They immediately realize the hazard into which the occasion of their visit—breaking the news about David plotting sex games involving their daughter—would put the boy, but get caught under the spell of Albert's terrible will. Soon enough the

---

26 See Freud, "Family Romance." For discussions of its exploitation in *Call It Sleep*, see Altenbernd 679; Sollors, "A World" 152-54.

27 Freud himself paved the way for this development. Departing from his earlier conviction that therapeutic work can ease but not heal a patient's psychic troubles, he ended his fifth and final Clark Lecture on a decidedly more optimistic, "Americanized" note: "Der energische und erfolgreiche Mensch ist der, der durch Arbeit seine Wunschphantasien in Realität umzusetzen vermag" (quoted in Illouz 84). Henceforth, the psychoanalytical search for the lost or buried self became reconcilable with the strife for self-realization that is quintessential to modern yearnings to belong—and, as Roth's novel shows, applicable with staggering universality.

tension becomes unbearable and David speaks up for himself, is attacked by his father, and flees the apartment.

Coinciding with this fateful chain reaction is a structural, or rather contractual dimension of the impact that David's transgressive narrative act has on the storytelling operation. In the immediate aftermath of the showdown in the Schearls' kitchen, focalization through his consciousness (the exclusive mediator of the novel's main narrative until now) is suspended for several short intervals—one focalized through the rabbi, another with the zero focalization of an auctorial narrator, and yet another with shifting focalizers and a pluralized narrative voice—with the effect of changing the terms of narrative transfer. The first two of these passages are strictly excursive; rather than furthering the narrative they neutralize focalization and arrest a narrative agency gone wild. After pages of interior discourse turning in circles, focalization through the boy winds down as his narrative capacity reaches degree zero:

The small sputter of words in his brain seemed no longer his own, no longer cramped by skull, but detached from him, the core of his surroundings. And he heard them again as though all space had compelled and were shattered in the framing, and they boomed in his ears, vast, delayed and alien. (409)

In this state of exhaustion, language exceeds him, but it also plants a thought in him: *"Now I gotta make it come out"* (409)—"*it*" being the redemptive light he wants to draw from the rail. The italic type in which the thought is set anticipates the typographical form in which David's exhausted consciousness continues to articulate itself while another part of the narrative ventures into the urban space surrounding him. Hence, as his hollow mind becomes occupied with a singular call to action, the dominant mode of telling the story is interrupted for a third and final time: In an unmistakable homage to the "Nighttown" chapters of *Ulysses*, it is broken up and pluralized. Pushing beyond the boy's consciousness that keeps driving the plot through the typographically separated sections, narration dissociates itself from the plotting operation, and meanders into the environment. In this expansive move, it gathers the random activities and vernacular-bent conversations of the multiethnic mix of urban dwellers peopling it: a rheumatic old watchman who talks to himself, a loud group of sailors, dock workers, promiscuous women in a nearby beer salon, the Irish motorman of the approaching streetcar ringing his bell, a leisurely Armenian peddler, a fainting woman, a policeman, a doctor. Here is a taste of how this works (411-12):

Over momentary, purple blossoms, down the soft incline, the far train slid like a trickle of gold. Behind and before, sparse auto headlights, belated or heralding dew on the bough of the night. "And George a'gappin' and me a'hollerin' and a'teching the ground with the toe of my boot and no wheels under me. Ha! Ha! Hmm! Wut cain't a man dream in his sleep . . . A wheel . . . A bike . . ." He turned away

seeking the clock. "And I ain't been on one . . . not sence . . . more'n thirty-five . . . forty years. Not since I uz a little shaver"
> *Clammy fingers traced the sharp edge of*
> *the dipper's scoop. Before his eyes*
> *the glitter on the car tracks whisked . . .*
> *reversed . . . whisked . . .*

"Say, listen O'Toole dere's a couple o' cozier in de back." The bar-keep pointed with the beer knife. "Jist yer speed!"
"Balls" Terse O'Toole retorted. "Wudjah think I jist took de Bull-durham sack off me pecker fer—nuttin'? I twisted all de pipes I wanna w'en I'm pissin!"
"No splinters in dese boxes, dough. Honst, O'Toole! Real clean—"
"Let 'im finish, will ye!" the hunchback interrupted sourly. "O'Toole don' have to buy his gash."
"Well, he says, yea. An' all de time dere wuz Steve an' Kekky unner de goiders belly-achin'—Hey trow us a rivert. An' I sez—"
  —*Nobody's commin'!*
Klang! Klang! Klang! Klang! Klang!
The fat bunion foot of Dan McIntyre the motorman pounded the bell.

This is more "found stuff" for the plotting operation for sure, but no *real* sense of community emerges from the polyvocal narration employed here. The "odds and ends" assembled in this experiment remain too disjointed for that; in fact, they converge only in the boy's yearning for a new way of belonging that drives narration toward and beyond the point of him losing consciousness when struck by the power drawn from the rail. The erratic passages articulating his hallucinating mind throughout this chapter (they are set in cursive, justified only on the left margin, and at times bracketed) are inserted into the text as a "boxed-in space or series of spaces" (McHale 98). Reminiscent of cinematic montage, these "textual enclosures" connect by way of separation, and just as in experimental cinema, this has the effect of foregrounding *procedural* matters. In loops of verbal and syntactical repetitions, language itself becomes tangible in both its referential and material dimension. But modernist experimentation with language and narrative is not boundless in this passage. Rather, the montage-like procedure advanced here allows Roth to exploit a transgressive aesthetics while keeping it safely confined to the boy's troubled mind. In doing so, Roth (like his fellow modernists Dos Passos and Lowry) "contains the Joycean poetics of reality pluralism by subjectivizing it" (McHale 98).[28] By the same token, however, the expansive narrative agency probed

---

28   I am following McHale's insightful reading here. He further elaborates this well-taken point as follows: "'Containment' here is not even a metaphor, but applies literally to the special typographical conventions of this episode, whereby David's hallucinations appear in italic type, inset from the rest of the text, justified to the left margin but not on the right, and even (for part of the episode, IV.xii.424-431) enclosed between parenthesis. The effect is to produce a kind

here in its capacity to generate a new way of belonging is not pluralized in actuality; the plurality of voices is the fantasy of a hallucinating mind, not the blueprint of a polyvocal mode of dwelling in and through language and narrative.

There is a political or even an ethical side to not endorsing fully a transgressive modernist aesthetics as the way to a better, truer state of belonging—a reluctance to retreat from the boy's developing sense of self, from his individual and particular need for change.[29] These narrative agents are decidedly not to be given up. Transformation is on its way, but it is not invoked by language spilling beyond the confines of the boy's emerging subjectivity with materializing effects. Rather, it takes shape in his exhausted consciousness while it becomes the locus of blending the urban environment projected into it with recurring images of light and dark, physical and metaphysical power, hammer, coal, the cellar, the Statue of Liberty, etc. And as narration expands, the boy's hermetic storytelling gives way to a narrative agency that engages with his environment in new and unprecedented ways. The novel's ending, reached ten pages later testifies to this transformation. Repeated like a mantra, the title-giving sentence opening the final paragraph—"He might as well call it sleep." (441)—is the emblem of David's newly found(ed) narrative capacities.

In the meantime, focalization through the boy has been resumed; he has been taken home, where the dreadful family constellation shows tacit cracks as the father shrinks under the actual possibility of his son's death, which David registers with silent but jubilant satisfaction. His first attempt at telling his life anew takes place in the family home, and this puts it to the hardest test right away. Responding to his mother's caring question "Sleepy, beloved?" (441), he refrains from imposing premature meaning on his exhausted state. "It was only toward sleep that every

---

of textual enclosure, a boxed-in space or series of spaces within which [...] the Circe principle is allowed free reign. But the walls of this textual enclosure are never breached. Nor, for that matter, are the ontological boundaries between the level of discursive figures and the level of the world, between the real world and the world of mystic archetypes. Nothing equivalent to the materialization, in 'Circe,' of the nymph Calypso [...] occurs in *Call It Sleep*, and the messenger angels on Roth's messianic subtext remain *discursive* angels only [...] Finally, there is here none of the 'ripple effect' of Joyce's 'Circe.' No trace of the Circe principle, even in Roth's attenuated and subjectivized version of it, is allowed to spread beyond the confines of Chapter IV (xxi) to any other chapter of the book" (97-98).

29 Ever since the novel's publication there have been heated debates about its political stakes, ranging from disappointed complaints about retreating into the sex phobias of the boy protagonist to insisting that the novel is focalized through the consciousness of a maturing political activist. For early reviews, see fn4 of this chapter. For two recent discussions of the novel as a political failure, see Lesser, "Revolutionary Energy," and Kerman, "Limits of Typicality." For an opposite discussion of this matter, including the transformative, community-building power of David's near self-electrocution, see Todorova.

wink of his eyelids could strike a spark into the cloudy tinder of the dark, kindle out of shadowy corners of the bathroom such myriad and such vivid jets of images" (441), he contemplates, pausing to let these images—all gathered during the novel's final day—take shape in his memory:

the glint on tilted beads, of the uneven shine of roller skates, of the dry light on green stone stoops, of the tapering glitter of rails, of the oils sheen on the night-smooth rivers, of the glow on thin blond hair, red faces, of the glow on outstretched, open palms of legions upon legions of hands hurtling towards him. (441)

Then the accident catches up with him, entering his psychosomatic narration in a stream of acoustic and visual sense data from the external world:

He might as well call it sleep. It was only towards sleep that ears had the power to cull again and reassemble the shrill cry, the hoarse voice, the scream of fear, the bells, the thick-breathing, the roar of crowds and all sounds that lay fermenting in the vats of silence and the past. It was only toward sleep one knew himself still lying on the cobbles, felt the cobble under him and over him and scudding ever toward him like a black foam, the perpetual blur of shod and running feet, the broken shoes, new shoes, stubby, pointed caked, polished, buniony, pavement-beveled, lumpish, under skirts, under trousers, shoes, over one and through one and feel them all and feel, not pain, not terror, but strangest triumph, strangest acquiescence. One might as well call it sleep. He shut his eyes. (441)

Only after an extensive process of feeling out his experience he tacitly distances himself from it. His final assurance of having prevailed, of having defied both fear and pain, may indicate a revised mode of self-narrative, a dawning possibility to change his place in the family and in the world revolving around it. But what does it mean that he feels "*strangest* triumph, *strangest* acquiescence"? That it is uncertain how these feelings will affect his world once he opens his eyes again? Toying with a new mode of giving voice and form to his need to belong may suggest that the young protagonist has, if not mastered, at least subsided in the rite of passage imposed on him; that there is hope to improve his displaced state in the life ahead of him. He may even be (as some have argued) on his way to becoming the poet who will eventually turn his experience into art. But could the strangeness of his feelings not also mean that drifting into this sleep-like state is a drift toward death? And if yes, what would this death "mean" within the narrative design of this tale? The futility of a herculean effort? The redemptive self-sacrifice of a New World messiah? That language persists where the need for a place in the world comes to an end? Where, in other words, does this suggestive, provisional ending leave us in terms of the boy's prospect of dwelling in the world?

YEARNINGS FOR AUTONOMY AND THE ACHING LIMITS OF BELONGING

If the novel's ending leaves us with an impenetrable uncertainty about the boy's future (and this is something that generations of scholars have failed to acknowledge when projecting their preferred "meaning" on David's journey), the search for meaning-as-form staged and engaged by the novel takes us back to the erratically plotted middle ground. And here it is difficult not to be struck, time and again, by the vast effort imposed on the boy by his need to belong. He may mature in ways that refine his remarkable talent for creative emplotment and equip him with the tools and techniques that it takes to narrate himself into a more comfortable state of belonging. But the Freudian subtext of the rite of passage plotted here turns matters of alleviating the boy's displaced state into a thoroughly individual(ized) responsibility. It is in this pivotal sense that *Call It Sleep* fathoms the immigrant's struggle—in a sad mix of exaltation and unease—as a strictly private affair.

In fact, the Oedipal script undergirding the novel's spatial order and rite of passage turns individual autonomy into the *sine qua non* of belonging. In doing so, *Call It Sleep* toys with a notion of belonging that is aligned with psychoanalytic redefinitions of autonomy as the freedom to decide for oneself what to do with one's life.[30] Prior to this shift, having a comfortable place in the world hinged on an autonomy of a different kind: the liberal investment in property—one's belongings—that we saw at work and contested in *Edgar Huntly* and *Pointed Firs*. Psychoanalysis maintains these conditional ties between belonging and autonomy, but in reframing the latter as an internal relation to the self, belonging now comes to rest on a highly mobilized, immaterial property in demand of constant readjustment. Exploring the stakes of this altered conjunction between belonging and autonomy is key to *Call It Sleep*'s narrative politics. The strategic weakness and vulnerability of the boy protagonist—and the immigrant population for which he synecdochically stands—maximizes the weight of his task to reach an autonomous state that may, in turn, redeem his painful lack of belonging. In telling us about the boy's struggle in terms of a world emerging from displacement, we are asked to closely participate in his erratic, fearful, and exhausting attempts of dwelling in the world. And if ambiguity is yet another technique of reconciliation—of artfully rendering uncertain what remains unsayable—underneath the ambiguous state

---

30 See Zaretsky 22-24, 235-38. Inherent to the philosophical and religious traditions of all civilizations, the project of individual autonomy was first secularized and universalized in Enlightenment thought. The Second Industrial Revolution, which provides the historical context for this novel, extended its meaning to ("extra-moral") realms such as creativity, love, and fortune; to explain why this new autonomy was so hard to attain, psychoanalysts invented concepts such as ambivalence, resistance, and sublimation. Previous notions of autonomy were "moral" in endorsing nineteenth-century understandings of property along with the liberal consensus that human beings could postpone individual interest for the sake of the common good.

of quiescence reached at the end, autonomous selfhood aches as a contemporary limit of belonging.

Yet again, things are not quite as simple. Throughout the novel autonomy as an endlessly malleable self-relation imposed with the freedom to dwell as one pleases is confronted with two other modes of autonomy: autonomy as the communal product of folk authenticity, which comes in tow with a promise of dwelling in the nourishing grounds of a shared ethnic culture; and autonomy as the property of an avant-garde aesthetics, which comes in tow with a promise of dwelling in grounds revitalized by modernist art. None of the three modes of autonomy is endorsed as a remedy for the deeply and multiply troubled state of belonging explored in this novel. The boy's effort is too staggering, ethnic culture is not a safe haven, aesthetic transcendence is warded in; in fact, none of the three modes is allowed to reign over the others at any given point. Rather, they create a force field of idle prospects and misguided hopes, wild dreams and sobering truths. Maybe we can say, then, that in the—modern, immigrant's—world of this novel, maturing in matters of belonging means shunning ideological alignment of any kind to dwell provisionally amidst conflicts, restraints, and imperfections.

5 Of Cranes and Brains
Richard Powers's *The Echo Maker*

With *The Echo Maker* (2006) these explorations of the novel's investment in giving narrative voice and form to concerns with belonging reach our late-modern present, depicted by Richard Powers in an intricate double perspective: as an encompassing ecosystem in which human troubles shrink in geological scale, and as a tenuous product of a specific narrative economy—that of the human brain. There is a striking congruence to these themes that begs to be read as counteracting the "hyper-liquefying" tendencies of late modernity. Speaking from a world in which daily routines and social relations have become intangible, short-lived and unpredictable to an unprecedented degree, the novel insists on the stoic materiality of that world and pairs it with a narrative activity that is located not in the lofty realm of the psyche but in the materiality of the brain. And if the brain's narrative capacity is firmly grounded in the materialist worldview of cognitive science, the novel renders it, quite naturalistically, as a product of evolutionary contingency.

Powers is known as a "content-intense" and "brainy" writer. He thinks of the novel as "a supreme connection machine—the most complex artifact of networking that we have developed" (Williams 104), and of connectivity as the baseline of late-modern problems with belonging.[1] His fiction seeks to enhance the novel's

---

1 His novels, says Powers with vast implications for their investment in matters of belonging, "work by saying you cannot understand a person minimally, you cannot understand a person simply as a function of his inability to get along with his wife, you cannot even understand a person through his supposedly causal psychological profile. You can't understand a person completely in any sense, unless that sense takes into consideration all of the contexts that that person inhabits. And a person at the end of the second millennium inhabits more contexts than any specialized discipline can easily name. We are shaped by runaway technology, by the apotheosis of business and markets, by sciences that occasionally seem on the verge of completing themselves or collapsing under its own runaway success. This is the world we live in. If you think of the novel as a supreme connection machine—the most complex artifact of networking that we've ever developed—then you have to ask how a novelist would dare leave out 95% of the picture" (Williams 104). Only recently, Powers has become an avid commentator of his own work. The many interviews published in the "second" phase of his productivity (since *The Time of Our Singing* in 2003)

connecting powers by blending novel-typical plotlines (of family trouble, ailing love, betrayed friendship, torturous disease) with scientific and other nonliterary discourses. *Three Farmers on Their Way to a Dance* engages with photography, *Prisoner's Dilemma* with mathematics, *Gold Bug Variations* with genetics, *Operation Wandering Soul* with medicine, *The Time of Our Singing* with quantum physics, and so on. In each case, Powers exploits "the elasticity of the novel to shift from strict dramatization to become essayistic, embedding the reader in a flood of data that extends beyond the boundary of the merely literary" (Burns xxviii), and that is not ornamental but essential to the act of giving narrative form. In *The Echo Maker*, the discursive matrix exploited with the aim of knitting a pervasive net of connections is neuroscience—specifically its recent efforts to reframe the cognitive operations of the human brain in terms of ontological narrative. In the words of Gerald Weber, the novel's eloquent expert in neuroscientific matters: "Consciousness works by telling a story, one that is whole, continuous and stable. When that story breaks, consciousness rewrites it. Each revised draft claims to be the original. And so, when disease or accident interrupts, we are often the last to know" (185).[2]

The Echo Maker both explicates and exploits the narrative drive of consciousness as "a networked ecology that mirrors the networked ecology of all life" (Harris 232).[3] Its narrative world arises from three intersecting and at times colliding acts of self-narration: those of the siblings Mark and Karin Schluter, and that of the star neurologist Gerald Weber. All three of these narrative acts are trapped in personal needs and self-delusions, struggling with the expectations, fears, hopes, and desires of the protagonists themselves and of those who happen to be in their lives. Drawing on the notion of identity as narratively produced and continuously revised over the course of a life, the novel allegorizes the process in which not one but three protagonists intermittently pursue their individual needs to belong in narrative

---

make up a powerful body of paratexts. I am engaging with them with mixed feelings. Powers has a gift of speaking about his work with insight that is of great resonance to our critical debates. But the frequency with which he is quoted in scholarly articles amounts to being imposing. In fact, while his commentary seems too relevant to be left out, it is difficult to escape the sense that the author is trying to control his reader and the discourse about his work. For a careful and differentiated take on the issue, see Ickstadt, "Asynchronous."

2 Quotations from *The Echo Maker* are cited parenthetically and refer to the William Heinemann Paperback Edition, London 2006. Weber, the characters through whom most neurological commentary is articulated, is modeled after a range of experts including the neurologist Oliver Sacks, the cognitive philosopher Daniel Dennett, and the Neural Darwinist Gerald Edelman. See Harris 230-32; Tabbi 225.

3 Some of Powers's earlier novels also deal with cognitive matters but without turning the theme into a major form-giving device. See for example *The Gold Bug Variations*, *Operation Wandering Soul*, and *Gallatea 2.2*.

acts that bounce off and seep into each other as "echo making."[4] And if making an echo presupposes a material entity from which sound waves can bounce off, the materiality of the human brain rendered as a "storytelling machine" provides this substance. Arguing against *The Echo Maker*'s frequent association with the genre of "psychological realism," Charles Harris makes the following important point:

> Whereas traditional psychological realism records the effect on the "inner self" of external forces or deep-seated neuroses, neurological realism foregrounds the effects of largely unconscious neurological activities. Whereas psychological realism affirms, indeed, requires, the concept of a solid, continuous "inner" self, Powers, drawing on contemporary neuroscience, challenges that concept at every turn, variously describing the self as "hundreds of separate subsystems" (171), "dozens of lost Scouts waving crappy flashlights in the woods at night" (415), "like coral reefs, [...] complex but fragile ecosystems" (186), a "division" (436), a "community" (383), a "committee of millions" (437). Whereas traditional psychological realism continues the longstanding reification of dualisms—inner and outer, mind and body, reason and emotion, self and other—Powers [...] dismantles such dualisms on neuroscientifical grounds. And whereas traditional novels of psychological realism view infringements of the boundaries between self and the world as threatening, Powers'sss novel of neuroscientifical realism exposes ego-boundaries as false demarcations, another illusion generated by the brains "spin-doctor subsystem" (444). (243-44)[5]

The thrust of *The Echo Maker*'s new brand of realism lies in its extraliterary foundations. In psycho-realism, psychological assumptions serve as the premises of narrative motives and mental states, and usually these assumptions are grounded in a notion of the psyche that (especially in the Freudian "geological" subdivision of the psyche into ego, super-ego, and id) harbors a personal "truth," buried as it may be by repression. *The Echo Maker*, however, is subtended by "*neuroscience, not psychology,*" which means that the mental states of its characters enact the "inner workings of the human brain" (243; my emphasis). This also means that the

---

4   See for example Ricoeur, "Narrative Identity;" Ezzy; Somers; Kraus; Keupp et al.; Kerby. Pragmatist models of identity formation (like Charles Herbert Mead's conception of the self, me and I) can be seen as forerunners of this concept. Yet, it was not until the concern with language unleashed by post-structuralism turned to narration as a highly significant form of language use that "narrative identity" began to be recognized as a scholarly concept. Today, its impact can be traced across many disciplines, ranging from sociology, psychology, philosophy, semiotics, and historiography to literary studies.
5   Harris situates this argument within the larger context of the evolution of the psychological novel: "*The Echo Maker* is character-driven and adapts the Jamesian central intelligence for its point of view. [...] Just as James, in inventing psychological realism, elevates to another level of the psychological novel, which had been around at least since Richardson, so does Powers, drawing on recent neurological research, nudge psychological realism into a different category. The result, I would argue, is the first fully realized novel of neurological realism" (243).

neuro-realism charted here does not rest on an ontological notion of a non-narrative "real" (be it situated in raw perceptions or unconscious desires) but in a neurologically authorized notion of ontological narrative that makes all forms of the "real" available to our consciousness by means of some form of emplotment. The inner workings of the human brain are fictional reenactments rather than reflections, for the novel's neuro-realism—despite its artfully crafted claims to transparency, achieved through what one may call, with Roland Barthes, its neurological "reality effects" ("L'Effet de Réel")—creates artificial textures and surfaces just as any other form of fictionalizing. It does not mirror its object of depiction but strategically stages and transforms it for specific purposes.

For classical American realism, these ends have been compellingly described as exploiting the depragmatized realm of narrative art to stage a conversation between text and reader; the ultimate function of its investment in intersubjective dialogue is to negotiate—and thus restore beyond the limits of the text—a community's values and beliefs as it faces a reality ruptured by the corrosive forces of modernization (Ickstadt, "Concepts of Society;" Fluck, *Inszenierte Wirklichkeit*; "Fiction and Fictionality"). In recent "returns" of realism, conversations between characters and between the text and the reader may have become epistemologically hollow or obsessed with semantic surfaces, but in Powers's novels, the commitment to this conversation—perceived as the social obligation of the novelist—persists. "Powers, whose books resonate with Dewey's pragmatist aesthetics, wants his fictions to be socially useful, he wants them to transform the awareness of the reader, and for that he has to rely on the reader's ability to read right," writes Heinz Ickstadt, quoting the author himself with the following weighty remark: "The only thing that is going to save us is better reading. Reading that knows when narrative is leading us away from the brink and when narrative is leading us headlong toward it. The future of the world depends upon our skill as readers" ("Asynchronous" 5). Powers's work as a novelist, a commentator of his own work and a teacher of creative writing and literature is committed to developing this skill with "a sense of urgency that has its origin in the discrepancy between the present state of scientific knowledge and the general state of social and ecological unawareness on which the global reign of corporate capitalism thrives" (Ickstadt, "Asynchronous" 3)—and that might threaten what Powers himself has called the novel's function as sanctuary from which "we reenter, more fully equipped, the world of reality" (quoted in Ickstadt, "Surviving").

Giving voice and form to contemporary concerns with belonging is closely, if not problematically, bound up with didactic "messaging" in *The Echo Maker*. The stakes of the conversation to be fostered among characters, and between text and reader, could hardly be higher: The novel exploits the recent approximation of cognitive science and narrative art not only to reframe the educational program of classical, psychological realism in neurological terms but also, and perhaps even more importantly, to propose a model of reality that is based on its participants' capacity to tell and listen. New insights in the cognitive operations of the human brain, described by Powers elsewhere as "the distributed, modular, massively preconscious, multiply recursive, *narrative-dependent model of the bundled 'I'*" (Burn 175; my emphasis), provide the extraliterary foundations for this narrative experiment. Expanding both the form and the scope of the novel in close dialogue with neurological discourse (and in ways structurally similar to and yet very different from the Freudian notion of "narrative therapy" that was part and parcel of the artistic enterprise of *Call It Sleep*), *The Echo Maker* posits and actively propagates a scientifically authorized notion of ontological narrative as the only viable means by which belonging can be pursued.

Making one's way across the plotted grounds unfolding from the intersecting narratives of the novel's multiple narrating agents is to familiarize oneselves with the neurological assumptions engrained into this world. And if Powers's novels can justly be described as pursuing "narrative therapy"—not only in the sense of "therapy through narrative, but also as therapy for narrative; […] an exploration of the possibilities of narrative, a recuperation of this currently much-maligned way of ordering the world" (Hurt 24)—*The Echo Maker* epitomizes this project while also exposing its limits.

CONNECTING MIDWEST AND MEDIAL CORTEX[6]

The Echo Maker takes us to the Midwest, a literary region that ever since *The Great Gastby* has been resonating with self-deluded longings for a world still in order. More concretely, it takes us to Kearney, Nebraska, a town on the outskirts of the Great American Desert. The place is home: to Mark and Karin Schluter, the siblings at the center of the novel, and to countless numbers of cranes that come to the shallow banks of the nearby Platte River for a few months every year to mate and breed. And as unremarkable a place as Kearney may be, the cranes' migratory routine enchants it once a year with a ritual of archaic beauty. Choosing the exceptional over the ordinary state of this place, the novel begins with the spectacle of the returning cranes, "the oldest flying thing on earth, one stutter-step away from pterodactyls" (3).

Cranes keep landing as night falls. Ribbons of them roll down, slack against the sky. They float in from all compass points, in kettles of a dozen, dropping with the dusk. Scores of *Grus Canadensis* settle on the thawing river. They gather on the island flats, grazing, beating their wings, trumpeting: the advance wave of a mass evacuation. More birds land by the minute, the air red with calls. (3)

---

6   The heading is inspired by a question asked to Powers by Michod in his interview for *The Believer*: "Can you talk about the role 'place'—be it the Midwest or the medial cortex—plays in your work, particularly in this book?" (n. pag.)

The homecoming scene is described with the awe of an enthralled spectator marveling at the secret script choreographing the eerily synchronized arrival of thousands and thousands of birds "tall as children, crowding together wing by wing on this stretch of river, one that they've learned to find by memory" (3). Year after year, the birds find this place through their mysterious capacities to remember and to recognize the route that takes them here at a secretly scheduled time. The time of the birds is mystic and ancient to the degree that it seems timeless. They "converge on the river at winter's end as they have for eons" (3). "This year's flight has always been" (4). But then, it is suddenly interrupted. "A squeal of brakes, the crunch of metal on asphalt, one broken scream and then another arouse the flock. The truck arcs through the air, corkscrewing into the field" (4). An accident must have happened, but after a short interlude of unrest, the cranes settle back into their well-worn routine as if nothing happened.

In another world, the disruptive force of the event rapidly spreads as Karin, torn from her sleep by a phone call and driving back to Kearney, finds out that her brother will survive the car crash but live on under the shadow of a rare brain injury known as the Capgras syndrome, which causes severe states of estrangement by interfering with what has just been introduced as the birds' mysterious mastery: making the right connections between recognition and memory. And so we arrive in Kearney twice within just a few hours, yet in vastly different lifeworlds. Both worlds belong to the same ecosystem but are separated by their different temporalities. One adheres to the age-old rhythm of migratory routines and the glacial pace of evolutionary changes with maps dating back to the Jurassic age; the other is sleepless, clock-timed, organized by networks of transport and communication, and sustained by modern medicine.[7] What connects the two in a violent flash is Mark's car shooting off the highway. Yet while the accident has dramatic repercussions in the human life-world, it is quickly bypassed in the world of the cranes. Formal differences dramatize this spatial antagonism. The time-space of the cranes is narrated in a meditative tone pregnant with an appreciation that seems to stem from the humble depths of knowledge. The present tense employed here underscores the archaic timelessness of the birds' migration routine, creating an aura of unmediated presence that sets the world of the cranes apart from the human world, which is narrated retrospectively in the past tense. Similar passages are placed at the beginning of each of the novel's five parts. Yet even though their rare occurrence and consecutive opening function disrupts the flow of the narrative, connections between the two time-spaces—through the missing parent crane that may have been killed by Mark's crashing car, through shared themes such

---

7 Powers's concern with ecological matters is the main topic of the interview that Scott Hermanson conducted with him and Tom LeClair. Ecocritical scholarship on Powers's work is nonetheless strikingly rare. An exception is Heise, whose essay predates *The Echo Maker* and discusses Powers's *Gain* and De Lillo's *White Noise* in dialogue with contemporary risk theory.

as orientation, place-making, or child-rearing—are unmistakable. But, while the "crane passages" are clearly construed to articulate an ecological conscience that exceeds human needs to belong, they are not focalized through the cranes. Instead of trying to familiarize us with these mysterious creatures by offering an imagined version of their perceptive world, they render the cranes as radically other. We are told about them in zero-focalized voice whose well-informed speculations draw from scientific sources, superstition, and myth with the effect of enhancing the mysteriousness of its object. "Something in their eyes must match symbols. But how it's done, no person knows and no bird can say" (277).

Within the narrative design of the novel, the crane passages are sanctuaries into which narration recurrently retreats from the dominant clock-timed, alarmed mode of storytelling. In fact, these insular passages, positioned in effective scarcity and uncovering utterly unfamiliar grounds, construe the time-space of the cranes as the ultimate "spatial other" to the sprawling time-space inhabited by the human characters of the novel. And if the by far larger share of the narrative presents us with (and confines us to) alternating worlds of individual, self-centered concerns, repeatedly reminding us that this time-space is indeed quintessentially molded from these concerns, the crane sections present us with the magical world of "feathered dinosaurs [...] , a last great reminder of *life before the self*" (277; my emphasis)—to project a distant future of *life after the self.*

What does a bird remember? Nothing that anything else might say. Its body is a map of where it has been, in this life and before. [...] Something in its brain learns this river, a world sixty million years older than speech, older even than this flat water. This world will carry when the river is gone. When the surface of the earth is parched and spoiled, when life is pressed down to near-nothing, this world will start its slow return. Extinction is short; migration is long. [...] Nothing will miss us. Hawks' offsprings will circle above the overgrown fields. Skimmers and plovers and sandpipers will nest in the thousand girded islands of Manhattan. Cranes or something like them will trace rivers again. When all else goes, birds will find water. (443)

In envisioning—celebrating—the *long durée* of geological time, the crane passages assume a heterotopian function within the imaginary geography of the novel. Not utopian but just as real as all other places in the novel, they are located outside of them, where they act as "counter-sites, a kind of effectively enacted utopia in which the real sites, all the other real sites that can be found within the culture, are simultaneously represented, contested, and inverted" (Foucault, "Other Spaces" 24). In fact, both the space inhabited by the cranes and the narrative interludes from which this space evolves relate to all other sites and narrative modes of the novel by means of what (again with Foucault) we may call "compensation": of creating "a space that is other, another real space, as perfect, as meticulous, as well arranged as ours is messy, ill constructed, and jumbled" (27). Departing from the temporal norm further enhances the crane-space's compensatory function. Its heterochronic temporality is indeed hyperpotent: It combines an "indefinitely accumulating time" (akin to the heterochronic temporality of the museum and the library) that produces a sense of eternity through the everlasting ritual of migration with its polar opposite, the "absolutely temporal" of the crane routine (in the fleeting, transitory sense that Foucault associates with the festival and the fairground) (26).

The heterotopian implications of the crane passages epitomize the novel's ecological concerns. And whereas articulating these concerns oscillates between enthusiastic celebrations of nature's mystic operations and Cassandra-like warnings of environmental destruction, the self-centered and clock-timed sections of the story unfolding from the novel's human-space explore the messy realities of late-modern life. Among them are the deceptive plans of a group of global investors and local realtors to build a crane-themed vacation resort that endangers the breeding grounds of the birds (ironically, the vacation village resembles the crane-space in drawing together the heterochronic extremes of extra- and fleeting temporality); personal struggles with the dictates of self-realization and professionalization, often in conjoined form, and thoroughly intertwined with the widespread use of mood-enhancing drugs that complicate the search for an "authentic" self; the mixed blessings of the time-space compression through digital technology and global travel; the media-enhanced post-9/11 fear of terrorism, the propagandistic protection of "homeland security" through missions such as Operation Iraqi Freedom, and their lure for young men with a lack of purpose like Mark Schluter and his friends. The heterotopian crane sections infuse these troubled realities with an ecological imagination—the notion of a shared ecosystem both sturdy and fragile that grounds matters of belonging in a thoroughly materialistic worldview. In fact, evolutionary biology provides a matrix of total connectivity that at once embeds concerns with belonging in a larger environmental scheme and relativizes them by insisting that life will go on after humankind has become extinct.

Rendering the novel's spatial imagination as systematically evolutionary and environmentalist as it is done here is significant for the narrative pursuit of belonging as a whole, for it widens the imaginative scope on the macro level in a similar way that the neurological perspective expands it on the micro level. In fact, the two levels are imagined as interacting ecosystems that conjointly create the novel's world, and they are most powerfully interlinked in the novel's conception of place. "Place has been important to me before in other stories but never quite like it was for this one," Powers notes, going on to expound:

The book is about memory and recognition, but those mental skills are themselves deeply linked to the brain's spatial abilities. The hippocampus—that portion of the brain that orchestrates the formation of new memories—seems to have developed in large part as a way of mastering place. Animals with the greatest navigational requirements also have the most developed memory. [...] Some neuroscientists have even proposed that the hippocampus may have originated as a processor of relations in space, a "spatial cognition machine," as it's been called. In some strange way, our capacity to form and retrieve memories—and with it, our ability to shape stories and construct a sense of self—may be a happy by-product of our sense of orientation. Even our social vocabulary reflects that connection, when we talk about who's in and who's out, who's up and who's down, who's at the center and who's marginalized. For that matter, our vocabulary for the elements of storytelling itself is also highly spatial: exposition, situation, plot, reverse, arrival ... (Michod n. pag.; ellipsis in the original)

Neurological assumptions thus serve as the foil to fuse memory, narrative, space, and place. They do so not only in the usual sense that storytelling unfolds a space (the imaginary geography of the novel) and unfolds in space (the space of the page, the space between book and reader, the mental space of the reader), but also in the sense of engaging narrative as a life-sustaining and distinctly spatial practice of orientation and emplacement. In exploiting the tacitly searching and categorically improvising narrative activity of the human brain as its main form-giving drive, place and self enter the world of the novel exclusively through some brain's more or less oriented storytelling operations. And because narrative acts affect the world in which they are conducted (either directly or through the "echoes" they make in other narrative acts), the need to belong depicted here engenders a complex and dynamic network of intersecting "narrative ecologies."

What does this mean for the novel's plotting operation? Throughout this study I have stressed how crucial emplotment is to matters of belonging. It is essential to conducting the search for meaning-as-form that is both the pragmatic and the artistic thrust of the narrative productivity engendered by the need to belong. It keeps the story on track or leads it astray, slows it down and speeds it up, connects characters and places, and in all of this it can be scarce or overpowering, subtle or imposing. But in whatever concrete way it molds the narrative operation, plot is what lays out the grounds to be traversed by a story unfolding in space and time. And hence it has substantial stakes in where the narrative "journey" takes us. In *The Echo Maker*, it takes us onto the intricately plotted and continually shifting grounds emerging from a plurality of narrative voices with notably different "spatial abilities" to remember and recognize. All three are caught up in specific narrative acts of orientation to be further spelled out later on. What can already be said at this point is that the story—brought to us by the indirect voices of three "narrating brains"—envisions a rite of passage that is made up of a compound simultaneity of rituals, conducted by storytellers who are also listeners. The intersecting acts of telling, receiving, and revising their stories accumulate in an erring and self-deluded, yet irreducibly dialogic practice of *conjoint* storytelling. And true to the evolutionary biologist's assumptions undergirding the neurological fusion of place, memory, and storytelling, a contingent course of *collision* is the trajectory along which the conjoint operations of emplacement and emplotment unfold.

Gaining momentum through the disruptive force of an accident—an event that is in itself an intriguing limit case of storytelling—collision is indeed the novel's primary connecting device. Making its first meteoritic occurrence in the opening passage, the accident that happens on the second page of the novel is surrounded by semantic gaps. The mystery about its cause sparks a hermeneutic desire of detection that generates the novel's most powerful plotline. In fact, in terms of narrative energy, it seems that only when the mystery around the accident's cause is resolved that the colliding, narrative-propelling forces emanating from this event weaken enough for the story to come to an end. Underscoring the novel's concern with emplacement, this transformation has a distinctly spatial dimension. As the reader is about to see, the network of social relations imagined here becomes decidedly more suitable for matters of dwelling toward the end. But just as crucial as the accident is in terms of engendering a narrative drive toward reaching a more comfortable state of dwelling, it stirs a chain of events that are both unpredictable and unstoppable. It is indeed through the haphazard contingency of colliding matter that concerns with belonging are made tangible in this novel.

The novel's "narrative ecology" revolves around Mark's accident: It connects crane-space and human-space; it distances Mark from his two closest friends; it brings his sister back to Kearney, causing further collisions between her life and the lives of two of her ex-boyfriends; it brings Gerald Weber there as well when one of these boyfriends finds out (in the endless connectivity of the world wide web) about Weber's expertise in Mark's rare brain condition, and encourages Karin to get in touch with him; it makes Barbara Gillespie, a burned-out journalist from New York, cause the accident in a moment of existential despair, take on a position as a nurse in the hospital where Mark is being treated, become entangled in Mark's and Karin's lives, and romantically involved with Weber. What takes shape in this web of lives randomly colliding with one another is an ecological version of Doreen Massey's notion of place as "formed out of a particular"—contingent, accidental—"set of social relations which interact at a particular location." Its singularity as an individual place is formed from a site-specific collision of forces—the needs and desire of individual characters, the reverberating trauma of 9/11, the global flow of finance capitalism, the mysterious migration routine of the cranes—"which occur at that location (nowhere else does this precise mixture occur)" and "will in turn produce new social effects" (168). In a world that is ecologically and materially grounded in the storytelling activity of the human brain, these effects are by default also narrative. By exploiting the accident as an event that not only makes *lives* collide but also the *stories* in which these lives are lived, *The Echo Maker* fuses concerns with place and narrative. It is the disruptive force of the accident that initiates and interconnects the three narratives that make up most of the story, and the resulting need for readjustment creates collisions with other "storied lives" with the effect of redirecting and molding through these stories the place evolving from their interaction, and the ways of dwelling that are possible at this place.

Being No One

In moving on to a closer analysis of the narrative fabric produced through these colliding forces, another interlocking place- and plot-making feature of the accident must be addressed: its providing the occasion for exploring the emotional dimension of the human brain's spatial and social intelligence—more precisely, the interaction of cognition with feeling in the imagined constitution of this most basic capacity of human survival.[8] Mark's recovery soon reveals that he suffers from a rare brain injury that eclipses his emotional intelligence and causes him to believe that those most familiar to him—his sister, his dog, his home—have been replaced "with lifelike robots, doubles or aliens. He properly identifies everyone else. The loved one's face elicits memory, but no feeling" (106).

> What did it feel like to be Mark Schluter? To live in this town, work in a slaughterhouse, then have the world fracture from one moment to the next. The raw chaos, the absolute bewilderment of the Capgras state twisted Webere's gut. To see the person closest to you in this world, and feel nothing. But that was the astonishment: nothing *inside* Mark felt changed. Improvising consciousness saw to that. *Mark* still felt familiar; only the world had gone strange. He needed his delusions, in order to close that gap. The self's whole end was self-continuation. (301; emphasis in the original)

The Capgras syndrome thus provides the imaginative matrix to defamiliarize what is most familiar to Mark through a narrative delusion produced by his injured brain as it struggles to provide his consciousness with a life-sustaining sense of continuity. The most daunting effect of Mark's condition is the strain that it puts on his social relations and the troubled sense of place evolving from them. There will be more to say about this later. For now, it is important to note that the impact of Mark's injured brain on the novel's conjoint operations of emplotment and emplacement is not confined to his particular troubles. Rather, Mark's condition allows Powers to illustrate how profoundly "the feeling of what happens" affects

---

8 Through its fictional mediation of the Capgras syndrome, the novel enhances academic discourses about space and narrative by connecting them to recent neurological attempts of reframing the relation of intellect and feeling. Coming to terms with this relation already played a major part in Hume's model of the human mind, which has been instrumental to conceiving the imagination as an indispensable motor of human belonging. For a longer discussion of the matter, see the Introduction and the "Historical Trajectories" section of Chapter 2. To my knowledge, *The Echo Maker* was the first novel to concern itself with Capgras. The fact that it was soon to be followed by two further American novels dealing with this condition, Nicole Krauss' *Man Walks Into a Room* and Rivka Galchen's *Atmospheric Disturbances*, underscores its capacity to articulate and fictionally mediate a collective, contemporary state of trouble.

the life-sustaining conjunction of orientation and narration for all human beings.[9] Exceeding an individual pathology, the Capgras syndrome is used to allegorize a collective state of alienation in which "the outline of life [...] still looks familiar," yet "the place no longer feels recognizable" (Michod n. pag.).[10]

In the materialist world and narrative ecology of the novel, Capgras spreads through the collision of lives and storylines. Again it is Weber, the character most frequently employed to articulate neurological ideas, who voices this option when observing, in the midst of his romantic involvement with Barbara, a distorted emotional resonance in himself. "He would write it up—first case ever of contagious Capgras—if he could still write" (430). There is a subtle irony to Weber's attempt to distance this troubling thought while still in the act of conceiving it. And although no one but the reader can hear it, its meaning spills over and "infects" the rest of the narrative. Similar to the trope of sleepwalking in *Edgar Huntly*) Capgras is not exploited as a stabilizing metaphor but as a metonymic trajectory, "the figure of contiguity and combination, the figure of syntagmatic relations" (Brooks, "Masterplot" 281) that destabilizes all certainty of "feeling right" about one's sense of self and place through the sheer circumstance of it being part and parcel of the novel's narrative world. As a looming threat of disjoining emotional and intellectual intelligence, its spread causes a "contagious" identity crisis. What kind of place evolves from the collateral encounters between such individuals? If the novel imagines place to a substantial degree as a shifting network of social relations, a sense of self that is troubled through the spread of Capgras must affect the place evolving from the particular set of social relations imagined here. Ricoeur's notion of self-identity is helpful for gasping this trouble. For Ricoeur, identity is a treacherous concept because it is used with two fundamentally different meanings: selfhood and sameness. Identity as *selfhood* responds to the question "who am I?" and is (like concepts such as "being-in-the-world," "care," or "being-with") characterized by the capacity "to question itself as to its own way of being and thus to relate itself to being *qua* being." Identity as *sameness*, on the other hand, answers to the question "what am I?" It belongs to the world of things that are "ready" or "present-to-hand" ("Narrative Identity" 190-92). Harking back to these different bearings, irritations within self-identity may best be described as a rift

---

9   Powers cites António Damásio with this phrase in the *Believer* interview with Michod. For an elaborate discussion of this topic, see Harris 231-38.

10 In the interview passage from which these quotes are taken, Powers ties this collective state of alienation to a distinctly national trauma: "Estrangement seems to have become the baseline condition for life in terrorized America. After November 2000, after September 2001, after the Patriot Act and the detainee bill, after Gitmo and Abu Ghraib, our stories—public and private—keep scrambling to keep America whole, continuous, and coherent, to *place* it" (Michod n. pag.). Sielke reads *The Echo Maker* as a post-9/11 novel, a qualification that is certainly apt, but limiting as a general label for a novel whose narrative scope so clearly exceeds this collective trauma.

between "being" and "having" that turns the social and psychic demand for identity into a troublesome affair.[11] And yet the two intersect in one matter that is vital for both: in the words of *The Echo Maker*'s eloquent neurologist, the "self's longing for self-continuation." For *selfhood* this means keeping one's promises and being accountable for former actions, for *sameness* it means maintaining a recognizable appearance. Hence, Ricoeur arrives at his influential notion of "narrative identity"—identity as the endlessly malleable product of self-narrativization—as a way of suturing this very gap.[12]

So yes, one's sense of self is constantly troubled by *having* the same properties versus *being* in the same relation to the world, but the resulting tension can be eased if selfhood is relieved from the burden of sameness. (In the late-modern world depicted here, this burden has increased through an growing specialization and compartmentalization of social life; responses to the question "who am I?" have multiplied, but flexible, pluralized, and contradictory as they may be, they still need to create what Powers has aptly called a "bundled I.") For Ricouer, the project of the modern novel is deeply engaged with the task of reducing the burden of sameness, with Robert Musil's "man without qualities" as an extreme case (a better translation would indeed be the "man without *properties*"); Max Frisch's Stiller or Nabokov's Humbert Humbert are other examples.[13] For Ricoeur, this literary phenomenon is significant because the loss or rejection of sameness-identity does *not* put an end to the problem of selfhood:

A non-subject is not nothing, with respect to the category of the subject. Indeed, we would not be interested in this drama of dissolution and would not be thrown into perplexity by it, if the non-subject were not still a figure of the subject, even in a negative mode. Suppose someone asks the question: Who am I? Nothing, or almost nothing is the reply. But it is still a reply to the question who, simply reduced to the starkness of the question itself. (196)

The heading of *The Echo Maker*'s first part—"I AM NO ONE"—seems to respond directly to Ricoeur's call for a rejection of sameness-identity. The line soon

---

11 Grounding subjectivity in a gap between "being" and "having" also features prominently in Lacan's "mirror stage." Despite their very different approaches to identity formation (visual and imaginary vs. narrative), both models are grappling with the same basic problem. In the mirror stage, identity is forever split along the lines of "being" (in front of the mirror), which in Ricoeur's reasoning can only confirm itself *"qua* being," and "'having' one's image in the mirror," which in Ricoeur's reasoning belongs to the order of the "present-to-hand," of things to be had in the sense of possessing (and, by extension, being possessed by) them.
12 For Ricoeur's most concise discussion of this concept, see "Life."
13 Musil is indeed one of the authors whom Powers credits as an influence on his own writing. See Williams 14.

reappears in the mysterious note that Karin finds next to Mark's bed in the trauma unit of the hospital.

No one could tell her when it had appeared. Some messenger had slipped it into the room unseen, even while Karin was shut out. The writing was spiderly, ethereal: an immigrant scrawl from a century ago.

> I am No One
> but Tonight on North Line Road
> GOD led me to you
> so You could Live
> and bring back someone else (10)

In its cryptic, "ethereal" act of messaging, the note projects a journey of self-erasure and spiritual recovery—a journey in which a subject with no claim to sameness-identity whatsoever gives up its life for a "You" that then brings back an enigmatic "someone else," possibly the transformed "I" or "You" of this note, possibly a third party "reborn" in their fateful encounter. A substantial part of the story is concerned with deciphering this enigmatic piece of writing and its connection to the accident. In fact, solving its mystery disperses the *horror vacui* of the missing cause haunting those who are accidently thrust together by it. The note's significance is amplified by using each of its lines as a heading for one of the novel's five parts, thus repeatedly (and somewhat pedantically) suggesting that it contains a secret "masterplot" for the unfolding narrative. But it is the note's first line with its rhetorical erasure of selfhood that is by far the most memorable. It looms over the story like a predicament. Anyone could have said it, and most of the characters do at some point in one way or another: Karin by calling herself "a stand-in [...] one of those chameleon people with nothing at the core" (327), Barbara by conceding that "she's finished, she's nothing now" (446), and Weber by realizing that he is "in reclamation," "nothing [...] left of him but these new eyes" (449). These multiple disclaimers of selfhood turn the capacity to question one's being into a recursive yet minimal assurance of one's existence (if I can ask a question does this not mean I am there?), but under the impact of this procedure selfhood becomes porous (what is the practical value of an empty account?).

Ironically, the only character who does not disclaim his selfhood is Mark. His shell-shocked insistence on being "the same" makes him immune to feeling that he might be nothing. In fact, Mark's insistence inverts the evacuation of selfhood and makes it spread. His stubborn refusal to recognize his sister turns *her* into being "not the same," a disclaimer that, once she begins to internalize it, turns her into "nothing." In the end we find out that he, who so obsessively tried to find the writer of the note, wrote it himself when caught between life and death but not yet unconscious—wrote it to address the woman standing next to his bed in the trauma unit of the hospital, and whom he had seen standing, apparition-like, in the middle of North Line Road just a few hours earlier. Seeing her for the second time shatters his former self, turning him into "no one"— and in this crucial sense the note literally *has no writer*. The medical records of Mark's brain activity bear a clear mark of this incident, yet it is not until the end of the novel that an actual event can be attached to it. Once this mark comes to index Barbara's guilt-laden presence at Mark's hospital bed, the traumatic fracturing of his former self, sealed off and denied through the Capgras state, takes on new meaning: Mark's brain damage is triggered not by the accident itself but by the shock of finding the person who caused it through her suicidal walk in the middle of the dark country road by his bedside upon walking up from his coma; and the accident is directly connected to 9/11. Barbara covered the terror attacks as a reporter, unsympathetically sticking her camera into people's faces in her desire for authentic coverage, thriving on the success of her work until she became so exhausted that her boss sent her off to Kearney for a human-interest story on the cranes. But instead of seizing her chance to recover, she tracks down another story of disaster: The breeding grounds of the cranes are threatened by deceitful plans to build a vacation resort whose wasteful use of water is bound to destroy the ancient ecosystem. Upon finding out about this complot, Barbara suffers a nervous breakdown, interrupts her nightly drive, and steps into the road.

The accident hence "erupts" from a troubled geography in which 9/11 terror and ecologic destruction collide with hazardous force; that these connections are recovered as the polyvocal narrative moves towards its end intertwines the needs for psychic and spatial recovery engrained into the world of the novel. Moreover, solving the mystery of the note relocates the source of contagion: Not Mark but Barbara is the damaged "cell" in the social organism from which the destructive force of emotional uprootedness spreads through the entire ecosystem. Her secret involvement in the mystery plot exempts her from being one of the focalizers. But leaving her voiceless creates a curious sense of indeterminacy, for she is at once central to the story and disconnected from the self-narratives gaining traction around her. How does she fit into the social network in which she operates with conspicuous ease? Where does she come from? Does she not seem overqualified for her job as a nurse? Why is she so committed to Mark's wellbeing even after he leaves the hospital? Barbara's voicelessness fuels both the "plot of action" driving the narrative forward (usually by creating some form of disturbance) and the "hermeneutic plot" that allows us to reconstruct what has happened.[14] Yet if Capgras is rendered "contagious" in this novel, the desire for *self-continuation*—conceived here as the narrative program that the evolution has engrained into the human brain to secure the surivial of the species—becomes instrumental in spreading the pathological state. In fact, it spreads through the collision of storylines fabricated for this very purpose.

---

14 The terms are drawn from Barthes, *SZ*.

Colliding Narratives, Conjoint Map-Making

Outside of the crane sections—read here as narrative manifestations of the desire for a spatialized, selfless Other—the story is told through the alternating narrative activities of Mark's, Karin's, and Weber's brains. As I have noted before, all of these activities are trapped within the confines of personal concerns and self-delusions. But regardless of these biases and limitations, each of these narratives depicts an inner state that is deeply entangled with the outer world and its inhabitants as it relentlessly seeks to process and integrate the narratives of the others. The form that results from interweaving these three voices—all of them indirect, and together adding up to the polyvocal texture that makes up most of the narrative—is the concern of this section. How does this kind of storytelling lend itself to giving voice and form to the need to belong depicted here? Does its disseminated yet conjoint act of voice- and form-giving project a viable mode of dwelling in narrative? What kinds of agency does it probe? What kinds of recovery does it pursue? In grappling with these questions it is important to note that the conception of the brain as a "storytelling machine" aligns the novel with the "narrative turn" in the social and natural sciences.[15] In fact, it is fair to say that Powers, true to his interest in merging science and fiction, lends his narrative art to exploring the convergence of social and narrative agency posited by proponents of ontological narrative. The novel's polyvocal narrative fictionalizes everyday acts of self-narration in a neuro-realist mode, and in doing so, it turns these everyday acts into the stuff of fictional world-making.

In this compound form, narrative agency is assumed and probed in every voice. Each voice is rendered in a specific way, with the effect of maximizing its impact on a world that exists only in and through the narrative acts that engage with it. Within the world of the novel, these acts and the agencies staged and performed by them, are not removed from the messiness of everyday life but closely entangled with it. Mark's rejection of his sister may be the best example for this. After awaking from his coma, his brain injury causes his consciousness to fabricate a story in which Karin plays the role of an identical-looking stranger who has replaced his real sister. As his life continues, the story prompts explanations for this odd situation that gradually grows into a full-blown conspiracy plot in which secret government agents are after him, having replaced not only his sister but also the entire neighborhood including his house while Karin's boyfriend trains cranes and other animals to spy on human beings.[16] A recursive double movement drives Mark's narrative: Implausible experiences need to be emplotted, but emplotment is continuously exposed to new experience, with exposure to other storylines (for instance, to Karin's repeated rejection of the fraud character he has construed

---

15 I discuss the topic in Chapter 1.
16 Keen elucidates this obviously paranoid kind of self-narration from a psychological perspective.

for her) being an inevitable part of the procedure. And while Karin's persistent rejections of the role ascribed to her must be integrated into Mark's story, her self-narrative has to cope with being exposed to Mark's tale of fraud and rejection—from being supposedly better looking than his "real" sister to wondering if she is indeed an impostor playing a part designed to please others rather than living a self-directed, authentic life. The self-doubt that being exposed to Mark's story stirs in her makes her turn to her ex-boyfriends, hoping that romantic entanglements will stabilize her (and finding out that the lover who makes her feel most like herself does so by virtue of taking mood-enhancing drugs). As readers of these interlacing self-narratives, we are inclined to observe and compare their respective world-making capacities and limitations, and to marvel at their artful revisions as lives and storylines keep colliding. In doing so, we may note that the separate accounts do not give seamless shape to the world in which they interact; that they indeed contradict and rival each other with the effect of continually undermining and transforming the selves for which they speak, and the lives they harbor and sustain. Yet while individual voices allow for an explication of different narrative modes and agencies, the polyvocality of the narrative makes its own claim in these matters. This latter feature of the novel—its art of connectivity and "narrative therapy" (Hurt 23)—is key to its vision of dwelling in the world; hence the need to trace its design.

The sections that are focalized through Mark initially map the recovery of his brain. That the first one of them is only half a page long replicates the fragility of its storytelling activity as Mark emerges from his coma. Perhaps the most striking feature about the highly fragmentary, impressionistic account of the accident given in this passage is the absence of self-asserting pronouns. While clearly speaking from Mark's subjective experience, its grammar bears no trace of selfhood.

A flock of birds, each one burning. Stars swoop down to bullets. Hot red specks take flesh, nest there, a body part, part body. Lasts forever: no change to measure. Flock of fiery cinders. When grey pain of them thins, then always water. Flattest width so slow it fails to liquid. Nothing in the end but flow. Nextless stream, lowest thing above knowing. A thing itself the cold and so can't feel it. (10)

The next section, already noticeably longer, is equally impressionistic, yet marked with first traits of subjectivity. In fact, these traits emerge precisely at the moment when Mark starts to feel again. "When sense returns, he's drowning" (18). The sensation stems from the depths of his childhood, reminding him of the unpleasant moment when his father taught him to swim. When this reawakening of sensation occurs, he cannot yet differentiate between past and present, but over the course of the novel's first part, and indicated by his increasing capacity of storytelling, his sense of self is more or less fully restored again. Yet even after the immediate effects of the accident are overcome, Mark's self-narration sounds curiously staccato-like. His sentences are short and often incomplete, reduced to a bare minimum of information. To the extent that he regains his strength, his irritations become more forceful and articulate with the effect of making his already mentioned conspiracy theories more and more elaborate. Rage is the dominant emotion he feels. Crying does not fit into his sense of self, but it does happen once during a visit to the farmhouse where the Schluters used to live when Mark and Karin were children. Mark's conviction that his sister is a fraud becomes porous at this site, and when she asks him what his real sister was like, he breaks down, emplotting what happens as "something must be wrong with Mark Schluter, something from the accident that not even the hospital knows about, because he stands there bawling like a goddamned child" (374).

Throughout these passages, Mark seems to be in conversation with himself, desperately trying to leave semantic marks of orientation in his defamiliarized lifeworld. And as his sister is the most important fixpoint in this world, he invents ever-new nicknames for her, "Kopy Karin," "Karin Two," "Karbon Karin," to name just a few. Mark's name—turned into "Marker" by his naïve girlfriend—puns on his obsession.

> [...] he needs to talk to someone, someone who can help to put all the facts together. Bonnie's out. Okay: she's still Bonnie-Baby. Call it love, whatever. But Kopy Karin has gotten her, turned her, as the federales say. Convinced her there is something wrong with him. Even when he lays out all the accumulated evidence—his missing sister, the fake Homestar, nobody admitting to the note, the new Karin hooking up with the old Daniel, the disguised Daniel following him around, training animals to watch him—she says she's not sure. (279)

Mark's biggest problem is that his interlocutors do not share the familiarity that he regains in his rampant quest for self-continuity. Paranoid narratives like his are cataclysmic in the sense that there is no "after," no social value to be gained from the story; "it will not be remembered, the suffering was for naught; the loss is absolute. There is no mourning, no analyzing, no commemorating; there is no redemption" (Keen 179). In fact, the constant rejection of his self-narration reifies Mark's aching sense of not belonging while making the narrative efforts of restoring his place in the world increasingly paranoid and self-destructive—to the point where the (com)plot of his own storytelling convinces him that he is already dead, and that suicide is hence the action he must undertake to set the story straight. As the plotting operations of Mark's shell-shocked brain go back and forth between his sense of self and his surroundings, they have indeed but one aim: to synchronize his inner and his outer world again. Eventually, Weber will find the medication that helps arrest this erring process by reconnecting Mark's cognitive operations to his emotional intelligence, thus "healing" his narrative capacities and the ways in which they emplot his self and emplace him in the world.

But Karin wonders if her brother's troubled sense of belonging could not be older than his accident. She recalls a phase in his life when Mark, still a child, was convinced that he was adopted, and that his only reliable childhood friend was the imaginary Mr. Thurman.[17] Karin's memory offers a view on Mark's condition that complicates the medical narrative. Maybe the accident disclosed or intensified a sense of alienation in her brother that stems from their troubled family history? Karin's counternarrative is too tenuous to unravel the medical diagnosis—"How much had Mark changed? The question dogged Karin, in that hot summer, a third of a year on [...] She no longer trusted her memory" (235)—and yet it subverts its authority. Moreover, the passage brings out a significant difference in Karin's and Mark's modes of self-narration. Mark's passages are invested in the immediate present. They claim authority by engaging with this present, and respectively, the narrative agency that gains shape in these passages is geared toward the present, driven by the rage about his distorted perceptions and rejected narratives crafted to set them straight again. Karin's narrative, in contrast, is withdrawn from the world around her. It tends to resort to the past, driven by a desire to retrieve memories in which it can ground itself, and often it is bound up in memories or emotions to an extent that makes it difficult for Karen to act.[18] Yet while her narrative is rife with empathy, it displays a striking lack of emotional distance. Karen constantly needs to feel herself against something, if this "other" is not given, she tends to dissolve into the environment. Smoking is one way of stabilizing the boundaries of her self, unhappy love is another.

Some days his rage was so bad that even lying still infuriated him. Then the therapist asked her to leave. Help out by vanishing. She camped out in Farview, in her brother's modular home. She fed his dog, paid his bills, ate off his plates, watched his television, slept in his bed. She smoked only out on the deck, in the frosty March wind, on a damp director's chair inscribed BORN SCHLUTER, so his living room wouldn't stink of cigarettes when he finally came home. She tried to keep it to one cigarette an hour. She forced herself to slow down, taste the smoke, close her eyes, and just listen. At dawn and dusk, as her ears sensitized, she could hear the sandhills' bugle call underneath the neighbors militant exercise videos and the long-haul eighteen-wheelers pounding up and down the interstate. She would hit the filter in seven, and be checking her watch again in fifteen minutes. (44)

Her cigarette addiction gives this passage an out-of-breath tone (other passages have much longer sentences), but it aptly captures the way in which her self-narrative circulates around others, how strongly and emphatically she feels, and how much she needs to express her emotions—always on the brink of dissolving into

---

17 This act of self-narration echoes the previous chapter as it can be read as Mark crafting his version of Freud's "family romance," which has been discussed with regards to David Schearl, tapping into what Freud specified as a child's early fantasy of exchanging the biological parents with made-up ones in search for an autonomous sense of self.
18 For an in-depth discussion of the relation of self-narrative and memory that surfaces here, see King.

her environment. A moment later, she calls an ex-lover: "Four numbers in she realized that she wasn't dead yet. Anything might still happen" (44). Alas, Karin's sense of self and the world around her are not disjointed; they are too attuned to the outer world. She is emotionally dependent on others, and this dependency impairs her narrative agency. She makes choices about the telling of her story based on what other people most likely want to hear. At one point Karin suggests that their father was sexually abusive when they were small ("Did Cappy [...] did he ever touch you?" [374])—a childhood trauma that might explain her difficulties to leave the past behind as well as her inclination toward unhealthy codependencies with the men around her. But the remark is tentative, more hint than proof, and as such not suitable as an anchor for her faltering sense of self. Compared to Mark, who stabilizes over the course of the novel and who is in the end finally treated with a medication that makes the Capgras symptoms disappear, Karin's longing for change is trapped and endlessly revolving around herself. She does, however, manage to shift her codependence from significant others (her brother, her lovers) to the cause of preserving the crane refuge—possibly a more livable form of dependency, and yet a merely superficial mode of change as such.

If Mark's tortured and torturing self-narration is eventually "healed" and Karin's evens out in a functional dysfunctionality (functional in terms of stabilizing her life, dysfunctional in terms of outgrowing emotional dependency), Weber's life narrative is in definite decline. He enters the story at the peak of his fame, a detached outsider, the eloquent expert flying in from New York, curious about the case yet snobbish and unwilling to commit himself truly to the wellbeing of his patient. The parts focalized through him enact this disengagement. They are strikingly rational, full of scientific jargon and sharp observations, and overall marked by a sense of humor that helps him keep emotionally challenging or messy situations at bay. He and his wife share a code that mimics this operation. That they call each other "Man" and "Woman," and refer to God as "tour director" testifies to a biologistic worldview, employed by the couple in ways that evacuates what is named of emotional resonance. But as Weber's reputation falters—he is reproached for exploiting his patients for their stories—this narrative mode and the emotional vacuum produced by it become a problem. His seemingly superior storytelling capacities, which once gained him fame beyond his scientific community, plunge into self-defeating registers of alienation, for instance when observing himself during a nervous breakdown:

He hated to read talks. Usually, he spoke from an outline, delivering free-wheeling, campfire performances. But when he wandered from the script that night, vertigo hit him. He stood high on a towering cliff, water pounding over it. What was acrophobia anyway if not the half-acknowledged desire to jump. (232)

During the night following this talk, his sense of crisis worsens:

> For a moment, Weber cannot find his shoulder. No sense of whether his hand was underneath or above him, palm up or down, flung out or drawn in. He panicked, and the alarm congealed him, bringing him almost alert enough to identify the mechanism: awareness before the return of the somatosensory cortex from sleep. But only when he forced his paralyzed side to move could he locate all his parts again. (258)

All of this happens when Weber is jetlagged, displaced to "an anonymous hotel, in another country" (258), and upset about the negative reviews of his latest book. But besides expressing his social and spatial sense of vertigo, this passage also illustrates the hollowness of Weber's splendid rationality. And along with it, it showcases the practical limitations of a narrative agency habitually employed to hold the world at bay. Only when he forces himself to move again can he break the haunting spell of dismemberment. This scene can thus be read as a *mise en abyme* of Weber's ailing mode of self-narration, and of the rational disposition from which it springs. For what initially presented itself as the most capable and advanced kind of cognition turns out to produce the most displaced and alienated sense of being in the world. And while Weber finds the right drug to treat Mark's brain condition, he fails to fathom a remedy for himself: He cannot restore his professional reputation, risks his rock-solid marriage when getting romantically involved with the enigmatic nurse who is really an investigative journalist, and when he returns to New York in the novel's final scene, who he is and where he belongs have become utterly unclear.

Distinct as they are, the three voices make for a neatly fitting sample of the basic types of self-narration posited by the narrative psychologists Kenneth and Mary Gergen: stabilizing (Karin), progressive (Mark), and regressive (Weber) ("Narrative and the Self" 23-26). The Gergens have developed these types by drawing from Northrup Frye's basic modes of storytelling, and from Joseph Campbell's idea of a fundamental, psychically grounded "monomyth" with countless local applications and an overarching capacity of emplotting negative events as harbingers of positive outcomes. Their interest is with the psychodynamics afforded by the three types rather than with the plotting operation driving them; in applying their model to the interlacing self-narratives of *The Echo Maker*, the conventionality of the three different modes of storytelling become clearly discernible along with their powerful impact on emplotting individual lives. Mark's self-narration can, indeed, not only be read as progressive but also as comic, captured in the above-quoted passage in his punning acts of name-giving ("Bonnie-Baby," "Kopy Karin," "the federales"), or in the hilarious accounts of his belief that his childhood friend Daniel Riegel trains wild animals to spy on him. In accord with the comic mode, Mark's narrative progresses towards a happy ending: Assisted by the drug that "heals" the Capgras symptoms, Mark crudely affirms his recovered senses of place and self. As he emerges from his nightmare and finds himself recognizing his long-lost sister, who cannot stop crying, he says to her with his unfaltering sense of humor:

"Hey. I know how you're feeling. Rough days, for us two. But look!" He twists around to the plate-glass window—a flat, overcast Platte afternoon. "It's not all so bad, huh? Just as good, in fact. In some ways even better."
   She fights to retrieve her voice. "What do you mean, Mark? As good as what?"
   "I mean, us. You. Me. Here." He points out the window, approvingly: the Great American Desert. The inch-deep river. Their next of kin, those circling birds. "Whatever you call this. Just as good as the real thing." (447)

As the story draws to a close, this hopeful statement is the end of Mark's active share in the narrative—and the only happy ending of three self-narratives. Karin's stabilizing mode of self-narration perpetuates her character's emotional dependency, shifting it merely from her brother and her boyfriends to the cause of saving the environment. Departing from Frye's scheme, the narration performed by Karin's consciousness may best be described as melodramatic. In fact, it thrives on a key feature of melodrama: "its compulsion to 'reconcile the irreconcilable'—that is, its tendency to find solutions to problems that cannot really be solved without challenging the older ideologies of moral certainty to which melodrama wishes to return" (Williams 37).[19] Karin's self-narrative thus confronts us with the "fundamental ambivalence of feelings" that is instrumental in providing the receptive parameters of the melodramatic mode of narration (Decker 14, quoted in Kelleter and Mayer 13; my translation). And if this ambivalence springs from an irresolvable tension between evoking and controlling affect, what would better describe the emotional deadlock of Karin's troubled state of belonging than her compulsive yearning to reconcile the irreconcilable? The siblings' final scene that has just been addressed stages the melodramatic drift in Karin's self-narration. As she visits her brother in the hospital after his suicide attempt and Weber's successful medication, the moment of their reunion is so precious to her that she wishes it might stay, or at least return in a reliable fashion. For once, he complies. "Hang where you know. Where else can you go with all hell breaking loose?" he sarcastically suggests, making "her nostrils quiver and her eyes burn."

---

19 The notion of the melodramatic employed here draws from Peter Brooks, Thomas Elsaesser, and Linda Williams, especially their proposition to understand it as a narrative mode. For a lucid discussion of this matter, see Kelleter and Mayer, "Revising."

She tries to say *nowhere*, but she can't.
"I mean, how many homes does one person get?" He waves his hand toward the gray window. It's not such a bad place to come back to."
"Best place on earth," she says. "Six weeks, every year." (447)

Indicating the proximity of the novel's ending, narration resorts to the present tense; it does so in the entire, very short fifth part, whose title "And Bring Back Someone Else" bears the promising lure of a successful rite of passage. Next to the obligatory crane section, the final part consists of one section that dialogically closes the narratives of Karin and Mark, and one section that closes Weber's narrative. In the above quote, whose final sentence is the end of Karin's self-narrative, she simultaneously dismisses and embraces the idea of having a home, wants to both stay and leave the place that is most prominently and painfully associated with it. In response, her storytelling resorts to the migratory routine of the cranes, her newly found "stabilizing other," for the right kind of storyline. ("Best place on earth [...] Six weeks every year.") The failure of saying *nowhere* preceding this reconciliation is grounded in a narrative act that thrives on the longing to leave the world unchanged in spite of its obvious flaws and corruptions.

Weber's mode of self-narration can be read as regressive and tragic. His lack of emotional involvement with others (including diagnosing himself as the first case of "contagious Capgras") has already been discussed. It is indeed his lack of attachment that serves as the main trajectory of Weber's decline—threatening to cost him his professional reputation, his popularity with patients and audiences, his romance with Barbara, and his marriage. The downward spiral culminates in the novel's final scene, in which Weber, arriving at a New York airport, anticipates his troubled homecoming:

A voice calls to disembark. In the rising crush, he stands and grapples for his carry-on, shedding himself on everything he touches. He stumbles down the jet bridge into another world, swapped out by impostors at every step. He needs her his wife to be out there, on the other side of the baggage claim, though he has lost all right to hope it. There, holding his name on a little card, printed clearly so he can read it. *Man*, the card must say. No: *Weber*. She will be the one holding it, and that's how he must find her. (451)

And while it is uncertain if Weber's life (and) narrative will recover, the unhampered course of decline that we have been witnessing gives these lines a cathartic ring. Weber is made to suffer for his snobby carelessness, and regardless of whether or not he can turn the tides we may feel for him in a way that makes it possible for *us* to learn from his mistakes. Powers seeks to capitalize on this possibility, it seems, by ending the narrative in a moment of surrender. In the closing paragraph, Weber feels that he needs his wife to be cured from the Capgras symptoms that have turned the inhabitants of his world into an army of impostors, and that he must leave his corrupted name (and self) behind in order to find her. Ending the novel with the unraveling neurologist arriving at an unnamed New York airport (a prototypical *non-place* in Augé's sense, and as such a hostile environment for matters of dwelling) capitalizes on the tragic implications of the decline imposed upon the presumably superior self that Weber embodies. As the splendid storyteller (for many the author's super-ego) surrenders to his longing for his wife, he also gives in to his desire to be received in and through his story.

Allegedly, Powers did not have the Gergens' model in mind when developing the three narrative voices at work in his novel, but MacLean's triune brain: "one part reptilian, one part limbic, one part cerebral, and all parts improvised, interdependent, perpetually revised, and mutually self-deluding" (Burn 178). In striking resonance with the crane sections, Mark's self-narration would then follow the "reptilian" mode (rage and basic survival), Karin's self-narration would be "limbic" (emotion and long-term memory), and Weber's "cerebral" (verbal eloquence and rationality). When combining this model with the Gergens', its evolutionary thrust merges with a progression of life narratives moving, in terms of their narrative sophistication, from "comic" via "melodramatic" to "tragic;" and, in terms of their implied psychodynamics, from "progressive" via "stabilizing" to "regressive." The question that remains, posing itself with amplified weight from this perspective, is what modes of dwelling are gained or lost by enlisting this particular narrative form and the kinds of agency that is afford.

BACK IN OZ AGAIN

The Echo Maker turns a naturalistic notion of narrative into the ultimate touchstone for matters of belonging: Emplacement, rendered here as a survival instinct engrained in the human brain, is determined by narrative. But narrative is presented as an utterly provisional and inescapably self-delusional enterprise in this novel. Ultimately, the narrative operations staged and performed on multiple levels and in manifold ways are only as good as their receivers—which brings me back to my earlier point about Powers's urge to educate his readers. *The Echo Maker* translates its author's desire for better readers into a self-reflexive, self-observing narrative operation, a virtual training ground to hone the skills of his readers, for which indirect voicedness of the self-narratives is instrumental. Throughout the narrative Powers opted for the third person, which has the paradoxical effect of creating both a sense of intimacy (through the first-hand insight into the characters' inner worlds) and of distance (because the innerness thus revealed is not expressed directly by the person possessing it). And as the three protagonists relentlessly alter their narratives to cohere their interdependent and socially embedded senses of self and place, the compound design of the narrative not only demands of the reader to move along with the constant shifts between different positions and individual struggles but also demands to continually bridge the structural gaps between intimacy and distance. The text thus creates a reading experience in which one can sympathize, partake, and identify, but never comfortably settle or even gain so much as a lasting sense of familiarity with one of the protagonists.

This constant destabilization undercuts the dire conventionality of the novel's three main characters: Weber, the male rational scientist; Karin, the emotional, caring and self-denying female, and Mark, the raging and rebellious male adolescent. What makes this inbuilt mechanism of "reader revision" all the more persuasive is that it takes shape from within the self-diluting, ever-shifting texture of the narrative. And this is indeed the nucleus of the novel's greatest achievement: to stage and explore the storied nature of human life and the need to belong around which it revolves as a practice of "echo making"—by telling one's story from a particular place that only becomes a place through the distorted versions of that story carried back to the teller. Echo makers, so the implied "message" of the novel goes, are at once sustained and trapped by their storied lives, and because they are trapped their senses of self and of place genuinely depend on mediation. Powers uses the trope of mapmaking to underscore this point: "There is no place *except* the map, and yet we make the map together, by reading ourselves into one another, through conventions and codes, all of them provisional" (178). The map envisioned here is inside as much as it is outside of those who make it. It is improvised and ever-changing, the basic form of all storytelling and the messy blueprint of all social engagement. The cranes are the ideal mapmakers in the novel's world. Instead of distorting the map with self-centered mediation, they embody it—even beyond their own lifespan.

Yet as productive as toying with notions of "echo making" and "mapmaking" are for the project of making tangible the inescapably emplaced and mediated nature of human being, the investment into these tropes gets daunting over the course of the narrative. In other words, the novel suffers from its author's didactic desire. What Heinz Ickstadt has aptly called his "asynchronous messaging" ("Asynchronous") becomes too synchronous in its relentless plea for communal and environmental values, too schematic in its idealization of a selfless, crane-like existence as the mystical, utopian opposite to the various late-modern struggles with selfhood. On the formal level, Powers's didactic urge tips the scales when the different narrative voices are merged toward the end. To the sophisticated reader (who certainly is the implied reader of this book), this move presents itself as a stylistic clue, indicating that the collective mapmaking has entered a new level of collaboration. And while the shift is subtle its effects are grave. Initially, the changing focalizations are used with great persistence and accuracy to produce the shifting, polyvocal narrative that has already been described—a narrative that has been crafted *for* a sophisticated reader, and that provides a dense, aesthetically rich, and challenging reading experience. Which is why this reader is likely to notice that half way through the part four, it becomes increasingly hard to tell whose "brain" is telling the story, and that focalizations are added that cannot be integrated into the previous pattern, for instance when Karin's ex-boyfriend Daniel calls Mark after the two have not been in touch since they were teenagers. Another passage seems to be focalized through Weber, yet the voice is notably less rational and in control than before, more like Karin's than Weber's. And sure enough, focalization shifts to Karin soon thereafter, yet again the narrative voice has lost some of its distinctive characteristics; it is strikingly less emotional and more coolly observant now. By the end of part four, a less subjective mode of narration is established, which remains in place until the end.

The gradual shift from exploring distinct psychological states and self-narratives to resolving the mysteries around the accident also entails a shift of gears in terms of emplotment. A closure-driven detective work, which favors the "hermeneutic code" over the "proairetic code," interpretation over action, takes over from now on.[20] And yet this artful maneuver aims for more than mere closure. In fact, the new zeal to find out what happened during the night of the accident is bound up with a *specific* quest for closure; the detective work conducted to this end is not that of a single individual but of a polyvocal collective. The merging of the different focalizations in the novel's final stretch hence invites to be read as a moment of synchronicity between different modes of being, feeling, and telling. It gives voice and form to a vision of narrative recovery, the possibility of mutually inhabiting a world in flux or even collision—by virtue of a narrative operation that is materially grounded, sufficiently permeable, and closely connected. The problem with this move, it should now be clear, is that it comes along with a didactical baggage that (even though one is likely to agree with Powers on ethical terms) diminishes much of the pleasure offered by the virtuoso composition of the narrative. Even so, what does it achieve in terms of giving voice and form to contemporary needs to belong?

Toward the end of the novel, "home" comes to provide the common ground for the enterprise of conjoint mapmaking; to return there (for Weber), to stay at home (for Mark), or to decide whether or not to leave this place again (for Karin) is the overarching concern in the novel's final pages. In fact, all three protagonists close their self-narratives (as far as they are still discernible at this point) by addressing this matter: Mark by affirming his recovered sense of self and place in a narrative act that seamlessly alternates between external dialogue and introspection; Karin by framing the relation to her hometown in terms of coming and going just like the cranes, and Weber by realizing that recovering his home will ultimately depend on his wife's forgiveness. Even though "home" has long ceased to be a promise of a security and become a destination or a fantasy instead, concerns with homecoming

---

20 Again, the terms are drawn from Roland Barthes, *S/Z*. Brooks discusses the conjoint operation of the two codes, one mobilizing the narrative, the other aiming at closure, as the constitutive antagonism of plot-making. See Brooks, *Reading* 16-17. In the context of this study, they have also been addressed with regard to Edgar Huntly's detective work. See Chapter 2, Fn. 24.

provide a shared horizon for all three stories—and for the narrative operation as a whole. For if, in the world of *The Echo Maker*, the productive nexus of belonging and narrative hinges on providing a kind of recovery that is imaginary and self-deluded rather than actual and material, narrative transfer is diegetically geared toward dissolving the individual, self-centered voices with which the novel begins. Notoriously erring and provisional as narration may be, the move from a self-absorbed to a communal mode of storytelling is fathomed and probed as a feasible dwelling ground. This prospect is nestled into and indeed artfully constructed through a polyvocal narrative that exposes the inadequacies and limitations of the self as the autonomous builder of that place called home. A while this place may or may not be called by that name, building it cannot do without a semantics of familiarity and attachment—just as it cannot escape the narrative forms and patterns that this semantics is inclined to assume.

In a way, then, *The Echo Maker* retells the lesson of the ruby red slippers with which this study (or story) began. Just as Dorothy, the main characters in Powers's novel come to find that calling out for one's home is a poetic act of taking measure. Mark's story ends happily because he gets to stay in Oz, which either replaces his Homestar or reinforces the Oz-like qualities already carried in its name. Karin and Weber are doomed if they do not find the way. *The Echo Maker* thus also affirms what is, for Salman Rushdie, the real secret of the ruby red slippers—"that there is no longer any such place as home: except, of course, for the homes we make, or the homes that are made for us: in Oz, which is anywhere and everywhere except the place from which we began" (Rushdie 57, quoted in Kaes 192). And who would know better than a diasporic writer in exile that there is no such place unless we build it, word by word, sentence by sentence, storyline by storyline. The construction material is mostly prefabricated, and much of it may even be bluntly imposed. But the need to belong draws us into the world, where it leaves us with at least some leeway of how to build a suitable dwelling place. And if getting home will not put an end to this need, perhaps we might say that dwelling in narrative is as good as the *next* story from which we build.

Works Cited

Aarons, Victoria. *A Measure of Memory: Storytelling and Identity in Jewish-American Fiction*. Athens and London: The U of Georgia U, 1996. Print.

Adams, Stephen J. "'The Noisiest Novel Ever Written': The Soundscape of Henry Roth's *Call It Sleep*." *Twentieth Century Literature*, Vol. 35.1 (1989): 43-64. *JSTOR*. Web. 25 June 2011.

Alber, Jan and Monika Fludernik, eds. *Postclassical Narratology. Approaches and Analyses*. Columbus: Ohio State UP, 2010. Print.

Allen, Walter. "Afterword." *Call It Sleep*. By Henry Roth. New York: Avon, 1964. 442-47. Print.

Altenbernd, Lynn. "An American Messiah: Myth in Henry Roth's Call It Sleep." *Modern Fiction Studies*, Vol. 35.4 (1989): 673-87. *Project MUSE*. Web. 25 June 2011.

Ammons, Elizabeth. "Material Culture, Empire, and Jewett's Country of the Pointed Firs." *New Essays on The Country of the Pointed Firs*. Ed. June Howard. Cambridge UK and New York: Cambridge UP, 1994. 81-100. Print.

---. "Jewett's Witches." *Critical Essays on Sarah Orne Jewett*. Ed. by Gwen L. Nagel. Boston: G.K. Hall & Co, 1984. 165-184. Print.

---. "Going in Circles: The Female Geography of *The Country of the Pointed Firs*." *SLITI* 16 (1983): 83-92. Print.

Appadurai, Arjun. "Global Ethnoscapes. Notes and Queries for a Transnational Anthropology." *Recapturing Anthropololy. Working in the Present*. Ed. Richard G. Fox. Santa Fe, NM: School for American Research Press, 1991. 192-210. Print.

Appleby, Joyce. *Capitalism and a New Social Order. The Republican Vision of the 1790s*. New York and London: New York UP, 1984. Print.

---. *Liberalism and Republicanism in the Historical Imagination*. Cambridge, Mass. and London: Harvard UP, 1992. Print.

Augé, Marc. *Non-Places: Introduction to an Anthropology of Supermodernity*. New York and London: Verso, 1995. Print.

Axtell, James, ed. *The Educational Writings of John Locke*. Cambridge UK: Cambridge UP, 1968. Print.

Bader, Julia. "The Dissolving Vision: Realism in Jewett, Freeman, and Gilman." *New Essays on American Realism*. Ed. Eric Sundquist. Baltimore: Johns Hopkins UP, 1982. 176-198. Print.

Bakhtin, M.M. "Epic and Novel. Toward a Methodology for the Study of the Novel." *The Dialogic Imagination. Four Essays*. By M.M. Bakhtin. Ed. Michael Holquist. Trans. by Caryl Emerson and Michael Holquist. Austin: U of Texas P, 1981. 3-40. Print.

Barnard, Philip, Mark L. Kamrath, and Stephen Shapiro, "Introduction." *Revising Charles Brockden Brown. Culture, Politics, and Sexuality in the Early Republic*. Ed. Philip Barnard, Mark L. Kamrath, and Stephen Shapiro. Knoxville: The U of Tennessee P, 2004. iii-xxi. Print.

Barthes, Roland. *The Pleasure of the Text*. Trans. Richard Miller. New York: Hill and Wang, 1975. Print.

---. *S/Z. An Essay*. Trans. Richard Miller. New York: Hill and Wang, 1974. Print.

---. "L'Effet de Réel." *Communications* 11 (1968): 84-89. Print.

Baude, Ann. *Radical Spirits. Spiritualism and Women's Rights in Nineteenth Century America*. Boston: Beacon Press, 1989. Print.

---. "Vorwort." Perspektiven der Weltgesellschaft. Ed. Ulrich Beck. Frankfurt/M.: Suhrkamp, 1998. 7-10. Print.

Baumgarten, Murray. *City Scriptures. Modern Jewish Writing*. Cambridge, Mass. and London: Harvard UP, 1982. Print.

Bell, Vicky. "Performativity and Belonging: An Introduction." Special Issue Performativity and Belonging, Vikki Bell, ed. *Theory, Culture & Society*. Vol. 16.2. (1999): 1-10. Print.

Bellis, Peter J. "Narrative Compulsion and Control in Charles Brockden Brown's *Edgar Huntly*." *South Atlantic Review*. 52.1 (1987): 43-57. JSTOR. Web. 8 Jan. 2010.

Benjamin, Walter. "The Storyteller. Reflections on the Works of Nicolai Leskov." *The Novel: An Anthology of Criticism and Theory 1900-2000*. Ed. Dorothy J. Hale. Malden, Mass.: Blackwell Publishing, 2006. 362-78. Print.

Bennett, Jane. *Vibrant Matter: A Political Ecology of Things*. Durham: Duke UP, 2010. Print.

Berkowitz, Leonard. *Advances in Experimental Social Psychology*. San Diego: Academic Press, 1988. Print.

Berthoff, Warner. "The Art of Jewett's *Pointed Firs*." *New England Quarterly* 32.1 (March 1959): 31-53. Print.

---. "A Lesson in Concealment: Charles Brockden Brown's Method in Fiction." *PQ* 37 (1958): 45-57. Print.

Berthold, Dennis. "Charles Brockden Brown, *Edgar Huntly*, and the Origins of the American Picturesque." *William and Mary Quarterly*, Vol. 41.1 (1984): 62-84. JSTOR. Web. 8 January 2010.

Bhabha, Homi K. "Narrating the Nation." *Nation and Narration.* Ed. Homi K. Bhabha. London and New York: Routledge, 1990. 1-7. Print.

Bieger, Laura. "Some Thoughts on the Spatial Forms and Practices of Storytelling." *Zeitschrift für Anglistik und Amerikanistik* 64.1 (2016): 11-16. Print.

---. "No Place Like Home; or, Dwelling in Narrative." *New Literary History* 46.1 (2015): 17-39. Print.

---. "'Look what they done done.' Property, Community and Belonging in Edward P. Jones' *The Known World*." *American Economies.* Ed. Eva Boesenberg, Reinhard Isensee and Martin Klepper. Heidelberg: Winter 2012, 403-31. Print.

---. "Transatlantic landscapes and living images: 'Marlboro Country' revisited." *Amerikastudien/American Studies*, Vol. 52.1. (2007): 21-139. Print.

Blum, Deborah. *Ghost Hunters. William James and the Search for Scientific Proof of Life After Death.* London: Century, 2007. Print.

Bodnar, John. *The Transplanted. The History of Immigrants in Urban America.* Bloomington: Indiana UP, 1985. Print.

Borchers, Hans. *Freud und die amerikanische Literatur (1920-1940). Zur Rezeption der Psychoanalyse in den literarischen Zeitschriften und den Werken von Aiken, Lewisohn und Dell.* München: Fink, 1987. Print.

Bray, Joe. *The Epistolary Novel. Representations of Consciousness.* London and New York: Routledge, 2003. Print.

Breen, T.H. "Creative Adaptations: Peoples and Cultures." *Colonial British American. Essays in the New History of the Early Modern American Era.* Ed. Jack P. Greene and J.R. Pole. Baltimore and London: Johns Hopkins UP, 1984. 195-232. Print.

Brodhead, Richard. *Cultures of Letters: Scenes of Reading and Writing in Nineteenth-Century America.* Chicago: U of Chicago P. 1993. Print.

Brooks, Peter. *Reading for the Plot. Design and Intention in Narrative.* New York: Alfred Knopf, 1984. Baltimore: Johns Hopkins UP, 1982. Print.

---. "Freud's Masterplot: Questions of Narrative." *Literature and Psychoanalysis. The Question of Reading: Otherwise.* Ed. Shoshana Felman. Baltimore and London: Johns Hopkins UP, 1982. 280-300. Print.

Brosch, Renate. *Krisen den Sehens. Henry James und die Veränderung der Wahrnehmung im 19. Jahrhundert.* Tübingen: Stauffenberg Verlag, 2000. Print.

Brown, Bill. *A Sense of Things: The Object Matter of American Literature.* Chicago: Chicago UP, 2003. Print.

---. "Regional Artifacts (The Life of Things in the Work of Sarah Orne Jewett)." *American Literary History* 14.2 (Summer 2002): 195-226. Print.

Brown, Charles Brockden. *Edgar Huntly; or, Memoirs of a Sleepwalker.* 1799. Ed. Sydney Krause and S.W. Reid. Bicentennial Edition. Kent, Ohio: Kent State UP, 1982. Print.

---. *Edgar Huntly; or, Memoirs of a Sleepwalker.* 1799. Ed. Philip Barnard and Stephen Shapiro. Indianapolis and Cambridge UK: Hackett, 2006. Print.

Buelens, Gert. "The Multivoiced Basis of Henry Roth's Literary Success in *Call It Sleep*." *Pluralism and the Limits of Authenticity in North American Literatures*. Ed. Winfried Siemerling and Kartin Schwenk. Iowa City: U of Iowa P, 1996. 124-50. Print.

Bulter, Judith. "Giving an Account of Oneself." *Diacritcis* 31.4 (2001): 22-40. Print.

---. *Subjects of Desire. Hegelian Reflections in Twentieth Century France*. New York: Columbia UP, 1987. Print.

Burgett, Bruce. *Sentimental Bodies. Sex, Gender, and Citizenship in the Early Republic*. Princeton: Princeton UP, 1998. Print.

Burn, Stephen J. "An Interview with Richard Powers." *Contemporary Literature* 49.2 (2008): 163-179. Print.

---. "Introduction." *Intersections: Essays on Richard Powers*. Ed. Stephen J. Burn and Peter Dempsey. Champaign, IL: Dalkey Archive Press, 2008. xvii-xxxix. Print.

Byerly, Alison. "Effortless Art: The Sketch in Nineteenth-Century Painting and Literature." *Criticism* 41.3 (Summer 1999): 349-364. Print.

Cappell, Ezra. *American Talmud:* The Cultural Work of Jewish American Fiction. Albany: State U of New York P, 2007. Print.

Carlin, Deborah. "Cather's Jewett: Relationship, Influence, and Representation." *Willa Cather and the Nineteenth Century*. Ed. Anne L. Kaufman and Richard H. Millington. Lincoln and London: U of Nebraska P, 2015. 169-188. Print.

Cary, Richard. "The Sculpture and the Spinster: Jewett's 'Influence' on Cather." *Colby Quarterly* 10.3 (September 1973): 168-178. Print.

----, ed. *Sarah Orne Jewett Letters*. Waterville ME: College Colby Press, 1967.

Casey, Edward. "David Carr on History, Time and Place." *Human Studies* 29.4 (2006): 445-462. Print.

Cassuto, Leonard. "'[Un]consciousness Itself Is the Malady': *Edgar Huntly* and the Discourse of the Other." *Modern Language Studies* 23.4 (1993): 118-130. *JSTOR*. Web. 8 January 2010.

Cather, Willa. "Miss Jewett." *Not Under Forty*. New York: Alfred A. Knopf, 1922. Print.

---. "Preface." *The Country of the Pointed Firs and Other Stories*. Ed. Willa Cather. Garden City, New York: Doubleday and Company, 1954. Print.

Cavarero, Adriana. *Relating Narratives. Storytelling and Seflhood*. Trans. Paul A. Kottman. New York: Routledge, 2000. Print.

Cavell, Stanley. "The Ordinary as the Uneventful." *The Cavell Reader*. Ed by Stephen Mulhall. Cambridge UK: Blackwell, 1996. 253-59. Print.

Chandler, Marilyn. *Dwelling in the Text. Houses in American Fiction*. Berkeley: The U of California P, 1991. Print.

Chapman, Seymour. Story and Discourse. Narrative Structure in Fiction and Film. Ithaca and London: Cornell UP, 1978. Print.

Chase, Richard. *The American Novel and Its Tradition*. Garden City, NY: Doubleday, 1957. Print.

Clemit, Pamela. *The Godwinian Novel: The Rational Fiction of Godwin, Brockden Brown and Mary Shelly*. Oxford: Clarendon P, 1993. Print.

Cox, James. "Regionalism: A Diminished Thing." *Columbia Literary History of the United States*. Ed. by Emory Elliott. New York: Columbia UP, 1988. 761-784. Print.

Currie, Mark. *About Time: Narrative, Fiction and the Philosophy of Time*. Edinburgh, Edinburgh UP, 2007. Print.

Davidson, Cathy N. *Revolution of the Word. The Rise of the Novel in America*. New York and Oxford: Oxford UP, 1986. Print.

Davitt Bell, Michael. "Gender and American Realism in *The Country of the Pointed Firs*." *New Essays on The Country of the Pointed Firs*. Ed. June Howard. Cambridge UK and New York: Cambridge UP, 1994. 61-80. Print.

Deleuze, Gilles and Felix Guattari. *A Thousand Plateaus. Capitalism and Schizophrenia*. Minneapolis: Minnesota UP, 1987. Print.

Diamant, Naomi. "Linguistic Universes in Henry Roth's *Call It Sleep*." *Contemporary Literature* 27.3 (1986): 336-355. JSTOR. Web. 25 June 2011.

Dillon, Elizabeth Maddock. *The Gender of Freedom. Fictions of Liberalism and the Literary Public Sphere*. Stanford: Stanford UP, 2004. Print.

Donovan, Josephine. "Jewett and Swedenborg." *American Literature* 65.4 (Dec. 1993): 731-750. Print.

---. "The Unpublished Love Poems of Sarah Orne Jewett." *Frontiers* 4.3 (1979). Reprinted in Gwen L. Nagel, ed., *Critical Essays on Sarah Orne Jewett*. Boston: K. G. Hall, 1984, 107-118. Print.

Douglas, Ann. "The Literature of Impoverishment: The Women Local Colorists in America, 1865-1914." *Women's Studies* 1 (1972): 2-40. Print.

Downes, Paul. "Sleep-Walking Out of the Revolution: Brown's *Edgar Huntly*." *Eighteenth Century Studies* 29.4 (1996): 413-431. Print.

Elliott, Emory. *Revolutionary Writers. Literature and Authority in the New Republic, 1725-1810*. New York and Oxford: Oxford UP, 1982. Print.

Engell, James. *The Creative Imagination. Enlightenment to Romanticism*. Cambridge, Mass. and London: Harvard UP, 1981. Print.

Ezzy, Douglas "Theorizing Narrative Identity: Symbolic Interactionism and Hermeneutics." *The Sociological Quarterly* 39.2 (1998): 239-252. Print.

Faderman, Lilan. *Surpassing the Love of Men: Friendship and Love between Women from the Renaissance to the Present*. New York: Morrow, 1990. Print.

Faherty, Duncan. *Remodeling the Nation. The Architecture of American Identity, 1776-1858*. Durham, NH: The U of New Hampshire P, 2007. Print.

Fein, Richard. "Fear, Fatherhood and Desire in *Call It Sleep*." *Yiddish* 5.4 (1984): 49-54. Print.

Felski, Rita. "Latour and Literary Studies." *PMLA* 130.3 (May 2015): 737-742. Print.

---. *Uses of Literature*. Malden, MA and Oxford: Blackwell, 2008. Print.

Ferraro, Thomas J. *Ethnic Passages. Literary Immigrants in Twentieth-Century America.* Chicago and London: The U of Chicago P, 1993. Print.
---. "Oedipus in Brownesville." *Ethnic Passages.* 87-122. Print.
Fetterley, Judith, and Marjorie Pryse. *Writing Out of Place: Regionalism, Women, and American Literary Culture.* Urbana: U of Illinois P, 2003. Print.
Fiedler, Leslie A. *Love and Death in the American Novel.* 1960. Dalkey Archive Edition, Third Printing, 2008. Print.
---. "The Many Myths of Henry Roth." *New Essays on Call It Sleep.* Ed. Hana Wirth-Nesher. Cambridge UK: Cambridge UP, 1996. 17-28. Print.
---. *The Jew in the American Novel.* New York: Herzl Press, 1966. Print.
Fields, Annie, ed. *Letters of Sarah Orne Jewett.* Boston: Hougton Mifflin, 1911. Print.
Fliegelman, Jay. *Prodigals and Pilgrims. The American Revolution Against Patriarchal Authority.* Cambridge UK, New York and Melbourne: Cambridge UP, 1982. Print.
Fluck, Winfried, *Romance with America? Essays on Culture, Literature, and American Studies.* Ed. Laura Bieger and Johannes Voelz. Heidelberg: Winter, 2009. Print.
---. *Inszenierte Wirklichkeit: Der amerikanische Realismus, 1865-1900.* Frankfurt/M.: Suhrkamp, 1992. Print.
Fludernik, Monika. *Toward a 'Natural' Narratology.* London and New York: Routledge, 1996. Print.
Folsom, Marica McClintock. "'Tact is a Kind of Mind-Reading': Emphatic Style in Sarah Orne Jewett's *The Country of the Pointed Firs.*" *Colby Library Quarterly* 18.1 (1982): 66-78. Print.
Foote, Stephanie. *Regional Fictions: Culture and Identity in Nineteenth-Century American Literature.* Madison: U of Wisconsin P, 2001. Print.
Foster, Hal. *The Return of the Real. The Avant-Garde at the End of the Century.* Cambridge, Mass. and London: MIT Press, 1996. Print.
Foucault, Michel. "Of Other Spaces." *Diacritics,* 16.1. (1986): 22-27. Print.
Frank, Armin Paul. "In der *romance* leben: Zu Charles Brockden Browns *Edgar Huntly* (1799) und einer alten 'modernistischen' Erzähltradition in Amerika." *Frühe Formen mehrperspektivischen Erzählens von der Edda bis Flaubert. Ein Problemaufriß.* Ed. Armin Paul Frank and Ulrich Mölk. Berlin: Erich Schmidt, 1991. Print.
Freedman, William. "Mystic Initiation and Experience in *Call It Sleep.*" *Studies in American Jewish Literature* Special Issue. Ed. Bonnie Lyons. 5.1 (1979): 27-36. Print.
---. "A Conversation with Henry Roth." *Literary Review* 19 (1975): 149-157. Print.
---. "Henry Roth and the Redemptive Imagination." *The Thirties: Fiction, Poetry, Drama.* Ed. Warren French. Deland, Fla: Everett Edwards, 1967. 107-114. Print.

Freud, Sigmund. *Beyond the Pleasure Principle [Jenseits des Lustprinzips]*. 1920. Trans. James Strachey. New York: Norton, 1961. Print.

---. "Family Romances." *The Standard Edition of the Complete Psychological Works of Sigmund Freud*. Ed. James Strachey. 24 vols. London: Hogarth, 1953. 9: 235-41. Print.

Freywald, Cartin. "Henry Roth, *Call It Sleep*." *Amerikastudien/American Studies* 35.4 (1990): 443-59. Print.

Fryer, Judith. "What Goes on in the Ladies Room? Sarah Orne Jewett, Annie Fields, and Their Community of Women." *The Massachusetts Review* 30.4 (1989): 610-628. Print.

Gabriel, Markus. *Transcendental Ontology. Essays in German Idealism*. London: Continuum, 2011. Print.

Garbo, Norman S. *The Coincidental Art of Charles Brocken Brown*. Chapel Hill: The U of North Carolina P, 1981. Print.

Gebhardt, Gunther, Oliver Geisler, and Steffen Schröter. "Heimatdenken: Konjunkturen und Konturen." *Heimat. Konturen und Konjunkturen eines umstrittenen Konzepts*. Ed. Gebhardt, Geisler and Schröter. Bielefeld: Transcript, 2007. 9-49. Print.

Gergen, Kenneth J. and Mary M. Gergen."Narrative and the self as relationship." *Advances in Experimental Social Psychology*. Ed. Leonard Berkowitz. San Diego: Academic Press, 1988. 17-56. Print.

Gibbons, Luke. "Ireland, America, and Gothic Memory: Transatlantic Terror in the Early Republic." *boundary 2* 31.1 (2004): 25-47. *Project MUSE*. Web. 23 March 2011.

Giddens, Anthony. *In Defense of Sociology. Essays, Interpretations and Rejoinders*. Cambridge UK: Cambridge UP, 1996. Print.

Gilmore, Michael T. "The Literature of the Revolutionary and Early National Periods." *The Cambridge History of American Literature*. Vol. I. 1590—1820. Ed. Sacvan Bercovitch. Cambridge UK, New York and Melbourne: Cambridge UP, 1994. 542-692. Print.

Goheen, Cynthia J. "Editorial Misinterpretations and the Unmaking of a Perfectly Good Story: The Publication History of The Country of the Pointed Firs." *American Literary Realism. 1870-1910*. 30.2 (Winter 1998): 28-42. Print.

Gomel, Elena. *Narrative Space and Time: Representing Impossible Topologies in Literature*. New York and London: Routledge, 2014. Print.

Grethlein, Jonas. "The Narrative Reconfiguration of Time Beyond Ricoeur." *Poetics Today* 31.2 (2010): 313-329. Print.

Hagenbüchle, Roland. "American Literature and the Nineteenth Century Crisis in Epistemology: The Example of Charles Brockden Brown." *Early American Literature* 23 (1988): 121-151. Print.

Hale, Jr. Nathan G. *Freud and the Americans. The Beginnings of Psychoanalysis in the United States, 1876-1917*. 2 Vols. New York: Oxford UP, 1971. Print.

Hamelman, Steve. "Rhapsodist in the Wilderness: Brown's Romantic Quest in *Edgar Huntly.*" *Studies in American Fiction* 21(1993): 171-190. Print.

Harmon, Graham. *Guerilla Metaphysics: Phenomenology and the Carpentry of Things.* Peru IL: Open Court, 2005. Print.

Harris, Charles. B. "The Story of the Self: The Echo Maker and Neurological Realism." *Intersections: Essays on Richard Powers.* Ed. Stephen J. Burn and Peter Dempsey. Champaign, IL: Dalkey Archive Press, 2008. 230-59. Print.

Harris, Karsten. *The Ethical Function of Architecture.* Cambirgde: MIT Press, 1996.

Hart, Curtis W. "William James' *The Varieties of Religious Experience* Revisited." *Journal of Religion and Health* 47.4 (Dec. 2008): 516-524. Print.

---. *Justice, Nature and the Geography of Difference.* Cambridge, MA: Wiley-Blackwell, 1996. Print.

Hedges, Elaine. "Introduction." *Quilts as Woman's Art: A Quilt Poetics.* By Radka Donnell. Vancouver: Gallerie Publications, 1990. ix-xi. Print.

Hedges, William. "Charles Brockden Brown and the Culture of Contradictions." *Early American Literature* 9.2, Charles Brockden Brown Number (1974): 107-142. *JSTOR.* Web. 8 January 2010.

Heidegger, Martin. *Being and Time.* 1927. Trans. Joan Stambaugh. Buffalo, NY: State U of New York P, 2010. Print.

---. "The Origin of the Work of Art."1935-36. *Poetry, Language, Thought.* Ed. and trans. Albert Hofstadter. New York: Harper Perennial, 2001. 15-86. Print.

---. "Was heißt denken?" 1952. *Vorträge und Aufsätze.* Stuttgart: Klett-Cotta, 1954. 123-38. Print.

---. "…Poetically Man Dwells…" 1954. *Poetry, Language, Thought.* Ed. and trans. Albert Hofstadter. New York: Harper Perennial, 2001. 209-27. Print.

---. "Building Dwelling Thinking." 1952. *Poetry, Language, Thought.* Ed. and trans. Albert Hofstadter. New York: Harper Perennial, 2001. 141-60. Print.

Heise, Ursula. K. "Toxins, Drugs, and Global Systems: Risk and Narrative in the Contemporary Novel." *American Literature* 74 (2002): 747-78. Print.

Hemmings, Clare. "Invoking Affect." *Cultural Studies* 19.5 (2005): 548-567. Web. 19 June 2012. Print.

Herman, David. *Story Logic: Problems and Possibilities of Narrative.* Lincoln and London: Nebraska UP, 2002. Print

---. *Narratologies. New Perspectives of Narrative Analysis.* Columbis: Ohio State UP, 1999. Print.

Hermanson, Scott. "Home: A Conversation of Richard Powers and Tom LeClair." *Electronic Book Review* (3 September 2008). Web. 3 March 2012. <http://www.electronicbookreview.com/thread/ fictionspresent/corporate>.

Hinds, Elizabeth Jane Wall. "Charles Brockden Brown and the Frontiers of Discourse." *Frontier Gothic. Terror and Wonder at the Frontier of American Literature.* Ed. David Morgan, Scott P. Sanders, and Joanne B. Karpinski. Rutherford: Fairleigh Dickenson UP, 1993. 109-25. Print.

---. "Charles Brockden Brown's Revenge Tragedy: *Edgar Huntly* and the Uses of Property." *Early American Literature*, 30.1 (1995): 51-70. Print.

---. *Private Property: Charles Brockden Brown's Genders Economics of Virtue*. Newark: U of Delaware P, 1997. Print.

Homestead, Melissa J. "Willa Cather, Sarah Orne Jewett, and the Historiography of Lesbian Sexuality." *Willa Cather and the Nineteenth Century*. Ed. Anne L. Kaufman and Richard H. Millington. Lincoln and London: U of Nebraska P, 2015. 3-37. Print.

Horstmannshoff, Kai. *The Loop. Chicago Architecture and the Social Imaginary*. Bielefeld: Transcript, 2017. Print.

Howard, Jane. "The Belated Success of Henry Roth." *Life* 53 (8 January 1965): 75-76. Print.

Howard, June. "Introduction: Sarah Orne Jewett's Traffic in Words." *New Essays on The Country of the Pointed Firs*. Ed. June Howard. Cambridge UK and New York: Cambridge UP, 1994, 1-38. Print.

---. *Form and History in American Literary Naturalism*. Chapel Hill: North Carolina UP, 1985. Print.

Howe, Irving. *The World of Our Fathers*. New York: Harcourt Brace Jovanovitch, 1976. Print.

---. "Life Never Let Up." *The New York Times Book Review*. 25 October 1964, 61-62. Print.

Howells, William Dean. *Fiction and Criticism and Other Essays*. Ed. by Clara Marburg Kirk and Rudolf Kirk. New York: New York University Press, 1959. Print.

Hühn, Peter, et al., eds. *The Living Handbook of Narratology*. Hamburg: Hamburg University. <http://www.lhn.uni-hamburg.de/article/narration-various-media> (October 5, 2015).

Hume, David. *A Treatise of Human Nature*. 1739-1740. Ed. L. A. Selby-Bigge. Oxford: Oxford at Clarendon Press, 1967. Print.

Hurt, James. "Narrative Powers: Richard Powers as Storyteller." *Review of Contemporary Fiction* 18.3 (1998): 24-41. Print.

Ickstadt, Heinz. "Asynchronous Messaging. The Multiple Functions of Richard Powers' Fictions." *Ideas of Order: Narrative Patterns in the Novels of Richard Powers*. Ed. Antje Kley and Jan D. Kucharzewski. Heidelberg: Winter, 2012. 25-46. Print.

---. "Surviving in the Particular? Uni(verali)ty and Multiplicity in the Novels of Richard Powers." *European Journal of American Studies* 1-2007. Web. 27 April 2007. 3 March 2012. <http://ejas.revues.org/1145>

---. "Concepts of Society and the Practice of Fiction. Symbolic Responses to the Experience of Change in Late-Nineteenth-Century America." *Faces of Fiction. Essays on American Literature and Culture from the Jacksonian Period to Postmodernity*. Ed. Susanne Rohr and Sabine Sielke. Heidelberg: Winter, 2002. Print.

---. "Toward a Pluralist Aesthetics." *Aesthetics in a Multicultural Age*. Ed. by Emory Elliot. Oxford: Oxford UP, 2002. 263-278.

Illouz, Eva. *Saving the Modern Soul: Therapy, Emotions, and the Culture of Self-Help*. Berkeley: The U California P, 2008. Print.

---. *Consuming the Romantic Utopia: Love and the Cultural Contradictions of Capitalism*. Berkeley: The U of California P, 1997. Print.

Iser, Wolfgang. *The Fictive and the Imaginary: Charting Literary Anthropology*. Baltimore: Johns Hopkins UP, 1993. Print.

---. *Prospecting. From Reader Response to Literary Anthropology*. Baltimore: Johns Hopkins UP, 1989. Print.

---. "Fictionalizing Acts." *Amerikastudien/American Studies* 31 (1986): 5-15. Print.

Jahn, Manfred. "Cognitive Narratology." *Routledge Encyclopedia of Narrative Theory*. Ed. David Herman, Manfred Jahn, and Marie-Laure Ryan. London: Routledge, 2005. Print-

James, Henry. "Mr. and Mrs. James T. Fields." *The Atlantic Monthly* 116 (July 1915): 21-31. Print.

---. "The Art of Fiction." *Theory of Fiction: Henry James*. Ed. James E. Miller, Jr. Lincoln: U of Nebraska P, 1972. 27-44. Print.

---. *The Portrait of a Lady* [1891]. London: Penguin Classics, 2011. Print.

James, William. *Varieties of Religious Experience*. New York: Longmans Green, 1902. Print.

---. "A World of Pure Experience." *Essays on Radical Empiricism* (1912). Cambridge Mass. and London: Harvard UP, 1976. 21-44. Print.

Jehlen, Myra. "The Literature of Colonialization." *The Cambridge History of American Literature*. Vol. I. 1590—1820. Ed. Sacvan Bercovitch. Cambridge UK, New York and Melbourne: Cambridge UP, 1994. 13-168. Print.

Jewett, Sarah Orne. *The Country of the Pointed Firs*. 1896. *Novels and Stories*. Ed. Michael Davitt Bell. New York: Library of America, 1994. 371-487. Print.

Kaes, Anton. "Leaving Home: Film, Migration, and the Urban Experience." *New German Critique* 74.1 (1998): 179-92. Print.

Kaplan, Amy. "Nation, Region, and Empire." *Columbia History of the American Novel*. Ed. Emory Elliott. New York: Columbia UP, 1991. 240-266. Print.

Kazin, Alfred. "Introduction." *Call It Sleep*. By Henry Roth. New York: Picador, 1991. Print.

---. *Starting Out in the Thirties*. London: Secker & Warburg, 1966. Print.

Kearney, Richard. „What is Carnal Hermeneutics?" *New Literary History* 46.1 (2015): 99-124. Print.

Keen, Ernest. "Paranoia and Cataclysmic Narrative." *Narrative Psychology. The Storied Nature of Human Conduct*. Ed. Theodore R. Sarbin. London: Praeger Press, 1986. 174-190. Print.

Kelleter, Frank. *Serial Agencies. The Wire and Its Readers*. Winchester: Zero Books, 2014. Print.

----, ed. *Media of Serial Narrative*. Columbus: Ohio State UP, 2017. Print.
---- and Ruth Mayer. "The Melodramatic Mode Revisited. An Introduction." Frank Kelleter et al., eds. *Melodrama! The Mode of Excess from Early America to Hollywood*, Heidelberg: Winter, 2001. 7-18. Print.
Kelly, Gary. *The English Jacobin Novel. 1780-1805*. Oxford: Oxford UP, 1976. Print.
---. *English Fiction of the Romantic Period. 1789-1830*. London: Longman, 1989. Print.
Kemp, Simon. "The Inescapable Metaphor: How Time and Meaning Become Space When We Think about Narrative." *Philosophy and Literature* 36.2 (2012): 391-403. Print.
Kerby, Anthony Paul. *Narrative and the Self*. Bloomington and Indianapolis: Indiana UP 1991. Print.
Kerman, Sarah. "Call It Sleep and the Limits of Typicality." *Journal of Modern Literature*, Vol. 33.2 (XXX): 47-69. Project MUSE. Web. 25 June 2011.
Kermode, Frank. *The Sense of an Ending. Studies in the Theory of Fiction*. New York: Oxford UP, 1967. Print.
Keupp, Heiner at al., *Identitätskonstruktionen. Das Patchwork der Identitäten in der Spätmoderne*. Reinbeck: Rowohldt, 1999. Print.
King, Nicola. *Memory, Narrative, Identity: Remembering the Self*. Edinburgh: Edinburgh UP, 2000. Print.
Kirschner, Suzanne R. *The Religious and Romantic Origins of Psychoanalysis. Individuation and Integration in Post-Freudian Theory*. New York: Cambridge UP, 1996. Print.
Kittler, Friedrich. "De Nostalgia." *Literatur und Provinz: Das Konzept 'Heimat' in der neueren Literatur*, ed. Hans-Georg Pott. Paderborn: Schöningh, 1986. 153-68. Print.
Kossmann, Herman, Suzanne Mulder, and Frank den Oudsten. *Narrative Space: On the Art of Exhibiting*. Rotterdam: 010 Publishers, 2012. Print.
Kraus, Wolfgang *Das Erzählte Selbst. Narrative Konstruktion von Identität in der Spätmoderne*. Pfaffenweiler: Centaurus, 1996. Print.
Krause Sydney J. "Penn's Elm and Edgar Huntly: Dark 'Instruction to the Heart'" *American Literature*, Vol. 66. 3 (1994): 463-484. JSTOR. Web. 23 March 2011.
Laplanche, Jean and J.-B. Pontalis. *Vocabulaire de la Psychoanalyse*. Paris: Presses des Universitaires de France, 1971. Print.
Latour, Bruno. *Reassembling the Social: An Introduction to Actor-Network-Theory*. New York: Oxford UP, 2005. Print.
Lefebvre, Henri. *The Production of Space*. Trans. Donald Nicholson-Smith. Malden, MA and Oxford: Blackwell, 1991. Print.
Levy, Helen Fiddyment. *Fictions of the Home Place. Jewett, Cather, Glasgow, Porter and Naylor*. Jackson and London: UP of Mississippi, 1992. Print.
Lewes, Darby. "Gynotopia. A Checklist of Nineteenth Century Utopias by American Women." *Legacy* 6.2 (Fall 1989): 29-41. Print.

Locke, John. *An Essay Concerning Human Understanding.* 1690. Ed. John W. Yolton. London: Dent, 1961. Print.

Lotman, Juri M. (1970). *The Structure of the Artistic Text.* Trans. Gail Lenhoff and Ronald Vroon. Ann Arbor: University of Michigan Press, 1977. Print.

Love, Heather. "Gyn/Apology: Sarah Orne Jewett's Spinster Aesthetics." *ESQ: A Journal of the American Renaissance* 55.3-4 (2009): 305-334. Print.

Luciano, Dana. "Perverse Nature": Edgar Huntly and the Novel's Reproductive Disorders." *American Literature,* 70.1 (1998): 1-27. *JSTOR.* Web. 23 March 2011.

Luck, Chad. "Re-Walking the Purchase: Edgar Huntly, David Hume, and the Origins of Ownership." *Early American Literature* 44.2 (2009): 271-306. Print.

Lueck, Beth L. "Charles Brockden Brown's *Edgar Huntly*: The Picturesque Traveler as Sleepwalker." *Studies in American Fiction* 15.1 (1987): 25-42. Print.

Lukács, Georg. *The Theory of the Novel. A Historico-Philosophical Essay on the Forms of Great Epic Literature.* Trans. Anna Bostock. Cambridge, MIT Press, 1971. Print.

Lyons, Bonnie. "Interview with Henry Roth, March, 1977." *Studies in American Jewish Literature* Special Issue. "Henry Roth's *Call It Sleep*: 1934-1979." Ed. Bonnie Lyons. 5.1 (1979): 50-61. Print.

---. *Henry Roth: The Man and His Work.* New York: Cooper Union, 1976. Print.

---. "The Symbolic Structure of Henry Roth's *Call It Sleep*." Contemporary Literature, Vol 13.2 (1972): 186-203. *JSTOR.* Web 26 June 2011.

Massey, Doreen. *For Space.* London: Sage, 2005. Print.

---. *Space, Place and Gender.* Cambridge UK: Polity Press, 1994. Print.

Matthiessen, F.O. *The American Renaissance: Art and Expression in the Age of Emerson and Whitman.* London: Oxford UP, 1941. Print.

McDonald, Henry. "Language and Being: Crossroads of Modern Literary Theory and Classical Ontology." *Philosophy & Social Criticism* 30.2 (2004): 187-220. Web. 3 June 2012.

---. "The Ontological Turn: Philosophical Sources of American Literary Theory." *Inquiry: An Interdisciplinary Journal of Philosophy* 45.1 (2002): 3-33. Web. 20 June 2012.

McGurl, Mark. "The New Cultural Geology." *Twentieth Century Literature* 57.4 (Fall/Winter 2011): 380-390. Print.

McHale, Brian. "Henry Roth in Nighttown, or, Containing Ulysses." *New Essays on Call It Sleep.* Ed. Hana Wirth-Nesher. Cambridge UK: Cambridge UP, 1996. 75-106. Print.

Meillassoux, Quentin. *After Finitude: An Essay on the Necessity of Contingency.* London: Continuum, 2009. Print.

Meretoja, Hanna. "Narrative and Human Existence. Ontology, Epistemology, and Ethics." *New Literary History* 45.1 (2014): 89-109. Print.

---. *The Narrative Turn in Fiction and Theory: The Crisis and Return of Storytelling from Robbe-Grillet to Tournier*. London and New York: Palgrave Macmillan, 2014. Print.

Messer, Stanly B., Louis A. Sass, and Robert L. Woolfolk, eds. *Hermeneutics and Psychological Theory. Interpretive Perspectives on Personality, Psychotherapy, and Psychopathology*. New Brunswick: Rutgers UP, 1988. Print.

Michod, Alec. "The Brain is the Ultimate Storytelling Machine, and Consciousness is the Ultimate Story. Interview with Richard Powers" *Believer* 5.1. (Feb. 2007). Web. 3 March 2012. <http://www.believermag.com/issues/200702/?read=interview_powers>.

Mikkonen, Kai. "The 'Narrative is Travel' Metaphor: Between Spatial Sequence and Open Consequence." *Narrative* 15.3 (2007): 286-305. Print.

Miller, D. A. *Narrative and Its Discontents. Problems of Closure in the Traditional Novel*. Princeton: Princeton UP, 1989. Print.

Minter, David. "The Search for Shared Purpose: Struggles on the Left." *The Cambridge History of American Literature*. Vol. 6. Ed. Sacvan Bercovitch. Cambridge UK: Cambridge UP, 2002. 225-40. Print.

Mitchell, W.J.T. "Imperial Landscape". *Landscape and Power*. 2nd Ed. Chicago and London: The U of Chicago P, 2002. Print.

Novalis. *Schriften*. Ed. Jacob Minor. Jena: Diedrichs, 1923. Vol 2. Print.

Nelson, Geoffrey K. *Spiritualism and Society*. London: Routledge and Kegan, 1969. Print.

Nünning, Ansgar. "On the Perspective Structure in Narrative Texts: Steps Toward a Constructivist Narratology." *Narrative Perspectives: Cognition and Emotion*. Ed. Seymour Chapman and Willie von Peer. Albany: State University of New York Press, 2000. 207-223. Print.

Nye, David. *Space and Narrative*. New York: Columbia UP, 1997. Print.

Pease, Donald. "Introduction: Remapping the Transnational Turn." *Reframing the Transnational Turn in American Studies*. Ed. Winfried Fluck, Donald E. Pease, and John Carlos Rowe. Hanover, NH: Dartmouth College Press, 2011, 1-46. Print.

Person, Leland S., Jr. "'My Good Mamma': Women in *Edgar Huntly* and *Arthur Mervyn*." *Studies in American Fiction*, 9.1 (1981): 33-46. Print.

Phelan, James. *Experiencing Fiction: Judgments, Progressions, and the Rhetorical Theory of Narrative*. Columbus: Ohio State UP, 2007. Print.

---. *Narrative as Rhetoric: Technique, Audiences, Ethics, Ideology*. Columbus: Ohio State Univ. Press, 1996. Print.

Plessner, Helmut. *Gesammelte Schriften* IV. Ed. Günter Dux. Frankfurt/M.: Suhrkamp, 1981. Print.

---. *Stufen des Organischen und der Mensch* [1929]. Berlin: DeGruyter, 1969. Print.

Powers, Richard. *The Echo Maker*. London: William Heinemann, 2006. Print.

Psarra, Sophia. *Architecture and Narrative. The Formation of Space and Cultural Meaning.* New York and London: Routledge, 2009. Print.

Rancière, Jacques. *The Politics of the Aesthetics. The Distribution of the Sensible.* London: Continuum, 2004. Print.

Ricoeur, Paul. *Time and Narrative.* 3 Vols. Trans. Kathleen McLaughlin and David Pellauer. Chicago: U of Chicago P, 1984-6. Print.

---. "Life in Quest of Narrative." *On Paul Ricoeur. Narrative and Interpretation.* Ed. David Wood. London, New York: Routledge, 1991. 20-33. Print.

----. "Narrative Identity." *On Paul Ricoeur. Narrative and Interpretation.* Ed. David Wood. London, New York: Routledge, 1991. 188-99. Print.

---. *Interpretation Theory. Discourse and the Surplus of Meaning.* Fort Worth: Texas Christian UP, 1976. Print.

Rideout, Walter. *The Radical Novel in the United States.* Cambridge, Mass.: Harvard UP, 1956. Print.

Ringe, Donald A. *American Gothic. Imagination and Reason in Nineteenth-Century Fiction.* Louisville, KT: University Press of Kentucky, 1982. Print.

Roazen, Paul. "Freud and America." *Social Research* 29.4 (1972): 720-32. Print.

Roman, Judith. "A Closer Look at the Jewett-Fields-Relationship." *Critical Essays on Sarah Orne Jewett.* Ed. By Gwen Nagel. Boston: G.K. Hall & Co, 1984, 119-134. Print.

Roth, Henry. *Call It Sleep.* New York: Picador, 1991. Print.

Rowe, John Carlos. "The Dream of Enlightenment and the Nightmare of Imperialism: Charles Brockden Brown's *Wieland* and *Edgar Huntly*." *Literary Culture and U.S. Imperialism. From the Revolution to World War II.* Oxford and New York: Oxford UP, 2000. 25-52. Print.

Rundum, David. "From Narrative Representation to Narrative Use: Towards the Limits of Definition." *Narrative* 13.2 (May 2005): 195-204. Print.

Ryan, Marie-Laure. "Space." *The Living Handbook of Narratology.* Ed. Peter Hühn et al. Hamburg: Hamburg University (2012/14). Web. 5 Oct. 2015. <www.lhn.uni-hamburg.de/article/space>.

Ryan, Marie-Laure. "Narration in Various Media." *The Living Handbook of Narratology.* Ed. Peter Hühn et al. Hamburg: Hamburg University (2012/14). Web. 5 Oct. 2015. <www.lhn.uni-hamburg.de/article/space>.

---- "Space, Place and Story." *Medienkonvergenz – Transdisziplinär.* Ed. Stefan Flüssel. Berlin and Boston: De Gruyter, 2012. 109-128. Print.

Ryan, Marie-Laure, Kenneth Foote, and Maoz Azaryahu. *Narrating Space / Spatializing Narrative. Where Narrative Theory and Geography Meet.* Columbus: Ohio State UP, 2016. Print.

Samet, Tom. "Henry Roth's Bull Story: Guilt and Betrayal in *Call It Sleep*." *Studies in the Novel* 7.4 (1975): 569-83. Print.

Sarbin, Theodore R., ed. *Narrative Psychology. The Storied Nature of Human Conduct.* New York: Praeger Press, 1986. Print.

---. "Introduction and Overview." *Narrative Psychology. The Storied Nature of Human Conduct.* Ed. Theorode R. Sarbin. New York: Praeger Press, 1986. ix-vxiii. Print.

---. "Root Metaphor." *Narrative Psychology. The Storied Nature of Human Conduct.* Ed. Theorode R. Sarbin. New York: Praeger Press, 1986. 3-21. Print.

---. *Being and Nothingness. An Essay on Phenomenological Ontology.* Trans. Hazel E. Barnes. New York: Taylor and Francis, 1956. Print.

Scheiding, Oliver. *Geschichte und Fiktion. Zum Funktionswandel des frühen amerikanischen Romans.* Paderborn: Schöningh, 2003. Print.

Schneck, Ernst-Peter. *Bilder der Erfahrung. Kulturelle Wahrnehmung im amerikanischen Realismus.* Frankfurt/M.: Campus, 1998. Print.

Schulz, Dieter. "*Edgar Huntly* as Quest Romance." *American Literature.* Vol. 43.3 (1971): 323-35. JSTOR. Web. 6 April 2009.

Schwab, Gabriele. *The Mirror and the Killer Queen. Otherness in Literary Language.* Bloomington: Indiana UP, 1996. Print.

---. *Subjects without Selves. Transitional Texts in Modern Fiction.* Cambridge, MA: Harvard UP, 1994. Print.

Seltzer, Mark. *Henry James and the Art of Power.* Ithaca NY: Cornell UP, 1984. Print.

Shannon, Laurie. "'The Country of Our Friendship:' Jewett's Intimist Art." *American Literature* 71.2 (Jun. 1999): 227-262. Print.

Shapiro, Stephen. *The Culture and Commerce of the Early American Novel. Reading the Atlantic World-System.* University Park: Pennsylvania State UP, 2008. Print.

Shklovsky, Victor. "Art as Technique." *Russian Formalist Criticism: Four Essays.* Trans. and with an Introduction by Lee T. Lemon and Marion J. Reiss. Lincoln: U of Nebraska P, 1965. 3-24. Print.

Sielke, Sabine. "(Re)Cognition in Richard Powers' (Science) Fiction." *Ideas of Order: Narrative Patterns in the Novels of Richard Powers.* Ed. Antje Kley and Jan D. Kucharzewski. Heidelberg: Winter, 2012. 241-64. Print.

Singh, Amrijit, Joseph T. Skerrett, Robert E. Hogan, "Introduction." *Memory, Narrative, Identity. New Essays in Ethnic American Literature.* Ed. Singh, Skerrett, Hogan. Boston: Northeastern UP, 1994. 3-25. Print.

Sivils, Matthew Wynn. "Native American Sovereignty and Old Deb in Charles Brockden Brown's *Edgar Huntly*." *American Transcendental Quarterly* 15 (2001): 293-326. Print.

Slotkin, Richard. *Regeneration Through Violence: The Mythology of the American Frontier, 1600-1860.* Middleton: Wesleyan UP, 1973. Print.

Smith, Barbara Herrnstein. *Contingencies of Value: Alternative Perspectives for Critical Theory.* Cambridge, MA: Harvard UP, 1991. Print.

Smith-Rosenberg, Carroll. "Captured Subjects / Savage Others: Violently Engendering the New American." *Gender & History* 5.2 (1993): 177-195. Print.

---. "The Female World of Love and Ritual. Relations between Women in Nineteenth Century America." *Signs* (Autumn 1975): 1-29. Print.

Soja, Edward. *Postmodern Geographies. The Reassertion of Space in Critical Social Theory.* London: Verso, 1989. Print.

Sollors, Werner. "'A world somewhere, somewhere else.' Language, Nostalgic Mournfulness, and Urban Immigrant Family Romance in *Call It Sleep*." *New Essays on Call It Sleep*. Ed. Hana Wirth-Nesher. Cambridge UK: Cambridge UP, 1996. 127-188. Print.

Somers, Margaret R. "The Narrative Constitution of Identity: A Relational and Network Approach." *Theory and Society* 23 (1994): 605-49. Print.

Stanzel, F.K. *Narrative Situations in the Novel. Tom Jones, Moby Dick, The Ambassadors, Ulysses.* 1955. Bloomington: Indiana UP, 1971. Print.

Sternberg, Mair. "How Narrative Makes a Difference." Narrative 9.2 (May 2001): 115-122. Print.

Stewart, Susan. *On Longing. Narratives of the Miniature, the Gigantic, the Souvenir, the Collection.* Durham and London: Duke UP, 1993. Print.

Tabbi, Joseph. "Afterthoughts on *The Echo Maker*." *Intersections: Essays on Richard Powers.* Ed. Stephen J. Burn and Peter Dempsey. Champaign, IL: Dalkey Archive Press, 2008. 219-29. Print.

Taylor, Charles. *Sources of the Self. The Making of the Modern Identity.* Cambridge: Cambridge UP, 1989. Print.

Taylor, Eugene. "The Spiritual Roots of James's Varieties of Religious Experience." *Varieties of Religious Experience: A Study in Human Nature.* By William James. Centenary Edition. London and New York: Routledge, 2002. xiii-xxxviii. Print.

Todorova, Kremena T. "'Oy, a good men!': Urban Voices and Democracy in Henry Roth's *Call It Sleep*." *Texas Studies in Literature and Language* 48.3 (2006): 250-72. Project MUSE. Web. 25 June 2011.

Tompkins, Jane. *Sensational Designs. The Cultural Work of American Fiction, 1790-1860.* New York and Oxford: Oxford UP, 1985. Print.

Torsney, Cheryl B. and Judy Elsley, *Quilt Culture. Tracing the Pattern.* Columbia and London: U of Missouri P, 1994. Print.

Turkle, Sherry. *Psychoanalytic Politics: Freud's French Revolution.* London: Burnett Books, 1979. Print.

Turner, Frederick Jackson. "The Significance of the Frontier in American History." 1893. Web. 30 June 2011.

Trilling, Lionel. "Manners, Morals, and the Novel." *The Liberal Imagination. Essays on Literature and Society.* Garden City, NY: Doubleday, 1950. 199-215. Print.

Valdés, Mario J. "Introduction: Paul Ricoeur's Post-Structuralist Hermeneutics." *A Ricoeur Reader: Reflection and Imagination.* Ed. Mario J. Valdés. New York: Harvester Wheatsheaf, 1991. 3-40. Print.

Voloshin, Beverly R. "*Edgar Huntly* and the Coherence of the Self." *Early American Literature* 23.3 (1988): 262-80. JSTOR. Web. 8 Jan. 2010.

Waggoner, Hyatt H. "The Unity of *The Country of the Pointed Firs*." *Twentieth Century Literature* 5.2 (1959): 67-73. Print.

Warner, Michael. *The Letters of the Republic. Publication and the Public Sphere in Eighteenth-Century America*. Cambridge, Mass. and London: Harvard UP, 1990. Print.

Waterman, Bryan. "Introduction: Reading Early American America with Charles Brockden Brown." *Early American Literature*, 44.2 (2009): 1-32. Print.

Watts, Steven. *The Republic Reborn. War and the Making of Liberal America, 1790-1820*. Baltimore and London: Johns Hopkins UP, 1987. Print.

Westbrook, Perry. *Acres of Flint: Writers of Rural New England, 1870-1900*. Washington, D.C.: Scarecrow Press, 1951. Print.

White, Hayden. *Metahistory: The Historical Imagination in Nineteenth-Century Europe*. Baltimore: Johns Hopkins UP, 1973. Print.

---. "The Historical Text as Literary Artifact" [1976]. *Tropics of Discourse: Essays in Cultural Criticism*. Baltimore and London: Johns Hopkins UP, 1978. 81-100. Print.

White, Stephen K. *Sustaining Affirmation. The Strengths of Weak Ontology in Political Thought*. Princeton and Oxford: Princeton UP, 2000. Print.

Williams, Jeffrey J. "The Last Generalist: An Interview with Richard Powers." *Minnesota Review* 52-54 (2001): 95-114. Print.

Williams, Linda. *Playing the Race Card: Melodrama of Black and White from Uncle Tom to O.J. Simpson*. Princeton: Princeton University Press, 2001. Print.

Winters, Laura. *Willa Cather: Landscape and Exile*. Selinsgrove: Susquehanna UP, 1993. Print.

Wirth-Nesher, Hana, "Introduction." *New Essays on Call It Sleep*. Ed. Hana Wirth-Nesher. Cambridge UK: Cambridge UP, 1996. 1-16. Print.

---. "Afterword. Between Mother Tongue and Native Language in *Call It Sleep*." *Call It Sleep*. By Henry Roth. New York: Picador, 1991. Print.

---. "The Modern Jewish Novel and the City: Kafka, Roth and Oz." *Modern Fiction Studies* 24 (1978): 91-110. Print.

Wisse, Ruth. "The Classic of Disinheritance." *New Essays on Call It Sleep*. Ed. Hana Wirth-Nesher. Cambridge UK: Cambridge UP, 1996. 60-74. Print.

Zaretsky, Eli. *Secrets of the Soul. A Social and Cultural History of Psychoanalysis*. New York: Alfred A. Knopf, 2004. Print.

Žižek, Slavoj. *Enjoy Your Symptom! Jacques Lacan in Hollywood and Out*. New York: Taylor and Francis, 2001. Print.

Zoran, Gabriel. "Towards a Theory of Space in Narrative." *Poetics Today* 5.2 (1984): 309-335. Print.

Cultural Studies

Gundolf S. Freyermuth
Games | Game Design | Game Studies
An Introduction
(With Contributions by André Czauderna,
Nathalie Pozzi and Eric Zimmerman)

2015, 296 p., pb.
19,99 € (DE), 978-3-8376-2983-5
E-Book: 17,99 € (DE), ISBN 978-3-8394-2983-9

Andréa Belliger, David J. Krieger
Network Publicy Governance
On Privacy and the Informational Self

February 2018, 170 p., pb.
29,99 € (DE), 978-3-8376-4213-1
E-Book: 26,99 € (DE), ISBN 978-3-8394-4213-5

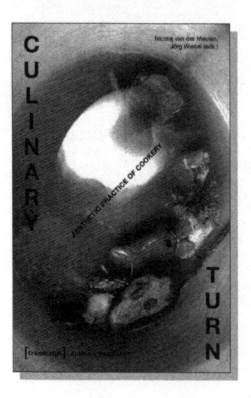

Nicolaj van der Meulen, Jörg Wiesel (eds.)
Culinary Turn
Aesthetic Practice of Cookery
(In collaboration with Anneli Käsmayr
and in editorial cooperation with Raphaela Reinmann)

2017, 328 p., pb., col. ill.
29,99 € (DE), 978-3-8376-3031-2
E-Book available as free open access publication
ISBN 978-3-8394-3031-6

**All print, e-book and open access versions of the titles in our list
are available in our online shop www.transcript-verlag.de/en!**

Cultural Studies

Martina Leeker, Imanuel Schipper, Timon Beyes (eds.)
Performing the Digital
Performativity and Performance Studies in Digital Cultures

2016, 304 p., pb.
29,99 € (DE), 978-3-8376-3355-9
E-Book available as free open access publication
ISBN 978-3-8394-3355-3

Suzi Mirgani
**Target Markets –
International Terrorism
Meets Global Capitalism in the Mall**

2016, 198 p., pb.
29,99 € (DE), 978-3-8376-3352-8
E-Book available as free open access publication
ISBN 978-3-8394-3352-2

Ramón Reichert, Annika Richterich,
Pablo Abend, Mathias Fuchs, Karin Wenz (eds.)
Digital Culture & Society (DCS)
Vol. 3, Issue 2/2017 – Mobile Digital Practices

January 2018, 272 p., pb.
29,99 € (DE), 978-3-8376-3821-9
E-Book: 29,99 € (DE), ISBN 978-3-8394-3821-3

**All print, e-book and open access versions of the titles in our list
are available in our online shop www.transcript-verlag.de/en!**